A
SNIPER
IN THE
TOWER

The
Charles
Whitman
Murders

Gary M. Lavergne

University of North Texas Press
Denton, Texas

First edition 1997

10 9 8 7 6

The paper in this book meets the minimum requirements of the American National Standard for Permanence of Paper for Printed Library Materials, Z39.48-1984.

Permissions
University of North Texas Press
1155 Union Circle #311336
Denton TX 76203

Library of Congress Cataloging-in-Publication Data

Lavergne, Gary M., 1955–
    A sniper in the tower : the Charles Whitman murders / Gary M. Lavergne.
        p.   cm.
    Includes bibliographical references and index.
    ISBN 1-57441-021-0 (cloth : alk. paper). —ISBN 1-57441-029-6 (pbk. : alk. paper)
        1. Whitman, Charles Joseph, 1941–1966. 2. Mass murderers—Texas—Austin—biography. I. title.
    HV6248.W477L39 1997
    364.15'0976431—dc21   96-50411
                                                       CIP

Cover design by Amy Layton
Interior Design by Accent Design and Communications
Cover photo used by permission
Prints & Photographic Collection #06517 The Center for American History
The University of Texas at Austin

ISBN-13: 978-1-57441-029-7 (pbk.)

For Laura Gwen

"In Lavergne's skillful hands . . . Whitman's moment of madness is chillingly re-created, and we come as close as possible to understanding the 'why' of mass murder."
—Gerald Posner, author of *Case Closed*

"A thorough and fascinating examination of one of the most shocking crimes of the century."
—Vincent Bugliosi, author of *Helter Skelter*

TABLE OF CONTENTS

PROLOGUE

Weathered Metal Plaques

U.S. Highway 59 in Texas spans both rural and urban areas. Through Houston the traffic can be murderous, but just south of the metro area, near Rosenberg, drivers breathe a sigh of relief. They are safely into the country-side. Rosenberg inhabitants, like many small-town Texans, worry about "planned communities" of deed-restricted, monotonous, brick homes creeping closer. They cling to an agrarian tradi-tion while welcoming vast riches from the oil and gas industry. Crops of all types carpet tracts of rich, dark soil, while oil-searching and oil-producing rigs dot the landscape.

Near the exit to Farm-to-Market Road 2218 are the Davis-Greenlawn Funeral Chapel and a large, well-manicured cemetery. Golf carts transport visitors and maintenance personnel. The main entrance is near the access road, but many visitors are attracted to a smaller, less ostentatious entrance on the northeast side. The bumpy path leads to an even smaller drive, where blades of grass struggle to grow through compacted gravel. At the confluence is a large white marble carving of Da Vinci's *The Last Supper*. That portion of the cemetery is nearly full, and unoccupied sites have long ago been sold and await their inhabitants. The graves are marked by weathered metal plaques on small marble slabs. Visitors are seldom distracted by the traffic noise from Highway 59; more noticeable are the chirping birds in a nearby wooded area. Here is peace.

Kathleen Leissner Whitman is buried here. Gothic lettering on her plaque indicates that she was born in 1943 and died in 1966. Far too young to have found the peace of a grave, she lies beneath an oak tree. Nearby, weak and rotted limbs from a towering pine fall to the ground as if to join the dead. The family service director of Davis-Greenlawn Cemetery steps off a golf cart and volunteers, "Hardly anyone ever comes here anymore, and few people around here even know who she is, but many of the old-timers tell me that reporters

Kathleen Leissner Whitman is buried in the Davis-Greenlawn Cemetery in Rosenberg, Texas. *Gary Lavergne.*

from all over the world were here for her funeral." Attached to the weathered plaque is a small black vase with nearly-fresh poinsettias. "I see to it that flowers are there, at least most of the time. I kind of adopted her. It just seems right."

Knowing what Kathy Whitman looked like makes the visit more tragic. She was beautiful. Knowing that she chose teaching as an honorable profession brings pointless questions of the lives she could have touched; the world was robbed of her grace, intellect and talent. Knowing that on her last day she fell asleep feeling safe and that her death came quickly and painlessly brings little comfort. She has occupied space five, lot forty-two of section H of Davis-Greenlawn Memorial Park since 3 August 1966.[1]

Approximately 1,200 miles away, via the Eisenhower Interstate System, in West Palm Beach, Florida, is Hillcrest Memorial Park. Across the street from a large, domed silver water storage tank, a life-size statue above a small columbarium depicts a mother and father looking down upon their young son and daughter with gentleness and kindness. At the base of the statue is inscribed "Family Protection." Here, too, is peace.

At Hillcrest narrow asphalt roads wind among the weathered metal plaques. Some of the plaques near the edges of the drive are bent, run over by indifferent and careless drivers. Well-manicured boxwoods and exotic trees dot the ground's rolling hills. In the very center of the cemetery, atop a stainless steel flagpole, the star-spangled banner flaps in a gentle breeze. Nearby, in section ten, is buried the man who killed Kathy Leissner Whitman—her husband, Charles Joseph Whitman. On the right lies Margaret E. Whitman, his mother. He killed her, too.

Charlie's plaque is adorned by an engraving of Saint Joseph, his patron saint. A rosary stretches across the top and around an opening where a vase should be. No one has adopted this grave. An engraving of the Virgin Mary and a rosary as well adorn Margaret's plaque. Yet another Whitman, John Michael, whom Charlie playfully called "Johnnie Mike," the victim of another tragedy, lies to the right. An angel with a spear adorns his plaque.

When Charles and Margaret Whitman were buried together on 5 August 1966, the world was only beginning to comprehend the horror of what he had done, and yet his gray metal casket was draped with the flag of the United States, and, like his devoutly religious mother, he was accorded full burial rites of the Roman Catholic Church. The celebrant of the funeral Mass, Father Tom Anglim of Lake Worth's Sacred Heart Church, asked the world to try to understand that Charlie was obviously deranged.

Charles Joseph Whitman is buried next to his first victim, his mother, Margaret Elizabeth Whitman, in section 10 of the Hillcrest Memorial Park in West Palm Beach, Florida. Both were afforded full burial rights of the Catholic Church and Charles's coffin was draped with the American flag. *Gary Lavergne.*

We trust that God in his mercy does not hold him responsible for these last actions. We trust that our nation, with its traditions for fairness and justice, will not judge his actions with harshness.[2]

But it was hard to understand. He had killed thirteen others earlier in the same week, and four days later another of his victims, a critically injured seventeen-year-old girl named Karen Griffith, would die. She would not return to Austin's Lanier High School to join a senior class filled with the former students of Kathy Whitman's biology classes. Instead, Karen has her own weathered metal plaque in Crestview Memorial Park in Wichita Falls, Texas. What should have been her senior yearbook was dedicated to her and Kathy Whitman.

Surely, Charlie Whitman had to have been an animal, void of virtue and conscience. But the *Austin American-Statesman* described him as "a good son, top Boy Scout, an excellent marine, an honor student, a hard worker, a loving husband, a fine scout master, a handsome man, a wonderful friend to all who knew him—and an expert sniper."[3] In articles that followed, the *Austin American-Statesman* and the media in general presented a more accurate and sober portrait, but no one would ever completely understand Charlie Whitman.

Twenty years after her death Kathy's father, Raymond W. Leissner, still referred to his son-in-law as "Charlie." Remarkably resigned to life without Kathy, Raymond Leissner harbored no ill will towards the man who murdered his only daughter. Instead, he believed that Charlie was driven to madness by a brain tumor discovered the day after his life ended as violently as that of his victims. "He was a brilliant boy," Leissner said, but he has given up trying to understand why it happened. "It's neither here nor there. It's done. It's over with; it's gone. There's no use trying to find out why. . . . I got my consolement [sic] from Almighty God. I kind of left it in his hands. That's the only way to live a decent life."[4]

It took Charles Whitman an hour and a half to turn the symbol of a premier university into a monument to madness and terror. With deadly efficiency he introduced America to public mass murder, and in the process forever changed our notions of safety in open spaces. Arguably, he introduced America to domestic terrorism, but it was terrorism without a cause.

In 1991 a University of Texas employee stated, "I can tell you now with total veracity that never once in the past twenty-five years have I looked at the Tower and not thought about Charles Whitman." Another UT alumnus who was present during the incident, William J. Helmer, lamented, "I can't quite shake an ever so slightly uneasy feeling that the Tower, somehow, is watching me." On the hundredth anniversary of the founding of Austin's Brackenridge Hospital, where so many lives were lost and saved because of Charles J. Whitman, one of the saved, Robert Heard, told the world of how he once suffered from recurring nightmares: "In my dreams, I'm looking through that scope at me, running. And I see the cross hairs right over my chest."

"He was our initiation into a terrible time," reflected a Guadalupe Street vendor. "[W]e grew numb. He was supposed to be an all-American boy. The sad thing is, maybe he really is."[5]

In an article in *Esquire* in August, 1977, noted author Harry Crews wrote of a visit to the University of Texas and how his host gave an unsolicited tour of the Tower massacre site. "That mindless slaughter was suddenly alive and real for me, as though it were happening again, and it was all I could do to keep from running for cover." Crews noticed his host glancing over his shoulder as they walked across UT's South Mall. Later in the evening Crews returned to the Tower and as he stared upwards, a disturbing personal revelation occurred:

> What I know is that all over the surface of the earth where humankind exists men and women are resisting climbing the Tower. All of us have a Tower to climb. Some are worse than others, but to deny that you have your Tower to climb and that you must resist it or succumb to the temptation to do it, to deny that is done at the peril of your heart and mind.[6]

In 1991, twenty-five years after the Charles Whitman murders, Catherine H. Cantieri summed up the danger of trivializing and forgetting the details of such a tragic story:

> After twenty-five years and the attendant anniversary requiems, the story loses something. The edges blur, the facts

lose meaning, the horror evaporates as it becomes just another media circus brought to you at six and ten by concerned-looking anchors. The salient points, the meat of the story, are tossed aside, although they are the stuff that will make you lose sleep.[7]

For individuals affected by the tragedy, like Raymond W. Leissner, there is wisdom in accepting what happened in Austin, Texas, on 1 August 1966, as something that can never be understood. Accepting the unknown as part of God's plan often brings peace and comfort to the faithful and the bereaved; it enables them to go on with their lives. But for society, and institutions, the crime looms too large to be forgotten. Periodic attempts to understand *what* happened and *why* are worthy; since 1 August 1966 there have been other Charles Whitmans, and there will certainly be more. Potential mass-murderers live among us; some of them are nice young men who climb their towers. It is no longer enough to look upon the University of Texas Tower and sigh, "This is where the bodies began to fall," because the story is larger than that. It is a story of how a nation discovered mass murder, and that nation's vulnerability to the destructive power of a determined individual.

Gary M. Lavergne
Cedar Park, Texas

---

[1] Greenlawn Memorial Park, *Internment Order*, Kathleen Frances Whitman, 3 August 1966. (The Greenlawn Memorial Park is now called the Davis-Greenlawn Memorial Park.)

[2] *Austin American-Statesman*, 4 August 1966; Father Tom Anglim quoted in *Palm Beach Post*, 6 August 1966; *Time*, 12 August 1966.

[3] *Austin American-Statesman*, 2 August 1966.

[4] Raymond Leissner quoted in *Austin American-Statesman*, 1 August 1986.

[5] Adrienne de Vergie quoted in *Daily Texan*, 1 August 1991; William J. Helmer quoted in *Texas Monthly*, August, 1986; Robert Heard quoted in Lisa Fahrenthold and Sara Rider, *Admissions: The Extraordinary History of Brackenridge Hospital* (Austin: City of Austin, 1984), p. 93; Guadalupe Street vendor quoted in *Dallas Morning News*, 1 August 1986.

[6] *Esquire*, August, 1977.

[7] *UTmost*, September 1991.

1

Two Very Different Upbringings

During the post-World War II era, middle class workers populated the community of Lake Worth, Florida, a seaside community along the Atlantic Coast. Hard-working entrepreneurs penetrated markets, cultivated clients, and grew rich while economic Darwinism and American free enterprise eliminated the weak. Lake Worth's population doubled from 7,408 in 1940 to 15,315 in 1955.[1] Charles Adolphus "C. A." Whitman flourished in such an environment. He became a successful plumbing contractor as well as an accomplished, affluent and admired businessman. It had not always been that way.

C. A. Whitman knew his mother, but he spent much of his childhood in the Bethesda Orphanage in Savannah, Georgia. He overcame a lack of formal education by sheer determination and by out-working his competitors. His ruddy, round face and neatly cut slicked-to-the-side hair complimented a stocky, solid body. His appearance suggested he had "paid his dues." Self-made and proud of it, he used his money to buy what he wanted, unapologetically. Some acquaintances, however, found his pride to be monumental egotism; he provided very well for his family—and never let them forget it.[2]

Early in his journey to financial security, he met and married Margaret Hodges. Though she lacked the determination and drive of her husband, she contributed to C. A.'s business success by running the office and keeping the books. For twenty-five years after its founding in 1941, the Whitman plumbing business grew consistently. By 1963, the firm owned four cars and twenty-one trucks, employed twenty-eight full-time workers and recorded gross annual sales of $303,433 on a net worth of $289,463. C. A. Whitman's prominence in the Lake Worth community paralleled the growth of his business. Driven to achieve greater social respectability, he joined nearly every public organization in the Lake Worth area. In his quest for upward mobility, he moved his family eight times between 1941 and 1947. In 1941 and 1942 their moves were between Georgia and Florida. After a brief move to Belle Glade, Florida, the Whitmans firmly settled in Lake Worth. C. A. became an acknowledged civic leader, popular enough to be elected president of the local Chamber of Commerce and the PTA.[3]

C. A. and Margaret Whitman became the parents of three sons: Charles Joseph, born in 1941; Patrick, born in 1945; and John, born in 1949. With his sons C. A. demanded strict discipline; he believed in and used corporal punishment. His marital relationship with Margaret was nearly as turbulent.

> I did on many occasions beat my wife, but I loved her. . . .
> I did and do have an awful temper, but my wife was awful
> stubborn, and we had some clashes over the more than
> twenty-five years of our life together. I have to admit it,
> because of my temper, I knocked her around.[4]

Charles J. Whitman during happier times with his family. Back row, L–R, his father, Charles A. Whitman, Jr.; Charles J. Whitman. Front row, L–R, his brother, John Michael; his mother, Margaret; and his other brother, Patrick. *UPI/Corbis-Bettmann.*

When discussing his relationships, C. A. Whitman had a propensity for mixing love and violence, often in the same sentence. He unashamedly pointed out that he used only paddles, his fists or a belt to discipline his sons, apparently believing that those restrictions were examples of his moderation.[5]

> With all three of my sons it was "yes, sir" and "no, sir." They minded me. The way I looked at it, I am not ashamed of any spankings. I don't think I spanked enough, if you want to know the truth about it. I think they should have been punished more than they were punished.[6]

In spite of his iron discipline, C. A. Whitman believed his sons were "spoiled rotten," and some Lake Worth neighbors agreed. He provided well for the material wants of his entire family, even his mother; he bought the house next door to his home for her. Later, C. A. provided each of the family members with new cars, and all of the boys had motorcycles. In return, however, he expected much. One Lake Worth neighbor characterized the elder Whitman as both "overly permissive" and "overly strict."[7]

Margaret Whitman also demanded strict discipline, although hers was a more gentle firmness. A devout Roman Catholic and a regular churchgoer, she insisted that her sons attend Mass with her. They attended Sacred Heart Catholic Church in Lake Worth, a rather small congregation that supported a grade school and Boy Scout Troop 119. One Lake Worth neighbor characterized Margaret as a "perfectly good mother." A Lake Worth police officer and family friend described her as one of the most gracious ladies he had ever known. Her eldest, Charlie, would become an altar boy, and win a five-dollar prize for "learning Latin the best." All of her children would attend Catholic parochial schools. She tried desperately to instill her deep religious devotion in her sons.

In June of 1947, the Whitman family moved into a comfortable home at 820 South L Street, eight blocks south of Lake Worth's business district. The neighborhood was distinctly middle class, and the Whitman home was one of the best in the area. Large awnings shielded the windows of the wood-framed house from Florida's radiant heat. The home's front yard had been expertly landscaped and dotted with tropical fruit trees. By the 1950s a swimming pool was installed in the backyard and an upstairs apartment rested above the large garage. By the 1960s the home was valued at $12,000–15,000. Every room was finely furnished. On almost every wall, along with the pictures, guns were displayed. C. A.'s admitted fanaticism for weapons provided his sons with the opportunity to become accustomed to instruments of hunting and aggression.[8]

Charles Joseph Whitman was born to eighteen-year-old Margaret in the Lake Worth office of Dr. Grady Brantley on 24 June 1941 after a full-term pregnancy and normal delivery. The Whitmans brought Charlie home to 2214 Ponce de Leon Street in West Palm Beach. The eldest Whitman son was a healthy boy who had the usual childhood diseases, suffering no long-term effects from any of them. Neighbors described him as "high-spirited" and fun, and never one to make trouble. While many neighbors found C. A. Whitman to be disagreeable, they nearly universally characterized Charlie, along with his brothers, as "good, normal boys." At ages three and four Charlie attended private kindergartens. In September of 1947, Margaret enrolled him in Sacred Heart's Catholic grade school, founded only three years earlier and staffed by the Sisters of Saint Joseph. Located next to the church, the barracks-like, two-story school resembled a small dorm or motel amid impeccably maintained and landscaped grounds.[9]

Shortly before entering grade school, Charlie began to take piano lessons, and by age twelve he excelled. Reportedly, C. A. placed a belt on the piano to guarantee Charlie's faithful and determined practice. The elder Whitman later denied the story, asserting that Charlie loved to play. Frank McCarty, a boyhood friend, did observe that Charlie loved to play the piano. For a time Charlie used his musical training to play in a teenage band run by Robert Vrooman; C. A. objected and made him quit.[10]

Even before Charlie began his musical training, he learned to handle guns. As soon as he could hold one, he did. One infamous photograph shows Charlie as a toddler holding two rifles—one a bolt action, the other a pump. In the photograph, taken at a beach with Charlie wearing a swimsuit that looks more like training pants, the rifles stand taller than Charlie. It must have struck other beachgoers as odd to witness a two-year-old playing in the sand with high-powered rifles. The Whitman boys received toy guns as gifts, followed shortly by real ones. C. A. boasted, "I'm a fanatic about guns. I raised my boys to know how to handle guns." In this, as in many other things, the elder Whitman insisted on excellence. He took pride in Charlie's prowess: "Charlie could plug a squirrel in the eye by the time he was sixteen." Given C. A.'s tutoring and the availability of so many firearms, Charlie was very proficient at a young age.[11]

C. A. Whitman had ambitions and wanted a better, more comfortable and accomplished life for his children than he had experienced. He may also have suffered from a need to relive his youth through his eldest son. Their experiences in the Boy Scouts of America provide a good example of the father's pressure on his son to excel. At age eight, Charlie joined the Cub Scouts where he attained the rank of Bear Scout. Two years later, the Lake Worth area experienced a shortage of Cub Scout leaders and Charlie was forced to drop out. In 1952, he attempted to join the Boy Scouts at age ten-and-a-half, but the minimum age for enrollment was eleven. He attended the meetings anyway and joined on or near his eleventh birthday. By that time he was prepared to earn a multitude of badges in a short time. According to Charlie himself, he reached the exalted rank of Eagle Scout and received national recognition for being the youngest Eagle Scout in the world at age twelve years and three months. The scout master, Father Joseph Gileus LeDuc, a close family friend, remembered that Charlie became an Eagle Scout so quickly because of constant pressure from his father. Harold Doerr, a Lake Worth scouting official, said, "This was a fine young man, a real Eagle Scout all the way." On the path to the rank of Eagle, Charlie and another scout named Michael Crook attended the 8 February 1954 meeting of the Lake Worth City Commission. The boys were dressed in full regalia when the Mayor of Lake Worth, James A. Stafford, asked them why they were there. Charlie and Michael stood at attention as they identified themselves and their troop numbers and responded that they were interested in learning about the operations of city government. A reporter covering the city beat was so impressed that he wrote, "They made a fine appearance and reminded the public just why this nation is great." Unfortunately, the two young, eager citizens could only have walked away confused; at the meeting it was revealed that Lake Worth had a zoning appeals board, but no zoning board.[12]

As a scout, Charlie earned twenty-one merit badges in fifteen months—an incredible accomplishment. He attended a National Boy Scout Jamboree in Santa Barbara, Florida, where he received the *Ad Altare Dei* Catholic Scout Award on 29 December 1953.[13] As a scout leader, the elder Whitman should have been extremely proud.

Sister Marie Loretta, a teacher at Sacred Heart School, described young Charles Whitman as "purposeful," a student who "seeks additional work," is "very capable" and "intelligent." His cumulative guidance record listed only one "B" in the first grade, and throughout the elementary grades (grades one to four) he consistently made the honor roll. On 5 December 1947 he was administered an IQ test and measured a 138.9, clearly a gifted student. During the middle school years (grades five to eight) he scored in the top five percent of students nationwide on standardized reading, language arts, and arithmetic.[14]

A preoccupation with making money started early for Charlie Whitman and remained constant throughout his life. He took responsibility for a very large, probably the largest, Lake Worth paper route for the *Miami Herald*. Customers noted that papers generally landed at or near doorsteps. During bad weather, the route became a Whitman family affair, and deliveries were made by automobile. Bob Everett, the *Herald*'s Lake Worth circulation manager, remembered Charlie as being very dependable, but not one to take criticism very well. He tended to personalize customer complaints and once asked Everett why his notes "sound so mean." A high school friend claimed, "He was always . . . busy working . . . and usually had some sort of job." By October of 1955 he had saved enough money to purchase a Harley-Davidson motorcycle for use on his route.[15]

On 1 September 1955, Charlie entered Saint Ann's High School. Founded in 1925 and located in West Palm Beach, the school was decidedly upscale. While not a campus leader or standout, he was modestly popular. At least one friend remembers that Charlie did not hang around with the most popular students and tried to draw attention to himself by exhibiting an eagerness to take dares: "They had a tower at Saint Ann's with some sort of a circus act. It was a real tower and someone bet him he wouldn't go up; we were in the tenth grade. He went all the way to the top."[16] He had normal friendships with many of the other boys and dated several girls, but had no steady relationships. Frank McCarty, a friend, stated, "He was completely normal. Just one of the guys." Sister Estelle, Saint Ann's principal, remembered Charlie as better behaved, and an overall better student than most others. She also recalled that he was popular. There appeared to be nothing peculiar about Charlie Whitman.[17] He pitched for the school baseball team and managed the football team. Ray Roy, a former classmate and later a football coach at Saint Ann's, recalled that Charlie enjoyed squirting players and bystanders with plastic bottles of water that were supposed to be reserved for thirsty players.[18]

Charlie's freshman and sophomore years were noticeably more successful than his junior and senior years. His standardized test scores were high and consistent throughout high school, but his grades dropped as he neared graduation. His grade point averages for the ninth and tenth grades were 3.30 and 3.46 (on a 4.0 scale) respectively; for the eleventh and twelfth grade they were 2.60 and 2.50. He had a mixed attendance record; perfect attendance during his sophomore year, but a total of twenty-six absences during his junior year, largely due to sixteen consecutive absences in February, 1958, when he underwent surgery to remove a blood clot on his left testicle. He graduated in 1959 with a cumulative GPA of 3.30, ranking seventh in a class of seventy-two, still a notable accomplishment in a small private school consisting of students from educated and wealthy households. But clearly, had Charlie been diligent through his junior and senior years he could have done even better.[19]

One evening, very near his eighteenth birthday, like many new high school graduates, Charlie went out with a number of friends and became very drunk. When he returned home, his father reportedly lost all control of his temper. In a conversation with Father LeDuc, Charlie alleged that the elder Whitman had administered a severe punishment and had thrown Charlie into the swimming pool, where he nearly drowned.[20] In spite of his intoxication, Charlie remembered the incident with bitterness. Whatever happened, Charlie finally had enough. Although it was widely reported that he had been accepted as an undergraduate student at Georgia Tech, he never associated himself in any way with the university. Instead, in an attempt to rid himself of his father's financial control and dominance, he applied for enlistment in the United States Marines on 27 June 1959, only three days after his eighteenth birthday. His mother Margaret, who undoubtedly witnessed the swimming pool incident, was the only person he told. She did not stand in his way. Charlie caught a bus to Jacksonville, Florida, and officially entered the marines on 6 July 1959 at the age of eighteen years and two weeks.[21]

Charlie Whitman had a very troubled childhood. While provided for in the material sense, he had little in the way of an emotional support system. In all significant pursuits, even as a very little boy, his father, himself the product of a broken and dysfunctional family (or arguably no family), sought relentlessly to instill a sense of excellence and near-perfection in his eldest. Charlie was never taught to handle failure; it simply was not an option. Few of his accomplishments were a consequence of intrinsic motivation. Success usually resulted from constant supervision, along with a desire to please, or avoid the wrath of, his overbearing father. His mother either did little to curb excessive expectations, or was powerless to do anything. For Charlie, mastery of one task simply meant that another awaited. Even after he had become a talented pianist, one of the youngest Eagle Scouts in the world, handled the largest paper route in Lake Worth, and could "plug the eye out of a squirrel" with a firearm, his father believed him to be spoiled and deserving of more punishment. Charlie escaped his father by joining the armed services. One problem remained, however—the United States Marines awaited the arrival of Charles Joseph Whitman.[22]

II

What Thomas Jefferson wanted for all of America—an agrarian culture, economy, and spirit—could be found in the little town of Needville, Texas, located thirty-five miles south of Houston. An historical marker gives a nearly-complete history while providing keen insights into what items are important to its citizens: God, work, and school. Needville's founder, August Schendel, opened a general store in 1892 and followed up with a blacksmith shop and cotton gin. By 1894, Needville officially became a village with the opening of a post office. The first church service had been conducted in 1891 and a school was opened in 1897. The village would become a trade center for widely scattered farmers and ranchers and the economy soon centered on their pursuits.[23] The boom of the petro-chemical industry of Texas engulfed Needville as well; its major sources of income changed during the 1920s, but agrarian values survived, evidenced by a Harvest Festival every third Saturday in October and an Annual Youth Fair and Rodeo in the spring.

When entering Needville, visitors in the 1950s and 1960s were greeted by a sign: "Needville Welcomes You" and just below those words, the town is described as "The Home of Friendly People." Another billboard described Needville as the home of the "Blue Jays" and listed state champs, finalists, and playoff teams. Eight public service, religious and business organizations sponsored the sign at a time when Needville's population was less than 1,000. There were many large churches of different denominations for a village that small. Needville held evidence of "traditional" family values: few wives worked outside of their homes and in print few were referred to by their own names. Instead, married women were "Mrs. John Doe." At the edge of the hamlet, another sign reminded visitors that they were leaving the home of friendly people—"Needville Thanks You."

Raymond W. Leissner was a well-known rice farmer and realtor who served the community as a member of many civic groups. He was once the president of the chamber of commerce. The Leissners were prominent members of the Needville Methodist Church, a congregation tracing its roots to the founding of Needville. Mrs. Leissner taught English in the local elementary school.

Kathleen Frances, the Leissner's eldest child and only daughter, was born on 12 July 1943. At that time the Leissner family lived in Freeport, but everyone in Needville knew of Kathy's arrival. "Mr. and Mrs. Raymond Leissner of Freeport are the proud parents of a baby girl. The little Miss is the granddaughter of Mr. and Mrs. H. A. Leissner [of Needville]," reported the *Rosenberg Herald-Coaster*.[24] Kathy grew to be pretty, vivacious, talented, and neat. Her activities in elementary and high school were typical: she liked volleyball, worked on the school newspaper and annual staff, and was a baton twirler and saxophone player for the band. Like most other girls of the era, she was a member of the Future Homemakers of America, wherein she learned skills to prepare her for domestic life. She was crowned queen of the 1960 Needville Youth Fair. But she was also driven to further her education and become a working professional. She liked science and usually read what friends called "big, thick volumes."[25]

Surrounded by good people who cared for one another, Kathy had a happy childhood. She was one of the original class members at Needville Elementary School in 1949's first grade. Her Needville High School classmates were supportive, more like brothers and sisters. The "village raised the children." Indeed, Needville *was* "the home of friendly people," and what neighbors did not know about each other could be learned in Lillian Brown's "News From Needville" column in the *Rosenberg Herald-Coaster*. One typical announcement involved Kathy: "Miss Kathy Leissner returned home Sunday from Huntsville where she visited with relatives this past week."[26] Needville was not a very good place to keep a secret.

Many of the town's social events centered around its public schools. On 18 May 1961 the Needville Methodist Women's Society of Christian Service honored Kathy and six other Methodist high school graduates with a breakfast at Volger's Restaurant. On 23 May 1961 the Blue Jay Twirlers were honored at the home of Mr. and Mrs. G. R. Wruck. Kathy and the other twirlers were treated to a buffet supper and mini batons were given "from those who would take their place."[27] On 29 May 1961, she graduated from Needville High School with fifty-three other classmates. By that time she had decided to major in science in the College of Education at the University of Texas at Austin. She had been inspired to teach.

The high schools of the Rosenberg-Needville area had a long tradition of publishing "Wills and Prophesies" of each year's senior classes in the local newspaper. References to Kathy stated:

> Continuing down the street, we observe Kathy Leissner trying in vain to purchase an automobile from a pair of crooked car dealers who go by the name of "Chiseling Lillie" and "Malicious Maggie."

> Kathy Leissner wills her ability to stick her foot in her mouth to Bettye Vaughn.[28]

Kathy Leissner was well prepared to enter the University of Texas, and would complete her degree program on time. She lived in a dorm and had an active social life. An attractive young woman, she measured five feet four inches tall, and while her weight fluctuated slightly, it hovered near 120 pounds. In February 1962, Francis Schuck, Jr., introduced her to his friend, a young, handsome marine named Charlie Whitman, who was mesmerized by her: "Her eyes are like twinkling stars, they are what fascinated me on our first meeting. . . . I can honestly say that she is the *most* versatile woman I have ever known." It was his first serious relationship, and he went to great lengths to get and keep her attention.[29]

Charlie occupied Room 706 in Goodall-Wooten Dorm, nicknamed "Goody Woo." Widely regarded as a party dorm and located in the heart of the "Drag" near the corner of Guadalupe and 21st Street, the private dorm provided ready access to the campus. Experienced pedestrians strolling the Drag always looked up before walking beneath the balconies of Goody Woo. Inexperienced pedestrians were *lucky* to be pelted with only water. Housing officials probably thought that in Charlie Whitman, marine on scholarship, they had a well-adjusted, mature young man who would make an ideal tenant and good floor counselor. They were wrong. On one occasion he telephoned Kathy at her dorm two blocks away and told her to go to the window of her room. Immediately he ran out to his seventh-floor balcony and, hanging by one arm, dangled over the side. He then waved to her with his free arm.[30]

Kathy and Charlie had a brief and intense courtship. On 19 July 1962 her parents published the announcement of her engagement in the *Rosenberg Herald-Coaster*. The young couple chose 17 August 1962 as their wedding day. Charlie's younger brother Patrick served as best man, and the entire Whitman family made the trip to Texas.

> Given in marriage by her father, the bride wore an original gown of white peau de soie and imported lace. The fitted bodice was fashioned with bateau neckline formed by scuppoped [sic] alencon lace and butterfly sleeves. The back of the bell-shaped skirt was highlighted with self roses. Multiple tiers of tulle formed the short bridal veil which was held in place by a lace cabbage rose. She carried white carnations and English Ivy surrounding a purple-throated orchid.[31]

They were married in Saint Michael's Catholic Church, a fairly large church for a predominately Protestant hamlet. Father Gileus LeDuc, a parish priest permanently assigned to the Houston area, performed the ceremony. Years earlier, in June of 1955, Charlie had served as an altar boy for Father LeDuc's very first Mass as a priest. Of course, Needville's sense of community was evident. Leissner family friends generally approved of and were impressed with Charlie. "[A] real nice boy. I understand he was what you call a brain," said a neighbor. Raymond Leissner seemed proud of the union. "He was just as normal as anyone I ever knew, and he worked awfully hard at his grades."[32] In reality, Charlie did not balance dating, marriage, and study very well. His grades were not good, and very soon he would lose the scholarship that had brought him to Austin.

The wedding of Kathy Leissner and Charlie Whitman and the reception that followed at the Leissner home should have been the beginning of a storybook marriage. The Whitman family traveled from Lake Worth to Needville for the union between a "real fine girl" and a "handsome young man." They were both intelligent and

Newlywed Charles J. Whitman is all smiles as he leaves St. Michael's Catholic Church in Needville, Texas, with his bride, Kathleen, after their marriage August 17, 1962. *UPI/Corbis-Bettmann.*

hard-working. She emerged from small-town America surrounded by the love of her family and friends. He was once America's youngest Eagle Scout, a talented musician, and now a marine. They both came from devout religious households, and at ages nineteen and twenty-one, they were both young and beautiful. They drove away from Needville on the evening of 17 August 1962, heading for a honeymoon in New Orleans and continuing to Lake Worth to visit family and friends; it should have been the start of a union that would last happily for decades.

---

[1] *Lake Worth Herald,* 26 May 1955.

[2] FBI Files: A Summary Report provided to the Austin Police Department and the Texas Department of Public Safety by Special Agent J. Myers Cole (hereafter cited as "FBI Files: *Cole Report,*" followed by date and page number). FBI Files: Statement by Father Gileus LeDuc, p. 2, (hereafter cited as "FBI Files: LeDuc Statement," and page number). Most of the FBI citations are part of the Texas Department of Public Safety Case File on Charles Whitman. Other FBI citations were made available to me by Daniel Barrera. C. A. Whitman, in a conversation with the author on

26 January 1995 (hereafter cited by name only). Editors of Time-Life Books, *True Crime: Mass Murders* (Alexandria, VA: Time-Life Books, 1992), p. 40 (hereafter cited as "Time-Life").

[3] Austin Police Department Files: *Autobiography of Charles Joseph Whitman*, 1 March 1956. (The Austin Police Department Files are hereafter cited as "APD Files" followed by a specific document citation. This particular document is hereafter cited as *"Autobiography."*) FBI Files: *Cole Report*, 17 August 1966, pp. 21–22; *Newsweek*, 15 August 1966; *Report to the Governor—Medical Aspects—Charles J. Whitman Catastrophe*, 8 September 1966 (hereafter cited as "Connally Report").

[4] Connally Report, p. 2; C. A. Whitman quoted in Time-Life, p. 40.

[5] American Justice Series, Arts and Entertainment Network. *Mass Murder: An American Tragedy*, broadcast 29 December 1993 (hereafter cited as "AJS"); C. A. Whitman.

[6] C. A. Whitman quoted in Time-Life, p. 42 and *Newsweek*, 15 August 1966.

[7] C. A. Whitman; *Palm Beach Post*, 3 August 1966; FBI Files: *Cole Report*, 17 August 1966, pp. 10–11.

[8] APD Files: *Autobiography*, 1 March 1956; FBI Files: *Cole Report*, 17 August 1966, pp. 3–5, 12, LeDuc Statement, pp. 2–6; *Austin American-Statesman*, 2 and 7 August 1966; Time-Life, p. 40.

[9] APD Files: *Autobiography*, 1 March 1956; Palm Beach County Health Department, *Certificate of Birth*, Charles Joseph Whitman, 24 June 1941; FBI Files: *Cole Report*, 17 August 1966, p. 22; Connally Report, p. 1.

[10] APD Files: *Autobiography*, 1 March 1956; Connally Report, p. 2; FBI Files: *Cole Report*, 17 August 1966, pp. 7–8, 28.

[11] This picture is in *Life*, 12 August 1966; C. A. Whitman quoted in *Time*, 12 August 1966; FBI Files: LeDuc Statement, p. 4; *Austin American-Statesman*, 2 August 1966.

[12] FBI Files: LeDuc Statement, pp. 2–3; *Lake Worth Herald*, 11 February 1954; Harold Doerr quoted in 4 August 1966; APD Files: *Autobiography*, 1 March 1956 and *Statement of Francis J. Schuck, Jr.*, 13 September 1966.

[13] APD Files: *Autobiography*, 1 March 1956; Time-Life, p. 40; *Lake Worth Herald*, 28 April 1955; *Austin American-Statesman*, 2 August 1966; Connally Report, p. 2; AJS.

[14] APD Files: *Florida Cumulative Guidance Record of Charles J. Whitman*, Sacred Heart School, Lake Worth, Florida.

[15] APD Files: *Autobiography*, 1 March 1956; FBI Files: *Cole Report*, 17 August 1966, p. 3; *Austin American-Statesman*, 2 August 1966; *Newsweek*, 15 August 1966.

[16] Ray Roy quoted in *Palm Beach Post*, 2 August 1966.

[17] Frank McCarty quoted in *Austin American-Statesman*, 2 August 1966; FBI Files: *Cole Report*, 9 August 1966, p. 2, and 17 August 1966, p. 2.

[18] *Palm Beach Post*, 2 August 1966.

[19] APD Files: *Florida Cumulative Guidance Record of Charles J. Whitman*, Saint Ann's High School, West Palm Beach, Florida. The GPAs cited were not part of the official record, but were computed by the author.

[20] FBI Files: LeDuc Statement, p. 4.

[21] FBI Files: *Cole Report*, 5 and 17 August 1966, p. 16, and Leduc Statement, p. 4; *Palm Beach Post*, 3 August 1966; *Austin American-Statesman*, 7 August 1966.

[22] *Palm Beach Post*, 3 August 1966.

[23] Historical marker, "Town of Needville."

[24] *Rosenberg Herald-Coaster*, 22 July 1943.

[25] Ibid., 7 February 1960; *Austin American-Statesman,* 7 August 1966.

[26] *Rosenberg Herald-Coaster,* 21 July 1960.

[27] Ibid., 25 May 1961.

[28] Ibid., 28 May 1961.

[29] *Austin American-Statesman,* 2 August 1966; *Newsweek,* 15 August 1966; APD Files: *Statement of Francis J. Schuck, Jr.,* 13 September 1966 and *The Daily Record of C. J. Whitman,* entry of 23 February 1964.

[30] Connally Report, p. 2; *Texas Observer,* 19 August 1966; *Life,* 12 August 1966.

[31] *Rosenberg Herald-Coaster,* 19 July and 19 August 1962.

[32] FBI Files: LeDuc Statement, pp. 3–5; unidentified Needville neighbor and Raymond W. Leissner quoted in *Austin American-Statesman,* 2 August 1966.

2

The Soldier
and the
Teacher

I

After basic training, Charlie was stationed at what was then one of the most troubled spots in the world—Guantanamo Naval Base, Cuba—beginning on 9 December 1959. At least one of his marine buddies believed that, above and beyond being in the marines, being at Guantanamo Bay placed a strain on Charlie.[1] Most likely, Charlie's desperation to free himself from his father's support and control made everything else secondary—even Cuba's drift toward Communism. Yet he had entered another life of regimentation; he would still have to take orders. He may have been drawn to another form of strict authority after becoming conditioned to taking orders. More likely, a hitch in the marines resulted from an attempt at a dramatic, irrefutable rite of passage into adulthood. No one, not even C. A. Whitman, could seriously argue that a United States Marine was anything less than a man. For Charlie Whitman, taking orders probably seemed like a small price to pay.

At eighteen, he looked more like a toy soldier than a real one. He stood nearly six feet tall and was not overly muscular, but rather thin and boyish. His long, narrow face and his large smile caused his eyes to squint, and his blond crew-cut accentuated his youthful features. At first, his uniform and his gear looked oversized, but marine life would fill him out considerably. Charlie shortly reached his adult height of six feet, and his weight hovered around 198 pounds. He had been branded with an unsolicited nickname—"Whit." As a young marine he was easy-going and prone to horseplay. During this first twenty-six-month period of active duty, Charlie underwent numerous routine physical examinations and each found him to be fit.[2]

Throughout his marine career, Charlie attended numerous classes ranging from sanitation to history. He kept precise notes on military protocol, law and justice. Not surprisingly, much of his notetaking involved offensive and defensive combat. On 8 October 1959 he noted:

> Individual movements while under enemy fire:
>   1) Rushing
>   2) Creeping
>   3) Crawling
> Four phases of offensive combat:
>   1) Movement to contact
>   2) Attack
>   3) Consolidation
>   4) Exploration
> Camouflage and concealment
>   Kinds
>   1) Natural
>   2) Artificial

Ways to Camof. [camouflage]
  1) Hide
  2) Blend
  3) Deceive[3]

Fairly early in his marine career, Charlie established himself as very proficient with a gun. He took copious notes on the care and techniques of firing a 30-caliber M-1 Carbine. At the end of the detailed notes he scribbled in large letters "World's Finest!!!" On the firing range he scored 215 out of a possible 250 points and earned a "sharp shooter" rating.[4] His Marine Corps Score Book documents high scores on "rapid" fire from long ranges. Remembered as "an excellent shot [who] appeared to be more accurate against moving targets during target practice sessions," he was also described as "the kind of guy you would want around if you went into combat."[5] Similar sentiments were echoed by Larry Phillips, who maintained that "Whit" was well-liked and would do anything for others in his squad. Once, Phillips and Charlie were involved in a serious jeep accident. Although it is not clear who was the driver, it would have been consistent with Charlie's history and personality to disregard dangers associated with the reckless operation of a vehicle. Regardless of who was driving, the vehicle rolled twenty-five feet down an embankment and pinned Phillips. Although stunned, Charlie is reputed to have single-handedly lifted the jeep, allowing Phillips to be freed. Charlie then fainted and remained unconscious for several hours. Charlie's readiness to take dares and his impatience with traffic laws and speed limits resulted in a number of traffic accidents and citations throughout his adult life as well. From 4 September 1957 to 17 November 1959 he received five traffic tickets for violations ranging from accidents to double parking.[6]

Charlie's service in the marines can best be understood in three phases. The first includes his basic training, infantry training, and subsequent service at Guantanamo Bay. The second consists of his non-active sojourn at the University of Texas at Austin. The third would be his return to active duty at Camp Lejeune, North Carolina, where he rejoined his outfit.

His first active duty hitch can only be described as successful. He evolved from a toy soldier to a marine sharpshooter. As in his relationship with his father, Charlie approached his orders dutifully. He earned a Good Conduct Medal, a Sharpshooter's Badge, and the Marine Corps Expeditionary Medal for his service in Cuba. Years later the Executive Officer of the 2nd Marine Division, Captain Joseph Stanton, would state, "He was a good marine. I was impressed with him. I was certain he'd make a good citizen." Charlie carried a card with these typed words:

YESTERDAY IS NOT MINE TO RECOVER, BUT TO-MORROW IS MINE TO LOSE. I AM RESOLVED THAT I SHALL WIN THE TOMORROWS BEFORE ME!!![7]

He tried desperately to live by the creed; numerous handwritten and typed copies of the quote were found throughout his personal effects.

While at Guantanamo Bay, Charlie learned of a scholarship program designed to increase the number of scientists in the United States Military. The Naval Enlisted Science Education Program (NESEP), begun after the Soviets successfully launched Sputnik I, was intended to train engineers who would later become commissioned officers. Charlie applied for a scholarship on 2 February 1961 and like all other scholarship candidates, took a competitive exam. He scored high enough to go before a selection committee who recommended him for a NESEP scholarship, which he eventually received. Marine Colonel M. H. LaGrone would later describe recipients of this prestigious scholarship: "Only the best are picked and located at various colleges."[8] Charlie was expected to earn an engineering degree, follow up with ten months of Officers' Candidate School, and then become a commissioned officer.

The marines sent Charlie to a preparatory school from 5 June to 31 July 1961 in Bainbridge, Maryland, for enrichment courses in math and physics. There he met and formed a lasting friendship with Francis Schuck, Jr., a fellow NESEP scholar. Schuck was a native Texan who helped Charlie with his trigonometry and algebra coursework. Upon arriving in Austin for the 1961 fall semester, they both reported to the Navy ROTC office. Afterwards, Charlie enrolled in the university with a major in mechanical engineering and was officially admitted on 15 September 1961.

NESEP scholars were generously rewarded. A civilian allowance supplemented their regular pay. According to a credit file cited in an FBI report, Charlie received $250 a month from the marines. Reportedly, C. A. Whitman chipped in an additional $140 a month. Tuition, books, and other campus fees also were paid.

During this time Charlie moved into Goodall-Wooten men's dorm. Francis Schuck, Jr., suggested to dorm officials that Charlie would make a good counselor. Schuck and Charlie were interviewed by the dean of men and the owner of the dorm and were offered jobs, which meant free boarding, and hence, extra money. Charlie had plenty of resources to live very well as a college student.[9]

What residence hall officials did not know was that Charlie was entering a second phase of his marine career. For the first time in his life, he would experience real freedom. He did not handle it very well. The first time Charlie ever exercised any significant control over his daily affairs should have been a cause for elation. But less than three months after his emancipation, he nearly got himself thrown into jail. He, Schuck, and another student named Jim Merritt ventured out into the Hill Country west of Austin, and in an area near the Lyndon B. Johnson Ranch, poached a deer by "jacklighting" it. A Hill Country resident observed the dead catch protruding from the trunk of Charlie's car, noted the license number and reported the incident to the Texas Game and Fish Commission. The game warden assigned to the case, Grover Simpson, with three policemen, followed a trail of deer blood from the entrance of the dorm to Charlie's room, where they caught Charlie and his cohorts skinning the catch in a shower. Charlie claimed to have wanted to send his father a supply of deer meat for Thanksgiving. Surprisingly, Simpson found in Charlie a cooperative and even likeable suspect, a "darn nice fellow."

Perhaps because he was new to Texas, a student, one of "our boys in uniform," or maybe because he could be charming, the incident was dropped after Charlie agreed to pay a $100 fine. Or maybe authorities found the spectacle of butchering a deer in a shower in a dorm inhabited by hundreds of college boys to be laughable. Regardless, he had been caught poaching in Texas, and he should have considered himself extremely fortunate at Travis County Court on 20 November 1961 when, as part of Case #69869, he was allowed to plead guilty, pay his fine plus court costs in the amount of $29.50, and go back to the dorm. Eight days later, however, he foolishly entered a motion for a new trial; the judge overruled him.[10]

The Charlie that Francis Schuck observed had good relations with his family. He kept a steady and faithful correspondence with them all and spoke of earning a degree in mechanical engineering so as to return to Florida and join C. A. in his business. He shared a love of guns and hunting with his father and looked forward to hunting trips they made together.[11] Charlie appeared to be a responsible student. "He seemed more mature than most students, and [was] very, very serious," stated Professor Leonardt Kreisle, Charlie's academic advisor. Schuck remembered him as well-mannered, good looking, well-dressed, and personable. But he had a distracting habit of biting his fingernails, which subtracted from his otherwise impeccable appearance.[12]

Today it is evident that Charlie had become a consummate actor. He could be a serious student, a contrite poacher, a daredevil, or a model marine. He considered himself a polished bluffer and a better-than-average gambler. In Charlie's circle of acquaintances, the stakes could get high, especially for college students with limited resources. Charlie and his friends often drove considerable distances to play poker. During one all-night poker game in San Antonio in March of 1962, a fellow dorm resident named Robert Ross bet $190 on a hand; Charlie called and lost. He had lost a total of $400 that night. The Texas State Bank check he wrote to settle the debt bounced. When Ross approached him with the bounced check, Charlie was lying on his dorm room bunk throwing a huge hunting knife into a closet door. "Look, kid, my family is loaded. I'll get you your money. Don't worry about it," he said.[13] Ross, considerably smaller than Whitman, would later decide the debt unworthy of pursuit. It would never be paid. The episode revealed Charlie to be obsessed with making quick money, to think nothing of dismissing a debt, to be able to revert to a dependence on his "loaded" family (i.e., C. A. Whitman), and to have little conscience when it came to intimidating the smaller and weaker.

Equally revealing was the manner in which Charlie dealt with characters who could intimidate *him*. After another night of gambling he owed a debt of $200, this time to two ex-con brothers well known in Austin circles as a very tough pair. Again he paid part of his debt by check but before it could be cashed Charlie put a stop on it; he claimed he had been cheated. Less than a day later, the men were at his dorm room threatening him with a knife. Charlie had been frightened enough to seek the advice of his former roommate, John Drolla, a first-year law student, who suggested going to the district attorney's office to report the matter. There Charlie swore out a "peace bond" against the ex-cons. He also wore a 357 magnum in a holster under his coat until he learned that his predators were incarcerated in the Dallas area for auto theft. Schuck later remembered: "It didn't take long after this incident and the urging of myself and Kathy, whom he was now dating steadily along with another girl . . . to stifle Charlie's interest in card playing.[14]

Not all instances of Charlie's immaturity were so sinister, though some could be cruel. David Pratt, a dorm resident, related that after a night of drinking, Charlie decided to try to get Nikita Khruschev on the phone in order to tell the Soviet General Secretary that he did not like him. He then engaged in a ridiculous exchange with a telephone operator.[15] On another occasion, Charlie and a friend named Jim were involved in an automobile accident. Charlie, bloodied, dirtied, and wet, returned to the dorm at about 5:00 A.M. Other dormmates had been playing poker when he arrived to announce that Jim had been "killed."

> Everyone was speechless. We called Jim's girlfriend on campus even though it was before dawn. Then we sat shaking our heads in disbelief. Suddenly Jim appeared around the corner of the door and said, "The ghost walks!" Charlie lay on the floor and couldn't move, he was so convulsed with laughter.[16]

Lost in their foolishness was the unnecessary grief that Jim's young girlfriend must have experienced. Charlie thought that was funny.

After a number of cruel jokes, gambling, instances with firearms, and butchering a deer in a shower, dorm residents concluded that there was little that Charlie could do anymore to surprise anyone. Consequently, Francis Schuck, Jr., while seated on the balcony of Charlie's dorm room, thought nothing of a remark Charlie was to make about the university's landmark Tower. "A person could stand off an army from atop of it before they got to him." The remark was followed by a description of how he would like to go to the observation deck and shoot people. As they gazed at the Tower, it never occurred to Schuck that Charlie could be serious.[17] Most of his acquaintances would conclude that Charlie thought that kind of remark was funny.

II

Kathy Leissner led a much less eventful dorm life. All indications were that she became a model student. She did spend enough time with Charlie Whitman, however, to witness a number of events that could have had serious consequences. One incident involved Charlie, Kathy, and three others in a car heading for a firing range west of Austin where Charlie wanted to try out a pistol he had just purchased. At the intersection of 21st and Red River Streets in Austin, he directed some pejorative remarks at a black man who appeared to be intoxicated. Then he pointed the pistol at the pedestrian about twenty feet away. John Daigle, a friend seated in the back seat with Charlie and Kathy, recalled that the pedestrian, rather than being intimidated, reached into his sweater as if to retrieve his own weapon. Kathy and the occupants ducked as the car sped away. Daigle and the others complained to Charlie that it was a stupid thing to do. Charlie thought that it was funny.[18]

Unlike Charlie, Kathy focused on her goals and remained studious, especially after Charlie was forced to leave Austin to return to active duty with the marines. Her degree program required her to complete courses on the university campus and then move on to an elementary or high school for a semester of student teaching under the careful watch of an experienced supervising teacher. Kathy was assigned to student teach at Sidney Lanier High School in north Austin where she completed her certification for teaching science in secondary schools in Texas.

Although she was very young—only three or four years older than the students of Lanier's senior class of 1965—Kathy's colleagues and administrators found her to be very mature and professional. As a student teacher Kathy became successful and popular with stu-

Kathy Whitman. She had a full smile which created a small dimple on her right cheek. Her hairdo betrayed her youth; unlike that of any of the other faculty women, her short blonde flip resembled the style worn by many of the senior girls. *Texas Department of Public Safety Files.*

dents, so much so that she accepted a position as a full-time faculty member for the next school year. She became close friends with several of the faculty members, like Eva Bayne, a typing teacher, and Mayda Tupper, the speech and drama teacher.[19]

Kathy taught biology to sophomores, and her success and popularity with students as a student teacher carried over to her professional tenure.[20] Consistent with tradition, as a first-year teacher she was not assigned the sponsorship of any clubs, but she worked diligently to establish herself as a professional. The *1966 Viking*, the Lanier annual, had only one picture of her; it was, of course, in the faculty section. She was very feminine and had a full smile which created a small dimple on her right cheek. Her hairdo betrayed her youth; unlike that of any of the other faculty women, her short blonde flip resembled the style worn by many of the senior girls.

III

One of Charlie's college English teachers, Roger C. Williams, described him as having "all the standard appellations of a high school yearbook. He was easily the 'Best Looking,' 'Friendliest,' and 'Most Mature.'"[21] In reality, during his first semester at the University of Texas at Austin, Charlie fell into academic trouble. With the exception of an "A" in algebra, he earned dismal grades. He failed general chemistry, made a "D" in an introductory economics course, and a "C" in three other courses. The good grade in algebra probably resulted from the refresher courses he had taken in Bainbridge, Maryland, during the first and most conscientious phase of his marine career. Clearly, during this second phase as a UT-Austin student, he studied little or not at all.

Charlie did not seem to appreciate the heavy investment the United States Marine Corps was making in him or the fact that the Corps expected him to become a commissioned officer. He was not under constant supervision and seldom took orders. He demonstrated no intrinsic motivation to succeed. He did not fit the NESEP profile of the brightest and the best, nor did he demonstrate conduct becoming of a potential officer. Charlie's grades did improve slightly and his tempestuous conduct tempered after his marriage to Kathy, but the marines did not consider his performance acceptable. During the 1963 spring semester, after a year and a half in Austin, he had his scholarship withdrawn by the marines. He responded by unceremoniously dropping out of the university on 12 February 1963 and returning to active duty by rejoining the 2nd Marine Division at Camp Lejeune, North Carolina.[22] He re-entered a life of regimentation and taking orders, but this time he would not find comfort. Rather than volunteering in order to leave behind someone he hated, this time he left behind someone he loved. Kathy remained in Austin to complete her degree program.

On 17 March 1966 Charlie attempted to recapture his NESEP scholarship, but the marines summarily dismissed his request. He became embittered and formed a hatred for the marines, especially after he was informed that his time spent in Austin would not count as part of his active duty enlistment. The return to active duty was quickly implemented, and in July Charlie was promoted to the rank of Lance Corporal.[23] The promotion was likely based on an excellent record at Guantanamo Bay, Cuba, and the fact that he was once a NESEP scholar.

The marines would soon conclude that the advancement was premature. In this third phase of Charlie's marine career, he became a troublemaker. His immaturity resurfaced. This phase, however, included fighting. On 7 October 1964 he and a friend named Edward Smith were "jumped" by four or five other marines. Charlie had been thrown to the ground and kicked about the head and face. His injuries required treatment for headaches and dizziness and he was taken to the camp dispensary and at 1:50 A.M. was given aspirin. He still considered himself a premier gambler, and his fascination with firearms could not be satisfied by government-issued guns. By late 1963, he got himself into serious trouble with the marines. He faced court martial on 26 November 1963 for gambling, usury, and the unauthorized possession of a non-military pistol. Charlie found a marine court martial far more difficult to deal with than a domineering father, a Texas game warden, or a helpless poker player in an Austin dorm. Testimony established he had threatened to "kick the teeth" out of another marine for failure to pay a thirty-dollar debt for which he demanded fifteen dollars of interest. On 27 November 1963 the guilty verdict on all counts resulted in a sentence of thirty days of confinement and ninety days of hard labor. Additionally, his rank reverted to private.[24]

While awaiting court martial Charlie began to transform his notebooks into a crude diary which began, "This book belongs to CPL. Charles J. Whitman." He would later scratch out CPL and write PVT. He clearly worried more about how Kathy would react to his being in the brig than any punishment the marines had in store for him:

> 7 Nov 63—Was made a "min" prisoner in Dorm #5 today, also received 3 letters. . . . I haven't heard from Kathy since she found out where I am. I am sure anxious to see how she feels and what she has to say. I hope she is "keeping her chin up."
>
> 8 Nov 63—Went on first wking [sic] party today. Received my watch and a letter from Kathy, she seems pretty disgusted with me. I wish I could talk with her.

"She seems pretty disgusted with me" was the first instance on record that Kathy ever got angry or grew weary with Charlie.

> 9 Nov 63—Received a call from home today. I am in very high spirits, I am glad that Kathy is only worried about my gambling, I will never gamble at anything again. I hope Kathy will believe and trust in this declaration.

Charlie apparently meant it; from that moment on there are no recorded episodes of serious gambling in his life.

> 10 Nov 63—Received a call from Kathy at 1510 [3:10 P.M.], it was fabulous, she sounds wonderful. I love her so much she sounded so pitiful when she cried that we were allowed to talk more than 3 minutes. It is so good to know that she loves and understands me. I will love her until the day I die. She is definitely the best thing I have in life, or as I say, "My Most Precious Possession."[25]

He now hated the marines and was desperate to get out. There was some confusion concerning his failure as a NESEP scholar and whether it meant that he was bound to the marines for five years after his return to Camp Lejeune. Significantly, Charlie turned to his father, C. A. Whitman, for help. Charlie's notes make it clear that the elder Whitman sought the intercession of Florida's Senator Spessard Holland, Congressman Paul Rogers and the Secretary of the Navy for an early discharge for his troubled son. In his notes from this time period, he referred to C. A. as "Daddy"; there are no denigrating references to his father. At that time one of Charlie's close friends, Edward Smith, knowing of the father and son's joint efforts to get Charlie out of the marines, assumed they were friendly.[26]

Writing in his notebook gave him comfort, and he would turn to writing as a source of solace for the rest of his life. He could write about deep, heavy topics: "I have thoughts [sic] very much about the concept of 'death.' When it overtakes me someday I must remember to observe closely and see if it is as I thought it would be."[27] Or, he could descend into the absurd: "Unless it is definitely advan-

SHE FEELS AND WHAT SHE HAS TO SAY. I HOPE SHE IS "KEEPING HER CHIN UP"

8 Nov '63 — WENT ON FIRST WORKING PARTY TODAY, RECEIVED MY WATCH AND A LETTER FROM KATHY, SHE SEEMS VERY DISGUSTED WITH ME. I WISH I COULD TALK WITH HER

9 Nov '63 — RECEIVED A CALL FROM HOME TODAY, I AM IN VERY HIGH SPIRITS, I AM GLAD THAT KATHY IS ONLY WORRIED ABOUT MY GAMBLING, I WILL NEVER GAMBLE AT ANYTHING AGAIN, I HOPE KATHY WILL BELIEVE AND TRUST IN THIS DECLARATION, HAD THE MARINE CORP BIRTHDAY

DINNER, IT WAS VERY GOOD AS M.C. CHOW GOES.

10 Nov '63 — RECEIVED A CALL FROM KATHY AT 1510, IT WAS FABULOUS, SHE SOUNDS WONDER- FUL, I LOVE HER SO MUCH WHEN SHE CRIED SHE SOUNDED SO "PITIFUL" THAT WE WERE ALLOWED TO TALK MORE THAN 3 MINUTES, IT IS SO GOOD TO KNOW THAT SHE LOVES AND UNDERSTANDS ME. I WILL LOVE HER UNTIL THE DAY I DIE, SHE IS DEFINIT- ELY THE BEST THING I HAVE IN LIFE, OR AS I SAY, "MY MOST PRECIOUS POSSESSION"

11 Nov '63 — THE DAY IS BEAUT- IFUL, THE SUN IS RADIANT AND WARM, BUT THE AIR HAS A CRISPNESS TO IT, I WONDER WHAT MY BEAUTIFUL WIFE IS DOING AT THIS TIME? I AM SO IN LOVE WITH HER, I THINK INTO THE FUTURE TRYING TO PICTURE OUR CHILD, HOW WONDERFUL IT WILL BE TO SEE KATHY FULL OF LIFE WITH OUR BABY, WHEN WILL THAT DAY COME? I SIT WRITING THIS WHISTLING "A TASTE OF HONEY" AND I WONDER IF I WILL EVER TASTE THE "SWEET HONEY" OF SUCCESS FOR MYSELF AND MY

LOVED ONES ———— AS I LOOK BACK OVER MY PAST FEW ADULT YEARS THEY SEEM SO WASTED, WILL I EVER ACCOMPLISH ANYTHING I SET FORTH TO DO? OH! BUT TO KNOW THE ANSWER TO THIS QUESTION — I NEVER REALIZED UP TILL NOW, THE PLEASURE OF TALKING TO ONES SELF IN A DIARY, I BELIEVE I WILL KEEP ONE FROM NOW ON —

12 Nov '63 — I HAVE BEEN IN A QUIET SULLEN MOOD ALL DAY, I AM ANXIOUS AS TO THE OUTCOME OF THIS INCIDENT, I HAVE

Selected passages from Whitman's diary written while he was in the brig at Camp Lejeune. *Austin Police Department Files.*

tageous health wise, I see no need for a brassiere except that now they are an accepted and social necessity."[28]

His notebook also betrayed what was for Kathy a very difficult period:

> Still don't know whether or not Kathy is pregnant. She might have conceived a baby on the night of Nov 23, '63 when she was here for my court martial. We were carefree that night, but in the depths of passion it is hard to be responsible and act rationally. I would not deliberately impregnate her at this stage of our life, but if she is going to have a child I can't describe the feeling of goodness or placidity it gives me to know that we share a child together. I would like to have my first-born be a boy, my son, but I hope (I don't pray anymore) most of all that, mother and child will be fine and healthy.[29]

In January, 1964, Charles Whitman's life was troubled. In Austin, Kathy wondered if she was pregnant; if so, her baby's father had been thrown in the brig, court martialed, and busted to private. At Camp Lejeune, Charlie was doing hard labor, and the Whitman family in Lake Worth was no better off:

> I just found out that Pat ran away from home a couple of days ago and had a car accident in Kissemme [sic], Fla. He was injured pretty bad. The boy has definite emotional and physcologial [sic] problems but as far as I know he won't go to anyone for help . . . until he puts forth some effort to make good I don't want anything to do with him.[30]

Those judgmental words would later haunt Charlie Whitman. In a fairly short time he would need help very badly, with his studies and his personal life, and he would make little effort to seek help. As days and weeks passed, his writing became less focused. "My mind is so broken up with thoughts, I never seem to consistently think of one plan for the future."[31]

Reminiscent of his matriculation at UT-Austin, Charlie could play different roles for different acquaintances. Ronald Russell, a friend at Camp Lejeune, observed:

> Whit had so much going for him, so much spirit, so much future. . . . [He] talked to Dorothy and me about marriage. He told us the good and the bad about getting married. He must have talked about three hours and we listened. He told us of his love for his wife Kathy, about how happy they were. Whit convinced us that we should get married.[32]

In early February 1964, Charlie purchased a green, bound volume and on the outside front cover under "Daily Record" he stenciled "of C. J. Whitman."

> I opened this diary of my daily events as a result of the peace of mind or release of feelings that I experienced when I started making notes of my daily events while in the Post Brig at Camp Lejeune, N.C., during the month of November 1963, where I was awaiting a Special Court Martial. At that time I seemed to have reached the pit of my life's experiences and it really relieved me to speak to myself in a diary. Unless it becomes a pain to uphold, I intend to make daily entries in this book or one similar continually in the future. Someday I hope to be in a brighter shade of life's light looking back on the drabness, with my wife, Kathy, sharing the pleasures and joys of life with me.[33]

On some evenings after lights were turned off he wrote by the light of a flashlight. Each entry was dated near the right margin; on the same line on the left was a number next to the acronym "DTDIC," which Charlie defined on 9 February 1964 as "Days to do in the Corps." On that date he had 902 days left. But in the meantime, Margaret and C. A. were working tirelessly to get him an early discharge. At this time Charlie wrote frequently and affectionately about his father:

> 7 February 1964
>
> I opened this diary of my daily events as a result of the peace of mind or release of feelings that I experienced when I started making notes of my daily events while in the Post Brig at Camp Lejeune, N.C., during the month of November 1963, where I was awaiting a Special Court Martial. At that time I seemed to have reached the pit of my life's experiences and it really relieved me to speak to myself in a diary. Unless it becomes a pain to uphold I intend to make daily entries into this book or one similar continually in the future. Someday I hope to be in a brighter estimate of life's light looking back on the darkness, with my wife, Kathy, sharing the pleasures and joys of life with me.
>
> *Charles J. Whitman*

The opening page of Whitman's "Daily Record." *Austin Police Department Files.*

12 February 1964
. . . I talked with Daddy (Mom was asleep in bed, she's been sick). He put me in a better frame of mind than I have been in a long time.

16 February 1964
Daddy definitely put me in a good frame of mind the other night. I have never even thought of letting the Corps get me down physically, but it never occurred to me that they were affecting me mentally until Daddy brought it out.

21 February 1964
Just before I left town I stopped in Dewey's for an order
of onion rings, and I was paid a compliment from an entirely unusual source. The owner of Dewey's asked me
how I managed to look so good and neat, as though I had
"just taken a shower" as he put it. I didn't answer but just
thought how glad I am to have been brought up right by
my parents. . . .[34]

Self-deprecating passages became more common. Charlie frequently lamented the obligation he felt towards his parents. He
blamed himself, quite rightly, for the problems he caused himself,
his parents and Kathy. He considered himself undisciplined and lazy,
but he also blamed the Marine Corps for many of his troubles.

Unlike Charlie's writings, which descended into a deeper and
deeper depression, Kathy's letters became more upbeat, becoming
the only source of cheer in Charlie's otherwise miserable life. The
couple spent an inordinate amount of time on the phone and the
long distance phone bills, apparently paid for by C. A. Whitman,
piled up. On 11 February 1964, C. A. Whitman asked Charlie to
cut down on the calls; his bill for the previous December and January was for $180.[35]

"Last Day on Hard Labor!" It was 25 February 1964. Hard labor
usually lasted until 11:00 P.M., and now it was over. Only two days
later Charlie visited Bernard's Men's Shop and applied for a job.
The manager gave him a chance and Charlie sold over $100 on his
first night. He got the job and worked a 5:00 P.M. to 10:00 P.M. shift,
but never made much money. He wanted to be out of the marines,
to return to Kathy in Austin, and to make his own fortune. A few
days later, he managed to get himself into trouble yet again, when
on 29 February 1964 he was charged with Article 92, "failure to
obey a lawful order," when he failed to carry his rifle on a hike.
Finally, good news came from Lake Worth:

I was given a message to call home to Fla [sic] immediately. I thought something was wrong with someone health

wise. When I called though I received some very good news. Daddy asked me how much a year of my life was worth. I couldn't think of a reasonable answer, but I suspected that they had received good news about my discharge. Sure enough Daddy received a call from Mr. Rogers [Congressman Paul Rogers] telling him that the Sec. of Navy had placed my EAS (Expiration of Active Service) at <u>6 December 1964</u>. That was just fabulous. I was so excited that I didn't know what to say.[36]

The news came just before the beginning of a leave for which he had been waiting for several months. Originally he was to meet Kathy in Mobile, Alabama. Her mother had even lent her fifty dollars to make the trip, but Charlie decided to go to Austin. He would surprise her with the good news there.[37]

The third phase of Charlie's marine career, his return to active duty after losing his NESEP scholarship, had been one of torment and misery. He had a bright, lovely and devoted small-town wife who adored him; and he gave her little more than grief. Surely it must have occurred to him that he had blown it. He began to believe his future was limited. He entertained the real possibility that he would never outdo his father economically or socially, and it may also have occurred to him that he would be supported by Kathy for some time.

Writing his thoughts seemed to tranquilize him, to give him comfort. He wrote of reaching "the pit of life's experiences." He was wrong; he did not know it, but this was only the beginning of the end for Charlie Whitman.

---

[1] *Palm Beach Post*, 3 August 1966; APD Files: *Statement of Francis J. Schuck, Jr.*, 13 September 1966; FBI Files: *Cole Report*, 17 August 1966, p. 16.

[2] *Texas Observer*, 19 August 1966; *Austin American-Statesman*, 7 August 1966.

[3] Connally Report, p. 2.

[4] In the Austin Police Department Files there are a number of small notebooks and calendars which belonged to Charles Whitman. Those that were contemporaneous to his service as a United States Marine are hereafter cited as APD Files: *Marine Notebooks*.

[5] APD Files: *Marine Notebooks*, undated entry; AJS.

[6] APD Files: *U.S. Marine Corps Score Book,* Cpl. Charles J. Whitman; Unidentified friend quoted in Time-Life, p. 48.

[7] FBI Files: *Cole Report,* 17 August 1966, p. 16; Connally Report, p. 3; Time-Life, p. 48.

[8] FBI Files: *Cole Report,* 17 August 1966, p. 16; Captain Joseph Stanton quoted in *Austin American-Statesman,* 7 August 1966. The card is in APD Files. Charles Whitman wrote many notes to himself. Information from those loose notes not contained in notebooks or diaries are hereafter cited as "Charles Whitman's Notes."

[9] Colonel LaGrone quoted in *Austin American-Statesman,* 7 August 1966; FBI Files: *Cole Report,* 4 August 1966; *Texas Observer,* 19 August 1966; Time-Life, p. 42.

[10] FBI Files: *Cole Report,* 17 August 1966, pp. 16 and 21; APD Files: *Statement of Francis J. Schuck, Jr.,* 13 September 1966; *Supplemental Offense Report (SOR)* by B. Hamm, 3 August 1966; *University of Texas Transcript,* Charles J. Whitman.

[11] Grover Simpson quoted in Time-Life, pp. 42–46; The Texas Department of Public Safety Intelligence File Number 4–38, The Charles Whitman Case (hereafter cited as "Texas DPS File" followed by a document title or description and date). Texas DPS Files: *Intelligence Report,* 12 August 1966; FBI Files: LeDuc Statement, pp. 5 and 7; APD Files: *SOR* by K. R. Herbert, 2 August 1966; *Austin American-Statesman,* 6 July 1986.

[12] APD Files: *Statement of Francis J. Schuck, Jr.,* 13 September 1966.

[13] Ibid.; Professor Leonardt Kreisle quoted in *Summer Texan,* 2 August 1966.

[14] *Life,* 12 August 1966; Time-Life, p. 42; Connally Report, p. 3; APD Files: *SOR* by Merle Wells, 2 August 1966.

[15] APD Files: *Statement of Francis J. Schuck, Jr.,* 13 September 1966; Time-Life, p. 42; Lawrence A. Fuess, interviewed by the author in Dallas, Texas, on 6 June 1996 (hereafter cited by name only).

[16] *Texas Observer,* 19 August 1966.

[17] David A. Pratt quoted in Time-Life, p. 46; Ibid.

[18] APD Files: *Statement of Francis J. Schuck, Jr.,* 13 September 1966; *Dallas Morning News,* 1 August 1986; Charlie Whitman quoted in Time-Life, p. 46.

[19] Texas DPS Files: *Intelligence Report,* 12 August 1966; *Texas Observer,* 19 August 1966; Time-Life, p. 46.

[20] *Austin American-Statesman,* 2 and 7 August 1966; APD Files: *SOR* by R. Kelton, 7 August 1966.

[21] *Austin American-Statesman,* 7 August 1966.

[22] Roger C. Williams quoted in *Austin American-Statesman,* 30 July 1967.

[23] Connally Report, p. 2; *Austin American-Statesman,* 2 and 7 August 1966; APD Files: *University of Texas Transcript,* Charles J. Whitman; AJS.

[24] FBI Files: *Cole Report,* 4 August 1966; Connally Report, p. 3.

[25] FBI Files: *Cole Report,* 4, 5, and 29 August 1966; APD Files: *Marine Notebooks,* entry of 27 November 1963; *Texas Observer,* 19 August 1966; Time-Life, p. 47; *Austin American-Statesman,* 7 August 1966; AJS.

[26] APD Files: *Marine Notebooks,* entries of 7–10 November 1963.

[27] Ibid., entries of 13 November 1963, 2 January 1964, and 11 February 1964; FBI Files: *Cole Report,* 29 August 1966.

[28] *Marine Notebooks,* entry of 13 November 1963.

[29] APD Files: *The Daily Record of C. J. Whitman,* entry of 21 January 1964.

[30] Ibid., entry of 2 January 1964.

[31] Ibid., entry of 22 January 1964.

[32] Ronald Russell quoted in *Austin American-Statesman,* 7 August 1966.

[33] APD Files: *The Daily Record of C. J. Whitman,* entry of 7 February 1964.

[34] Ibid., entries of 10, 12, 16, 21, and 24 February 1964.

[35] Ibid., passim in February, 1964.

[36] Ibid., 26 and 29 February and 12 March 1964; FBI Files: *Cole Reports*, 4 and 8 August 1966.

[37] Ibid., passim.

3

Austin is Different

I

Metropolitan Austin has always had a large representation of families who are relatively new to the area, with roots spread throughout the United States. "Native Texans" call them "naturalized Texans." Many people relocate believing in the Texas stereotype: a state filled with cowboys, good-ole-boys, and rich oilmen; where music is country-and-western and western swing; politics are conservative and crooked; the land is dry and flat; food means meat; law enforcement is strict and effective, and if it is not, the Rangers are called to straighten everything out. Naturalized Texans soon discover that Austin, at least, is different from all that.

Charles Whitman might have fallen for the Texas stereotype, but he lived in Austin, where—as John T. Davis and J. B. Colson have written—equally stubborn influences of southern nostalgia and western idealism meet and battle.[1] Added to the mixture are rich Latino and African-American influences with literate and articulate leaders. Throughout Austin's history, incredulous observers have been entertained by some of the nation's most memorable city council and school board meetings. Like it has in the rest of Texas, legend has infiltrated much of Austin's history. Austin has always been different.

Mirabeau Lamar, one of Texas's founding fathers, first visited the area that would become the City of Austin while on a buffalo-hunting trip. The beauty of the area stunned him. A four-family settlement called Waterloo had been situated there near the Balcones Escarpment, better known as the Balcones Fault, a dramatic topographical boundary separating dark, fertile alluvial bottoms on the Coastal Plains to the east from thin rocky sediments on the Edwards Plateau and the Texas Hill Country to the west. The confluence at the fault would not be limited to a geographical dichotomy; it would become the scene of cultural clashes as well.

In May of 1839, Edwin Waller headed a surveying team that mapped out the original capital city. The team designed a 120-foot-wide street named Congress Avenue to serve as the main street. In September, government archives and furniture for the struggling Republic of Texas were transported from Houston City by fifty ox-drawn wagons. By that time Waterloo had been renamed Austin to honor the just-deceased Stephen F. Austin, often called the "father of Texas," sometimes ironically since he was a bachelor. Sam Houston, the first president of the Republic, was disturbed to learn of the capital's relocation; he considered Austin remote and impossible to defend, and it was both. Nevertheless, on 11 November the Fourth Congress of the Republic of Texas met there.[2]

Sam Houston never liked Austin, and during the first violent years of the Republic of Texas he tried to maneuver a relocation of the capital. Evidently, elected officials considered the physical location of the archives to be the *de facto* seat of government. During the war with Mexico a ludicrous struggle ensued between Houston City, Washington-on-the-Brazos, and Austin for control of the archives. The three cities struggled less over the prestige of having the seat of government than what the capital's location could do to the value of the surrounding property. Sam determined that the papers and furniture should be moved out of Austin to the more secure Washington-on-the-Brazos. He succeeded in moving his wife and the furniture, but once Austinites heard that the papers were being removed, an unruly mob at Kenny's Fort on Brushy Creek hijacked the cargo and returned it. A disgruntled Sam Houston announced shortly afterwards that he was no longer personally responsible for the archives, and thus Austin remained the capital of Texas.[3]

The early history of Austin is inextricably connected to the history of the young Republic of Texas, and again, legend has embellished an already colorful story. Only France established a legation in Austin. On the verge of bankruptcy, Texas needed French financial assistance, and the arrival of Jean Pierre Isidore Alphonse Dubois de Saligny, the *Chargé d'Affaires*, should have been an occasion of great joy. Instead, Saligny and his Texan innkeeper, Richard Bullock, began to bicker over debts, and Saligny moved next door into a spacious residence that became the French Legation. By 1841, Saligny and Bullock's feud reportedly took a ridiculous turn when a new dispute erupted over Bullock's pigs. The Frenchman's temper flared when the Texan's pigs persistently invaded the garden of the legation. The subsequent controversy has been ingloriously called "The Pig Wars." Legend has it that Saligny ordered his servant to kill any trespassing pig. Bullock then beat the hapless servant and threatened Saligny. When Saligny demanded immediate justice, Texas officials were slow to act, claiming Bullock had rights of due process. (And besides, Bullock was a Texan!) Saligny responded by breaking off diplomatic relations with Texas, putting a stop to a proposed five-million-dollar loan to the financially-starved republic, and moving to the more exotic and entertaining New Orleans.[4] The incident was not atypical of Austin's colorful history. Austin is different.

Austin began to look more like a state capital towards the end of the nineteenth century. Although decades behind schedule, construction began on the capitol building and the new University of Texas. Both would become monuments to size. The capitol dome was intentionally built seven feet taller than the Capitol in Washington, D. C. Construction at the University of Texas at Austin did not begin until 1882, a year after Tillotson Collegiate and Normal Institute, a college for black students, opened in Austin with an enrollment of 250.[5] Thus, the first seed of higher education in Austin produced a predominately black institution.

East of Austin, productive farmlands yielded a diversity of crops; to the west huge ranches with panoramic Hill Country views raised fine breeds of cattle. From its beginning Austin became a cultural, intellectual, economic, and geographic center of staggering diversity. Because of its position as a topographical crossroad and the mass of people attracted to and employed by a large university, Austin became multicultural—and liberal, even radical, by Texas standards. A popular saying around town is, "Put two Austinites in a room, and you're likely to get three opinions."[6]

Austin's criminal history tended to focus on a few infamous cases. In a case eerily similar to that of Jack the Ripper, the "Servant Girl Annihilator" terrorized Austin from 1884–85. The serial killer hacked young girls while they slept. At the time, City Marshal James E. Lucy had a police squad of fourteen men. The force, citizen patrols, and several posses with bloodhounds never caught the killer. The last two Annihilator murders occurred on Christmas Day, 1885, when two women were hacked and their bodies dragged from their homes. During the reign of terror thirteen women were killed. The crimes have never been solved.[7]

In 1925, E. E. Engler, his wife, and their twenty-five-year-old daughter were victims of a brutal ritual-like torture and murder. They were found shot to death in their modest farmhouse near Del Valle, a small suburb south and east of Austin.[8]

In all of 1965 Austin would have only nineteen homicides. James C. Cross, Jr., of Fort Worth confessed to the two best known of the murders. He strangled two University of Texas coeds and dumped their bodies in a field in north Austin. Cross was sentenced to life in prison.[9] The crime was still the talk of the campus when Charlie and Kathy Whitman returned to make a home for themselves. While the Austin community grieved the loss of the young coeds, Austin was still thought of as a good and safe place to live. Murder was seen as an infrequent crime committed by stalkers who crept up on their victims in the dark of night. Killing was done in private so that there would be no witnesses. Few could conceive of murderers who might make no attempt to escape and might be willing to pay for their crimes with their own lives. Shortly, more people would begin to accept those notions, not only in Austin, but in all of America.

II

The University of Texas at Austin had 25,511 students enrolled in 1966, but only 13,000 for the summer session. Its campus was comprised of 232 acres of Spanish-style buildings with red terra cotta tiled roofs and wide, tree-lined walkways called malls. Elaborate fountains greeted visitors at the entrance of each mall, and a consistent architectural style gave the campus character. The West Mall connected Guadalupe Street, also known as the "Drag," with the center of the campus. The larger South Mall ran from 21st Street to the center of the campus, past the famous Littlefield Fountain and statues of American, Confederate, and Texan heroes. Each mall led to the Main Building, from which rose the symbol of the university—the Tower.

The campus, located just a few blocks north of the state capitol, was very near the center of the city. In 1966, it already had serious parking and traffic problems. The Drag formed the western border of the campus. There, small shops catered to a student and faculty clientele. Bookstores, dress shops, music stores, theaters and barber shops lined the street that by 1968 would also boast street vendors peddling cheap "stuff." Musicians played in doorways and on street corners with instrument cases opened, hoping pedestrians would throw in some change. But the Drag was not part of the campus—not officially anyway.

The University of Texas Tower, Austin's tallest building, rose 307 feet above an area of Austin which was itself 606 feet above sea level; the state capitol rose 311 feet above an area 600 feet above sea level. This meant that the Tower was taller by two feet, and for some Texans this was significant. Should any of UT's athletic teams win a national championship, all four sides of the structure were (and still are) lighted orange, and selected rooms are lit to form a "1." The top of the Tower is also lit to celebrate Texas Independence Day and other holidays. During World War II the Tower became a symbol of potential combat by housing Austin's air raid warning system, but on V-J Day its huge carillon played "America" while students and others in the area stood silently.[10] After the war, people remembered the Tower as a source of melodious euphony emitted from its caril-

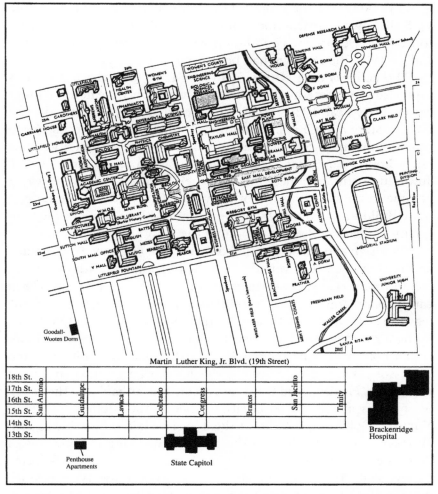

The above map is not drawn to scale nor are all of the buildings near or on the University of Texas campus depicted. The map is meant to give the reader an idea of where some of the events occurred on the University of Texas campus in 1966.

lon as the world wept and greeted peace. War and peace! How much more diverse can a symbol be? Such diversity was very "Austin."

The genesis of the Tower was similar to that of many public buildings of the era. During the early 1930s, when university officials identified a need for a new main building and library complex, the Great Depression and Franklin Roosevelt's New Deal response provided an opportunity for the university to expand its physical plant. The Public Works Administration (PWA) allotted $1,633,000.00 for the project, but nearly a year would pass before W. S. Bellows Construction Company of Oklahoma City signed a construction contract. Foundation work began shortly afterwards, and by 1937 the building had been occupied.[11]

The collaborative efforts of Robert L. White, the university's supervising architect, and Paul Cret of Philadelphia, created the Tower design in typical 1930s style, where colossal skyscrapers like the Empire State and Chrysler Buildings rose above cities to dominate urban landscapes. Smaller versions of the architectural style, like Huey Long's Louisiana state capitol in Baton Rouge and the UT Tower in Austin, became symbols of their locales. In the same way it became impossible to think of New York City without the Empire State Building, it eventually became impossible to think of the University of Texas without envisioning the Tower.

Its design and construction, however, were not universally lauded and in some quarters were derided. Self-appointed critics were uncomfortable because the style fit no convenient category; it has been called many things from "modified Spanish Renaissance" to the oxymoronic "Modern Classical."[12] In a 1947 article, Thad W. Riker, Professor of Modern European History, called the Tower "a mongrel, a hybrid. It is partly classical, partly Spanish." Folklorist and Professor J. Frank Dobie became the Tower's best known and most vocal critic. He described the style as "Late Bastardian" and the crown of columns above the observation deck as the "Temple of Vestal Virgins." Dobie suggested that the Tower be laid on its side so that all rooms would be close to the ground. Speaking to a southwest literature class during the building's construction, Dobie was reported to have said: "It's the most ridiculous thing I ever saw. With as much room as there is in Texas and as many acres of land as the University owns, we have to put up a building like those in New York."[13]

Defenders of the Tower had a simple response. So what if the Tower reached for the sky! It was big—like Texas itself. Professors like Riker and Dobie could hardly deny the building became a source of pride for their students or for Texas. Almost immediately tourists began to visit the Tower in order to step out onto the observation deck on the twenty-eighth floor. By 1966 visitors reached the deck at an annual rate of about 20,000. University officials found the spectacular view useful; the deck became a convenient observation point to direct traffic by radio after UT football games. Some Tower visitors wanted a close-up view of the famous clock which served as the principal time piece for the campus community. First set when it arrived in 1936, its four faces, one on each side of the Tower, had a diameter of more than twelve feet. Quarter-hours were marked by four bells of the Westminster Chime, a bell weighing three-and-a-half tons marked each hour, and a carillon of seventeen bells allowed musicians to ring out holiday music on special occasions.[14]

The first death associated with the Tower occurred in the fall of 1935 during the construction of the building. Charles Vernon Tanner, a construction worker, accidentally slipped off a scaffold and fell twelve floors to his death. The first suicide did not occur until nine years later on 11 June 1945 when an English professor and faculty member, Dr. A. P. Thomason, leapt to his death after slashing his wrists, ankles, and throat. Four years later a UT sophomore named Edward Graydon Grounds leapt from a window on the nineteenth floor. Less than a year later Benny Utense Seller accidentally fell from a window ledge in an apparent attempt to regain entrance to the building. The 1950s was a safe decade for Tower visitors; the next death did not occur until 3 March 1961 when Harry Julius Rosenstein jumped from the twenty-first floor after learning he was three academic hours short of graduation.[15]

III

While Charlie Whitman languished in Camp Lejeune waiting for his enlistment to expire, he became distressed about his own mental state.

> I wish so much that the Marine Corps would quit hindering my life and give me a discharge so that I could start

leading a normal life. I have so much I want to accomplish. It seems I'll never get started. I hope I am able to discipline myself to keeping up with my correspondence courses. It seems like Kathy and I will never live together and have the troubles of normal people. God, I can't stand the Corps. My love for Kathy and my sense of responsibility to our unborn children is the only thing that keeps me from going berserk. At times it seems as if I am <u>going to explode</u>.[16]

Charlie was lonesome. He missed Kathy, and in his own unusual way he loved her. There were signs that she feared him and had been assaulted by him during his leaves. Her roommate later remembered that Kathy feared Charlie's violence and dreaded an accidental pregnancy, especially after her close call in November of 1963. Motherhood would delay the completion of her studies. Her landlady later reported that Kathy feared handing over one of Charlie's guns for safekeeping. "He'll beat me again," she was reported to have said. But Charlie wrote in his diary:

I think so much of Kathy, but when I really start to concentrate on what we have done in the past and what I would like for us to do in the future I seem to explode. Or rather I seem to think I am going to explode. I wonder how long I can go on keeping to myself (I don't associate with very many people here now, and when I do I hardly ever discuss anything serious or my true feelings with them) without going nuts. I wonder if I will ever amount to anything in this world? I have great plans and dreams. . . . [17]

He loved his wife, but seemed incapable of healthy or normal demonstrations of love. Charlie Whitman had never witnessed a successful married relationship void of violence. To him a large part of being a good husband and father meant providing liberally for the material wants of his family. C. A. Whitman had succeeded at that, but Charlie certainly had not, a fact that contributed to the pressures he placed upon himself to outdo his father, and explained his obsession with making money. He discovered that success in adult life differed from becoming an Eagle Scout in less than two years; it required endurance and patience.

A fixation with money plagued Charlie for the rest of his life. He continued to gamble and believe in his poker prowess, although he lowered the stakes. His friends give testimony of his willingness to engage in schemes to make a quick buck. Although there is no evidence to support the claim, he bragged that he made enough money gambling to put Kathy through college. Kathy did much to put herself through college, and she and Charlie would continue to live as "poor" students. She served as the major provider of the Whitman household.

Charlie had shown potential for becoming a serious student when he enrolled in a course entitled "American History from 1865" during the summer of 1961 at East Carolina College.[18] His loneliness and the stark reality of Camp Lejeune's brig may have rekindled a determination to succeed, but he was still a troubled young man and his insecurity manifested itself in doubts over Kathy's love for him.

> I think she is just neglecting me, as she says she is getting lazy. She doesn't like me writing in my diary and wants me to come home on the 26th. I am undecided what to do. But I definitely feel as though there is something unusual in my mental state. I don't know if it is my imagination or if my feelings are valid. But I notice an unusual uneasiness inside myself. However, I am quieter externally than I have ever been. And I seem to think more before making a statement or decision. . . . [19]

Kathy joined Charlie for a short time in North Carolina, and surely that eased his troubled state, for a while.

Kathy resumed her studies during the 1964 fall semester. She neared the end of her undergraduate degree program, and when Charlie returned to Austin, he, for all practical purposes, soon began his. During the following spring he would change his major from mechanical engineering to the more aesthetic architectural engineering, a major he believed to be better suited to his artistic interests. He arrived with a great sense of urgency, sensing it was his last real chance for success at the University of Texas. He had learned a hard

Members of the American Association of Architectural Engineers posed for a group picture for the 1966 *Cactus*, UT's annual. Charlie Whitman is sixth from the left on the fourth row. Some students pictured here remembered Whitman's use of drugs to stay awake for projects and exams. Others reportedly complained of how difficult he could be in study groups. *Cactus, CN08901, The Center for American History, The University of Texas at Austin.*

but valuable lesson—an engineering degree at UT required serious work and study.

Upon his return, finding a job became his first task. In September he settled for a position as a bill collector for Standard Finance Company. Because it paid little, the Whitmans lived on a tight budget. Charlie did not handle the mundane job very well. He was relieved when other distractions, such as his volunteer activities, interfered with work. But the young couple had healthy priorities and a strong work ethic. They saw a college education for both of them as a necessity and were willing to sacrifice to get it. Charlie did not attend UT during the spring semester of 1965. Technically, he was still a marine, and during that time he underwent routine physicals which found him to be healthy. The last of his physicals took place in November, just before his honorable discharge on 4 December 1964. Charlie held reserve status for the next eight months, and on 18 July 1965, he received his honorable discharge as a Private 1st Class (E-2) with a military specialty as "0211–Rifleman."[20]

Once completely out of the military, Charlie re-enrolled in the University of Texas. He did not schedule a particularly heavy course load. His new major and a healthier attitude about work and study served him well. He earned three Cs, one B, and one A at the end of the spring of 1965. He worked for Standard Finance until April, when he left to take a more convenient job as a bank teller at Austin National Bank, working afternoons for $1.25 an hour. Either Charlie did not find the job fulfilling enough or, more likely, he became dissatisfied with the pay. He left only three months later. His supervisor at the bank, Eddie R. Hendricks, later described Charlie as "an outstanding person, very likeable, neat and nice looking."[21]

Charlie and Kathy moved into Apartment A at 1001 Shelley Avenue in a section across Shoal Creek from downtown Austin. Small but neat houses crowded the neighborhood, where overgrown shrubs landscaped the yards of some of the older homes. The inhabitants were diverse. Neighbors concluded that the Whitmans loved music; they often heard it blaring from the apartment. Soon there would be an addition to the young family—Charlie bought a little dog that Kathy would name Schocie. He had long been a lover of animals. Many Lake Worth neighbors remembered his attachment to a favorite dog named "Lady," so much so that Lady was generally referred to as "Charlie's Dog."[22] Schocie remained with the Whitmans until it mysteriously disappeared on 1 August 1966.

True to her upbringing, Kathy continued to be a devout Methodist, worshipping with the congregation of the First Methodist Church of Austin. She managed to involve Charlie in at least some of the services; he sang in the choir, but never exhibited deep religious devotion. Carole Barnfield, a friend of both Whitmans, recalled that on one occasion a minister from the church went over to see Charlie at home. Determined not to see or speak to the minister, Charlie ran out the back door.[23]

Charlie's experience with the Boy Scout troop of the Methodist Church represented a more comfortable and significant contact with the congregation. He had been recruited as an Assistant Scout Master in January, 1965. By February he had become the Scout Master of Troop 5. As a former Eagle Scout and Marine Corps reservist, Charlie should have been ideally suited to lead and counsel young boys, but in reality he had limited success. Some of the other adults involved with the troop remember that at times he had little patience, and on one occasion he got angry with another scouting associate over whether the troop had been made to do too many calisthenics. Even though Charlie did not take constructive criticism well, he could be quite an effective leader. Nearly everyone associated with the scouts remembered how well he taught the safety and care of firearms. At Camp Tom Wooten, Charlie demonstrated the use of a 22-caliber rifle by hanging a clothespin on a line, and from a distance of about seventy to eighty feet, shooting it so that it spun continuously until it fell apart.

Others began to notice that Charlie often had very severe headaches, perspired profusely (even on cold days), and had the nervous habit of chewing on his fingernails. He ate constantly, and since his discharge from the marines, he probably exercised less. Predictably, he put on weight. The kids began to call him "Porky." His service as a scout master ended by January of 1966, after only a few months of involvement. He is reported to have asked to be relieved because of the pressures of work and studies.[24]

Kathy spent the spring of 1965 student-teaching at Lanier High School. She graduated with the UT-Austin Class of 1965 with a B.S. in Science Education. Meanwhile, Charlie got more frustrated and impatient. Racked with insecurity, he was haunted by a short rhetorical question he had written in his diary eighteen months earlier: "As I look back over my past few adult years they seem so wasted. Will I ever accomplish anything I set out to do?"[25]

---

[1] John T. Davis and J. B. Colson, *Austin: Lone Star Rising* (Memphis: Towery Publishing, Inc., 1994), p. 19.

[2] Ibid., pp. 4, 19–21; Clifford Hopewell, *Sam Houston: Man of Destiny* (Austin: Eakin Press, 1987), p. 253–54.

[3] Hopewell, pp. 270–75.

[4] Davis and Colson, p. 103; Richard Zelade, *Austin* (Austin: Texas Monthly Press, 1984), p. 50.

[5] Davis and Colson, p. 21.

[6] Ibid., p. 44.

[7] Austin History Center, File AF Murders–Mass M8960 (1), unidentified clipping. Hereafter cited as "AHC"; *Austin American-Statesman*, 3 August 1966; Zelade, p. 65.

[8] *Austin American-Statesman*, 3 August 1966.

[9] Ibid.; *Dallas Morning News*, 4 September 1966.

[10] *Austin American-Statesman*, 7 August 1966, 1 August 1976; *Newsweek*, 15 August 1966; AJS; *UTMost*, September, 1991; *Time*, 12 August 1966; Davis and Colson, p. 11; Mary Catherine Berry, *UT Austin: Traditions and Nostalgia* (Austin: Eakin Press, 1992), p. 27; *Dallas Morning News*, 2 August 1966.

[11] Davis and Colson, p. 21; Berry, p. 27; *Austin American-Statesman*, 1 August 1976.

[12] *Austin American-Statesman*, 1 August 1976.

[13] Unidentified clipping in AHC; *Austin American-Statesman*, 1 August 1976. J. Frank Dobie quoted in Berry, p. 30.

[14] Berry, pp. 27, 29; *Dallas Morning News*, 2 August 1966. A complete carillon has 35 bells. Today the Knicker Carillon has 56 bells.

[15] *Summer Texan*, 2 August 1966; *Austin American-Statesman*, 1 August 1976.

[16] APD Files: *The Daily Record of C. J. Whitman*, entry of 6 February 1964.

[17] Texas DPS Files: *Intelligence Report*, 18 August 1966; APD Files: *The Daily Record of C. J. Whitman*, entry of 6 February 1964; *Life*, 12 August 1966.

[18] Lawrence A. Fuess; FBI Files: *Cole Report*, 17 August 1966, p. 16; Time-Life, p. 42; *Austin American-Statesman*, 7 August 1966.

[19] APD Files: *The Daily Record of C. J. Whitman*, entry of 11 February 1964.

[20] FBI Files: *Cole Report*, 17 August 1966, p. 17; APD Files: *Certificate of Service, Armed Forces of the United States*, Charles J. Whitman; Connally Report, pp. 2–3; Texas DPS Files: *Intelligence Report*, n.d.; *Austin American-Statesman*, 2 August 1966; *Texas Observer*, 19 August 1966; *Summer Texan*, 2 August 1966.

[21] *Summer Texan*, 2 August 1966; Eddie R. Hendricks quoted in *Austin American-Statesman*, 7 August 1966; Time-Life, p. 48; Connally Report, pp. 3–4.

[22] FBI Files: *Cole Report*, 17 August 1966, pp. 24 and 28; *Austin American-Statesman*, 2 August 1966.

[23] *Texas Observer*, 19 August 1966; *Austin American-Statesman*, 2 August 1966.

[24] *Austin American-Statesman*, 2 August 1966; APD Files: *SORs* by V. McBee, 2 August 1966 and H. F. Moore, 2 August 1966; Connally Report, p. 4; Time-Life, p. 48.

[25] APD Files: *The Daily Record of C. J. Whitman*, entry of 11 November 1963.

4

The Nice Facade

Charlie's involvement with Boy Scout Troop 5 of the Methodist Church and his reported membership in the Lion's Club suggest some openness to camaraderie, but he struggled to establish relationships. Members of study groups in the College of Engineering found him difficult to deal with. His life was complicated. He convinced himself that he had too much to do, and he seemed incapable of establishing priorities. A lifelong friend described him as a thinker and a planner, but he had serious problems deciding what to do with his life.

50

In early 1964, Charlie wrote in his diary, "I would definitely like to develop an interest in electronics. . . ." He used the word "definitely" frequently in his notebooks and diary, yet he seldom displayed definitiveness. Perhaps Kathy's academic success and her timely graduation inspired his renewed drive towards finishing his degree program as early as possible. Or he may have interpreted her success in teaching as a blow to his ego. She provided most of the income and all of the health care coverage in their household.[1] Regardless, he took moderate to heavy course loads for the remaining semesters of his academic career.

Charlie indicated to Frank Greenshaw, a friend and fellow student, that he planned to graduate in May of 1967 and then enroll in law school. Another close friend, a very bright engineering student named Lawrence "Larry" Fuess, believed that Charlie was interested in becoming an attorney with an engineering degree. Charlie, according to Fuess, struggled in engineering mostly because he was not a very good math student. "That will kill you in engineering," Fuess said.[2] Curiously, Charlie's life and educational experiences may have prepared him for a scientific or artistic career, but not for success in law school. Charlie's ambitions concerned money. In the combination of engineering and law, he saw a route to wealth.

While her success may have intimidated him, Kathy, nonetheless, was a source of pride for Charlie. He saw her as an asset. Smart, accomplished, and beautiful, he made sure to introduce her to his teachers at UT and to friends in Florida. He kept a card in his wallet of her measurements and clothes sizes: "My Girl, Kathleen Whitman, wears. . . ." The card listed a size 7 shoe, a 7-1/4 hat, a size 10 dress, 34C bra and fifteen other sizes of various accessories. The card also recorded her birthday and their wedding anniversary.[3] He seemed happy and in love. Both Fuess and Greenshaw observed that he wanted only the best for himself and Kathy.

People used the word "nice" *ad nauseam* to describe Charlie. But for Charlie, *pretending* to be nice proved easier than actually *being* nice. He developed a benevolent facade to hide his inner turmoil. Patience and kindness did not come naturally. Even with Kathy, the only person he genuinely loved, he found it necessary to make strenuous efforts to improve his attitude. During the summer he worked as a NASA assistant, he and Kathy had a fight serious enough to give their friends, John and Fran Morgan, the impression that Kathy had decided to seek a divorce. Such fights, however, are common among young married couples. On an index card he characteristically typed a list of things he needed to do to enhance his relationship with her:

GOOD POINTS TO REMEMBER WITH KATHY
1. Don't nag
2. Don't try to make your partner over
3. Don't criticize
4. Give honest appreciation
5. Pay little attentions
6. Be courteous
7. BE GENTLE[4]

Most husbands do not find it necessary to list being courteous and gentle to their wives as a goal or a special effort. However, Charlie did sincerely struggle to control himself. Larry Fuess observed: "Originally when he first got married he was like his father, subject to violence, but he had improved. He suppressed hostilities."[5]

While he knew little about intimacy and normal demonstrations of love in a marital relationship, he did love Kathy. Other relationships and responsibilities caused more problems, and he compensated with a nice pretense. "Everybody is uptight when they go to school,

Charles Whitman at the University of Texas. *Prints and Photographs Collection, CN06517, The Center for American History, The University of Texas at Austin.*

but Charles was really high strung. He really got uptight about things, courses and tests," commented a friend.[6] "Nice" became a mask that hid frustration and anger. As he came closer to a decision to surrender to his anger, the facade became larger and more unwieldy. He continued to chew his fingernails even though that habit bothered him because he considered it childish. "Charlie was like a computer. He would install his own values into a machine, then program the things he had to do, and out would come the results," said Larry Fuess.[7] And so, Charlie Whitman programmed himself to be nice.

Sometimes, however, Charlie suspended the acting and the nice front fell. Barton D. Riley, an architecture instructor and confidant of Charlie, related how Charlie lost his temper when he made a "C" on a project because he misunderstood the directions.

> He hit the table with his fist and, without a word, just walked out. Charlie was used to excelling. He later came back and apologized and always in the future made certain he knew what I was talking about.

Larry Fuess remembered an incident where Charlie nearly got into a fight in the middle of the streets of Austin. Charlie and the driver of the car in front of them apparently aggravated each other enough for Charlie to have interpreted their exchange as a challenge. Larry, unaccustomed to public fighting, sat stunned as Charlie ripped off his rings and threw them on the dashboard of his car, then ran out of the car for an encounter on the street. To Larry's relief, the driver sped away. "I thought he wanted to get out; I was ready," Charlie said as he returned to his seat.[8]

For the most part, however, Charlie continued to play the nice role. His teachers believed him to be more mature than most students his age, and his classmates liked him. "About all I can say is that the Charles I know is just a nice guy," claimed the wife of a friend. But Whitman also seemed to enjoy watching others squirm. On one occasion, Riley, a former military man, lost his temper with a classmate of Charlie's and gave him a military-style tongue lashing. Afterwards, he happened to look at Charlie and observed "the most contented grin on his face."[9] One of Charlie's more astute academic advisors described him as an "overstriver." He believed Charlie had to work harder to get what he wanted, and what he wanted was to surpass the accomplishments of his father. "He had hoped he would someday be able to financially, politically, and socially outdo me," said C. A. Whitman, claiming to quote from a letter written by his son.[10]

Charlie spent an inordinate amount of time setting goals, making lists, and laboring over details. The bulk of his efforts at most endeavors consisted of thought and organization. Actual results and closure were rare. Minor setbacks bothered him immensely, mostly because he worked so hard. His architectural designs were much like his temperament—not original, but competent and efficient. Riley described his designs as "strong, nothing wasteful—direct. Although not particularly creative, they answered the problem. As a result he was an 'A' student."[11]

In spite of his preoccupation with making money and outdoing his father, Charlie accepted monthly allowances from C. A. Whitman. Reports varied, but during this period he routinely received from $180 to $380 a month. The elder Whitman continued to purchase new cars for his family. He bought a new, black, two-door, hardtop Chevrolet Impala for Charlie's use. C. A. presented the car, along with other new cars, to members of his family during the Christmas holidays of 1965. Charlie and Kathy had been using a tan Dodge, a model that their friend Elaine Fuess had once called the ugliest car ever made. It ran well, however, and Charlie did not want the new Impala. "He hated that car," said Larry Fuess. And Charlie would hate that car as long as he had it. According to Charlie, his father bought a number of cars at a very good price; Charlie apparently felt that he had been forced by his father to take a new car he could not afford. Charlie and Kathy would later borrow $3,400 from the Austin Teachers' Federal Credit Union to pay for it.[12] Most likely it reminded him of his father's success, something that eluded the ever-impatient son. Moreover, the car probably became a constant reminder of his seeming inability to stand up to his father. By the latter part of 1965, Charlie's attitude toward his father turned into a consuming hatred.

As in much of the rest of his day-to-day life, his outwardly cordial relationship with his father appeared to be an act. Charlie's friends could not comprehend how C. A. Whitman could possibly believe he had a good relationship with his son. But occasionally, Charlie and his father spent time together, appearing to enjoy each other's company. They had a mutual love of guns and hunting. Sometime in 1965, while visiting Charlie and Kathy in Austin, C. A. Whitman and Charlie visited Chuck's Gun Shop. On that trip Charlie ordered a 6mm Remington with a four-power scope, and the elder Whitman placed an order for a .243-caliber Winchester Sako bolt-action rifle. C. A. Whitman told the store employee that they were going deer hunting. Charlie would return to the shop several times to make payments on the rifles. On one of the trips, he indicated that his father sent money to pay the notes on the purchases, but Kathy used the occasion to inflict a good-natured "guilt trip." Shortly afterwards, during a visit by their friend Francis Schuck, Kathy showed off her "deer rifle," a new fur coat.[13]

Charlie first related a smoldering resentment of his father during an unusual friendship he formed with A. J. Vincik, one of very few people with whom Charlie ever had long conversations. Vincik ran a trailer sales firm at 4810 Burnet Road in Austin. His business interests included insurance, real estate, and mechanics. Vincik, who met Charlie through scouting, confirmed Charlie's obsessions with money and proving himself. He also provided keen insight into some of Whitman's other beliefs and thoughts. With Vincik, Charlie never indicated an outright hatred for his father, but rather a shame. In spite of C. A.'s remarkable road to success, he embarrassed Charlie. It bothered him that his father grew rich cleaning cesspools. With Vincik, Charlie shared the fiction that he did not have enough time to devote to his various ambitions. In reality, his problem was not time but his inability to set priorities. Charlie saw himself as driven and achievement-oriented, and he bitterly resented others who were less so. In that respect he greatly resembled his father. "[P]eople should have more initiative, get more things done, be recognized, and step up in life," Charlie said.

After his brief employment at NASA, he held government employees in very low regard, seeing them as unproductive and unambitious. Charlie maintained that he could do the work of eight NASA employees in thirty minutes.[14] But Charlie could hardly deny that he fit much of the description of what he despised. He may have been ambitious, but he did not produce. His ever-changing

goals and an inability to make up his mind limited his accomplish-
ing anything. He showed no patience to persevere. Vincik helped
Charlie get his real estate license, and Charlie would become bonded
as an insurance agent and real estate broker on 1 May 1965, but he
never sold anything.[15] In truth he had achieved little and had excelled at nothing since becoming the nation's youngest Eagle Scout
at age twelve and being rated a sharpshooter in the marines. He
accepted money from and thus still partially depended on a man he
considered a source of embarrassment. He could not have been
pleased with himself and the uncertainty of what he would become.
It tortured him.

Kathy continued to focus on becoming an effective science
teacher.

II

During a long conversation with A. J. Vincik, Charlie expounded
on his religious beliefs. Vincik concluded that despite his friend's
strict Roman Catholic upbringing, Charlie did not practice the Catholic faith because of the Papacy and its condemnation of birth control.
He did believe in heaven, but in a departure from Catholicism he
doubted the existence of hell. Instead, to Charlie, life on earth was
hell. He saw God not as a single entity or a Blessed Trinity but as a
strange combination of pantheism in the Hindu tradition, and a
corruption of St. Thomas Aquinas's proof of the existence of God—
the Uncaused Cause.

The Whitman theophany held God to be energy, and since energy is essentially the movement of molecules and all matter is made
up of molecules, God is everywhere. Followers of the Hindu tradition believe that God can be found in everything. No record of
Charlie's involvement in the study of comparative religious dogma
exists; he probably pondered the existence of a God, and in his rebellion against Catholicism, developed his own pantheistic folklore.
According to Charlie's logic, God (energy) can neither be created
nor destroyed, ergo, God is omnipotent. Being reared in Catholic
traditions and educated in Catholic schools, Charlie may have been
exposed to St. Thomas Aquinas's argument from motion, which asserts that our senses make the world's motion evident. Further, no

object can move itself; instead, every movement has been caused by a prior movement. Equally evident is that there can be no infinite regress in which things move other things; there must be a first mover. Thomism asserts that the cause of the first movement is the Prime Mover—God.[16]

But Charlie saw energy as God. He maintained that since mankind was a form of energy, God must be within mankind. God was each man's conscience, and since energy can neither be created nor destroyed, an afterlife must exist as a destination for a person's energy following death.[17]

Charlie's religious beliefs may simply have sprung from guilt and simple rationalization. During most of his life he found comfort in being dutiful. Abandoning the Catholic faith required a justification. The Whitman rationalization could be logically and dangerously extended; maybe death does not exist except as a change in the form of energy. If this life is hell, then the afterlife must be better. For Charlie Whitman, the moral basis for the value of life slowly began to erode.

III

Even a childless couple like Charlie and Kathy Whitman must have found the apartment at 1001-A Shelley small. In the spring of 1966, Charlie heard of a tiny house available for rent in south Austin across from Town Lake (the Colorado River) and the couple arranged to rent it. Charlie surprised everyone by buying a couple of rooms of fine furniture, including a wooden dining room set. Shortly afterwards he and Kathy moved to 906 Jewell Street.

The five-room bungalow had a small front and back yard; behind and to the right of the house stood a one-car garage that resembled a workshop. The Jewell Street area teemed with families and children, and both Charlie and Kathy seemed to enjoy the youngsters. "He loved children and they loved him," stated a neighbor. The children, especially the young boys, felt comfortable playing in the Whitmans' yard. Charlie tied a rope to a large oak tree in the backyard and used it to exercise. He taught the boys of the neighborhood how to climb the rope hand-over-hand as marines are trained to do. A twelve-year-old, Mark Nowotny, knew the Whitmans well.

"Both were real nice," he said. Mark's older sister Judy said of Charlie: "He was the nicest person I know at the university. He was always a lot of fun—always joking." The adults of the area admired the young couple. "He was such a handsome young man, husky and strong," said Mark and Judy's mother. And after his landlord chimed yet another "nice," he observed that Charlie appeared worried at times, "but you know how students are, they have a lot on their minds." Judy Nowotny made the same observation. Mike Merino, another neighborhood kid, noticed that Charlie loved guns and made frequent trips to the rifle range. More than a few of the neighbors knew of the collection of military paraphernalia in the garage in his back yard.[18]

The Jewell Street neighbors also observed a hardworking couple. Their move to Jewell Street took place towards the end of Kathy's first year as a teacher at Lanier High School. During the previous summer she had worked as a bookkeeper at Clear Lake Yacht Basin near NASA, and during the summer of 1966, after her first year of teaching, Kathy applied for and obtained a part-time position as an information operator for Southwestern Bell Telephone Company. She listed her banker, the Superintendent of Schools, and a pharmacist in Needville as references.[19]

Kathy's ability to learn quickly and work hard universally impressed her co-workers at Southwestern Bell. "She acted a lot older than she looked," said Patricia Barber. Kathy's station was located on the third floor of the telephone building on the corner of Colorado and 9th Streets in downtown Austin. On 6 June 1966 she reported for her first day of training and met Linda Damereau, a co-worker who became her close friend. Damereau discovered what everyone else knew: Kathy was quick, alert, and very easy to get along with.[20] Southwestern Bell supervisors saw her as a well-adjusted and happy young wife. No one suspected that Kathy had ever been abused by Charlie in any way.

The Whitman marriage held a mystery. Without question the young couple had arguments, shed tears and entertained notions of breaking up—even divorcing. But most acquaintances of the young couple find it hard to believe that Charlie ever laid a hand on Kathy. "I just can't believe he ever beat her. If he did, she certainly hid it well," an operator supervisor would later say.[21] No one in the

Whitman or Leissner families ever related any direct knowledge of abuse. All of their mutual friends considered them a fun couple. They remember trips to Austin's famous Barton Springs, the picturesque Highland Lakes north and west of Austin, and visits to the historic sites of nearby San Antonio. Surviving pictures of their home life suggest a laid-back Charlie enjoying the company of Kathy, friends, and their little dog Schocie. Curiously, the most credible references to Charlie ever getting physical with Kathy come from Charlie himself. He claimed to have attacked her on two occasions. Certainly, he often lost his temper and would rant at her; given his size and power, she must have been frightened. Kathy would confide to her parents that she feared Charlie's temper, which was so explosive she thought he could actually kill her. On one occasion close friends witnessed an embarrassing verbal shot at Kathy. "Wouldn't you think we would have enough self-discipline to exercise every day?" Again, Charlie fit the description of what he appeared to detest. Kathy was disciplined and as a result had a fine figure; Charlie was the one who ate too much and was getting fat.[22] One close friend of the couple, Elaine Fuess, observed:

Whitman often fit the description of the very traits he claimed to despise in others. He considered being overweight a sign of a lack of will power, yet overlooked his own inability to keep off excess pounds. *Austin Police Department Files, from film left in one of Whitman's cameras.*

Even when he looked perfectly normal, he gave you the feeling of trying to control something in himself. He knew he had a temper, and he hated this in himself. He hated the idea of cruelty in himself and tried to suppress it. He had seen cruelty before and he didn't want it in his own house.[23]

But the Whitman house on Jewell Street did hold cruelty, and Charlie seemed incapable of preventing it. Their marriage probably survived only through Kathy's remarkable patience and loyalty and her belief that Charlie made real attempts to control himself. She may have feared his emotional outbursts, but she stood by him. While others nodded in agreement, one of her colleagues at Southwestern Bell would later comment: "She loved him, there's no doubt about that."[24]

IV

On 17 June 1966, two weeks after Kathy began her training as an information operator for Southwestern Bell Telephone, Charlie abandoned plans to sell insurance or real estate and applied for a job as an engineering laboratory assistant. He had just completed nineteen hours of coursework in the 1966 spring semester, a heavier than average load. He then enrolled for the 1966 summer semester and scheduled fourteen semester hours of courses—a very heavy load. He wanted to get his coursework out of the way. The combination of the summer job and school work added to pressures he placed on himself.[25]

Charlie's supervisor, Dr. Clyde Lee, an associate professor of civil engineering, headed a team engaged in a highway research project entitled "Evaluation of Traffic Control at Hiway Intersections." The twenty-five-hour-a-week job paid $160 a month. On the job Charlie proved himself reliable. He impressed Lee with his maturity and thoughtful questions about the objectives of the project. Lee stated, "He was an unusually good worker."[26]

Charlie's breakneck pace seemed to include his driving. He received at least two traffic tickets in a two-week period during the spring of 1966. He could not have been pleased to pay the fines. As a result of running a red light and being ticketed yet again, he contested the citation on 9 July 1966. He defended himself in a manner that the Austin Chief of Police, Bob Miles, would later characterize as brilliant, but he still lost the case and had to pay the fine. It may have been the onset of his interest in the law. In an odd coincidence, Charlie's brother, John, had been arrested in Lake Worth for "physical possession of alcohol" on the same day. Johnnie Mike's relationship with his father had by this time nearly ceased to exist. He had left the Whitman residence altogether, preferring instead to live at the home of friends. A judge offered to suspend the fine if John moved back to 820 South L Street; John refused and paid the fine instead.[27]

Charlie's adult life consisted largely of tribulations that he brought upon himself. He maintained slightly above-average grades, but because of the dismal grades he had earned before the revocation of his NESEP scholarship, his overall GPA never reached the 2.0 mark. He did dependable work, and became popular with his teachers, some of his fellow students and neighbors. But he had no direction. Inner insecurities and obsessions to make money began to take their toll. While in the brig at Camp Lejeune, he wrote lovingly about both of his parents, his father in particular. But after his return to Austin he began to feel alternately embarrassed and indifferent towards his father.

Meanwhile, the Florida Whitman family began to disintegrate. Patrick had married Patricia Smith of Lake Worth on 14 July 1965 and was now the head of his own household. Widely considered the kindest of the Whitmans, Patrick could not escape the turmoil that would envelope his parents and brothers. As the youngest brother John reached his late teens and his rebellion grew more serious, he wanted nothing to do with his father. Very soon Margaret would no longer have the presence of children as a motivating factor to sustain her marriage. But as unhappy as every Whitman was, each of them knew that they were nearly wholly dependent on C. A. Whitman for their financial and material support. And, at least according to some observers, he never let them forget it.[28] Unfortunately, by the end of 1965 Charlie's attitude evolved into embittered hatred towards his father. Very soon more troubles would be imported from Lake Worth, Florida, the pressures would increase, and the nice facade would disappear altogether.

[1] Statement of the University of Texas Health Center, 2 August 1966, hereafter cited as "UT Health Center"; APD Files: *The Daily Record of C. J. Whitman*, entry of 22 February 1964, and *Blue Cross/Blue Shield of Texas Membership Card*, Kathleen Whitman, effective date 1 November 1965; Lawrence A. Fuess.

[2] Lawrence A. Fuess; *Austin American-Statesman*, 2 and 7 August 1966.

[3] APD Files: Card found in Charles Whitman's wallet, 1 August 1966.

[4] APD Files: Charles Whitman's Notes, n.d.; Texas DPS Files: *Intelligence Report*, 3 August 1966.

[5] APD Files: *Details of Investigation* (DOI), Interview of Lawrence A. Fuess, 8 August 1966.

[6] Unidentified friend quoted in Time-Life, p. 48.

[7] Larry Fuess quoted in *Austin American-Statesman*, 7 August 1966.

[8] Barton Riley quoted in Time-Life, p. 48; Larry Fuess; *Texas Observer*, 19 August 1966.

[9] Carole Barnfield quoted in *Texas Observer*, 19 August 1966; *Austin American-Statesman*, 7 August 1966.

[10] *Daily Texan*, 1 August 1986; C. A. Whitman quoted in *Austin American-Statesman*, 1 August 1976.

[11] *Texas Observer*, 19 August 1966.

[12] Lawrence A. Fuess; APD Files: *Vehicle Impounding Report*, 1 August 1966; Texas DPS Files: *Intelligence Report*, 2 August 1966; *Newsweek*, 15 August 1966; *Dallas Morning News*, 1 August 1986; *Austin American-Statesman*, 1 August 1976; Time-Life, p. 48.

[13] FBI Files: *Cole Report*, 17 August 1966, p. 14; APD Files: *Statement of Francis J. Schuck, Jr.*, 13 September 1966; Time-Life, p. 32; *Austin American-Statesman*, 6 July 1986.

[14] *Texas Observer*, 19 August 1966; Time-Life, p. 48; APD Files: *SOR* by V. McBee, 1 August 1966.

[15] APD Files: *Real Estate Salesman ID.*, License # 117338, Charles J. Whitman, 1 January 1966; *Texas Observer*, 19 August 1966.

[16] For a review of St. Thomas Aquinas's Five Proofs see George Brant, ed., *Catholicism* (New York: George Braziller, 1962), pp. 30–32; *Texas Observer*, 19 August 1966.

[17] *Texas Observer*, 19 August 1966.

[18] Lawrence A. Fuess; APD Files: *Invoice—Central Freight Lines, Inc.*, 5 April 1966; Merino and various Nowotny quotes are from *Austin American Statesman*, 2, 4, and 7 August 1966; Time-Life, p. 32.

[19] *Austin American-Statesman*, 7 August 1966.

[20] Patricia Barber quoted in *Austin American-Statesman*, 7 August 1966.

[21] *Austin American-Statesman*, 7 August 1966.

[22] Texas DPS Files: *Summary of Detailed Reports*, 15 August 1966. The summary of the intelligence report clearly states that Kathy believed that Charlie could kill her if he lost his temper. The "detailed" report, i.e., the DPS Intelligence Report, however, is not in the Whitman file; *Life*, 12 August 1966; *Austin American-Statesman*, 4 August 1966.

[23] Elaine Fuess quoted in *Texas Observer*, 19 August 1966.

[24] *Austin American-Statesman*, 7 August 1966.

[25] APD Files: University of Texas, *Application for Employment* by Charles J. Whitman, 17 June 1966; *Daily Texan*, 1 August 1991; UT Health Center; Ibid.; *Summer Texan*, 2 August 1966; Connally Report, p. 4.

[26] Texas DPS Files: *Intelligence Report*, 3 August 1966; Dr. Clyde Lee quoted in *Summer Texan*, 2 August 1966.

[27] APD Files: *Statement of Francis J. Schuck, Jr.*, 13 September 1966; Connally Report, p. 4; FBI Files: *Cole Report*, 17 August 1966, pp. 5–6; *Austin American-Statesman*, 2 and 7 August 1966.

[28] FBI Files: *Cole Report*, 17 August 1966, pp. 4–6 and 18–19.

5

Oozing with Hostility

I

Some of the finest behavioral scientists in the world would one day conclude that Charlie Whitman was "intelligent, intense, and driven," qualities that should result in success and satisfaction. But Charlie found frustration instead. The nice facade became harder for him to maintain; eventually he concluded that he could not master the forces working against real achievement. He took no initiative to seek meaningful help for his academic or psychological problems. He behaved inconsistently towards Kathy, although his serious loss of control was more infrequent. His bouts of depression were probably more troubling to Kathy; it would have been in her nature to try to keep Charlie happy. During the spring of 1966, she began to gently guide him towards professional counseling.

Charlie believed he suffered from some physical malady. Specifically, he thought something was wrong with his head; and he also feared that he was sterile.[1] Those suspicions seemed to torture his mind, but there exists no evidence of his wanting professional help. Instead, he chose to wallow in self-doubt and personal dissatisfaction. For all his talk about the need for others to achieve and get ahead and in spite of his harsh words for his brother Patrick's refusal to get help for his problems, Charlie Whitman stalled himself by his own inability to deal with self-inflicted problems. Other sources of stress would result in a complete surrender to his frustrations and anger—and in tragedy.

The grades Charlie earned in his courses during the spring and fall of 1965 were significantly improved from his earlier matriculation at the University of Texas. In the spring he made three Cs, one B, and one A. During the fall, after his summer at NASA, he earned three As and one B, but had to drop calculus. Charlie had, at last, become an honor student.[2] He had learned hard lessons and paid for his foolishness, and he now had Kathy. For some time she had been universally lauded by Lanier students, fellow teachers, school administrators, and Southwestern Bell Telephone operators and supervisors. Her loyalty and determination to make her marriage work and her emotional support for Charlie were extraordinary.

In Lake Worth, Florida, a different Whitman wife had given up. After enduring more than twenty-five years of a difficult marriage, Margaret decided she could take no more. On 2 March 1966 at 9:30 P.M. someone called the Lake Worth Police Department reporting a disturbance at 820 South L Street. "They are going to kill each other" the complainant said. But by the time officers arrived all was quiet. Less than two hours later, at 11:20 P.M., LWPD received another call, but this time the caller identified himself as Charles J. Whitman of 1001 Shelley Avenue, Austin, Texas. According to the police report, Charlie informed the dispatcher that "Mr. Charles A. Whitman of 820 South L Street had threatened to do bodily harm to his mother. He advises that he is enroute to this city at this time to pick up his mother." Obviously, Margaret had called Charlie for help. Most likely he convinced her to leave his father and once she agreed he immediately set out to cover the 1,400 mile trip to Lake Worth. He arrived on 4 March to find his entire family in complete disarray. By 4:05 P.M. Margaret had been firmly convinced of the wisdom of moving to Austin. She called the LWPD and requested that an officer be dispatched to 820 South L Street to stand by while she removed some of her personal effects. The two officers, Lieutenant Sargent and Officer Arbour, reported standing by for an hour and fifteen minutes observing C. A. and Margaret arguing and "giving each other all kinds of trouble for the entire time, all nonsense."[3]

Very shortly Charlie and Margaret were in Austin. Charlie reputedly made the entire trip without any sleep. Soon afterwards Patrick arrived; before the end of March he had moved in with Charlie and Kathy. Within a few weeks Pat relocated to 1404 West 12th Street, an apartment very near Margaret. He found a job as a truck driver and salesman for Big Three Welding and Gas Equipment Company. While in Austin, however, Patrick began to feel neglected, and developed a feeling that Margaret favored Charlie. Anger and strained relations haunted the Whitmans even in the absence of C. A.; after a few weeks Patrick returned to Florida.[4]

The troubled family was dysfunctional, at best. The whole messy affair just added to the pressures of a tormented young Charles Whitman. The Lake Worth problems had moved to Austin and had become inescapable.

By May, Margaret made a firm decision to make a complete break. At that time she returned to Lake Worth to get more of her things. Evidently, another painful clash took place between the elder Whitmans. An unidentified neighbor recalled that C. A. tried to remove Margaret's ring before she left him, but he could not get it off her finger. Whether or not Charlie witnessed the struggle is not known. The elder Whitman did make repeated and serious attempts to get Margaret to return to him, including a barrage of phone calls to Charlie.

> I'm not ashamed of the fact I spent a thousand dollars a month on the phone bill, begging her to come back. I loved

my wife dearly, my sons dearly, and I wanted our home to
be happy. I kept begging Charlie to come back to me, too.
I promised Charlie that if he'd only persuade his mama to
come back, I'd swear never to lay a hand on her. But my
wife was a fine woman, and she understood my nature,
and even when she left me in May—we'd had a clash and
she said to me, "I'm leaving because you've been too good
to us all." She told me that was where the thing had gone
wrong.[5]

And so again, C. A. Whitman associated love with brutality. In his
mind, his goodness and generosity caused his family's problems.
Charlie and Margaret both lived in Austin with new cars purchased
by C. A. Whitman, but Margaret could justifiably argue that she
was responsible for a good part of the success of the Whitman business. Through her brother, she contacted a West Palm Beach attorney
to begin negotiations with C. A. to arrive at a property settlement.

Despite evidence of his generosity, C. A's admitted domineering
and overbearing personality should not be underestimated. On 5
June 1966, Margaret wrote to her father: "I don't know whether you
know it yet or not but Charles and I have separated and I am getting
a divorce. I hate it but I just couldn't take it any longer." She never
mailed the unfinished letter.

Margaret's Austin roots grew deeper when she applied for and
accepted a position as a cashier at Wyatt's Cafeteria in the Hancock
Shopping Center. She reported for her first day of work on 8 April
1966. Three months earlier the University of Texas had reclassified
Charlie as a resident of Texas. The Whitmans were becoming naturalized Texans.[6]

Kathy knew how depressed Charlie could get and she was afraid
to leave him alone. He could get frighteningly unhappy and often
languished in a state of anxiety. Dr. Dana L. Farnsworth, a Hygiene
Professor and Health Services Director of Harvard University, would
later observe:

He indicated to friends that he had been depressed from
time to time because he felt that something was going on
inside him he did not understand. He had a fear of his

impulsive behavior. He became more and more vulnerable to the accumulated stresses with which he was dealing in a less and less satisfactory manner.[7]

During one serious attack of depression, Charlie showed up after 10:30 P.M. at the home of one of his teachers, Barton Riley. He dropped a bundle of papers on the living room floor. The strain on his face produced a familiar film of sweat that distressed Riley. "What's the trouble, Charlie?" Charlie replied that he was carrying too much of a load. During the lamentation he finally shared the real reason for his anxious state. "I've got problems." A vicious tirade of how much he hated his father followed.

> "I just despise my father. I hate him. If my father walked through that door, I'd kill him."
> "Charles, you don't mean that," Riley replied in a quiet tone.
> "I certainly do."

They had been talking quietly for some time, and just when Charlie seemed to have calmed down, he surprised Riley by saying, "I can't resist it anymore." Walking quickly to a baby grand piano, Charlie seated himself, and without request, played *Clair de Lune*. The tune, familiar to all pianists, is normally played in a soft and lyrical style, but Charlie's loud and strong rendition woke Mrs. Riley, who had been sleeping upstairs. As he played he seemed to mellow. The power with which he played seemed to drain his tension. Riley recalled that he played very well. Music could have been a source of relaxation and peace, but tragically, for some unknown reason he normally refused to play—even for friends.[8]

Soon there would be another anxiety attack during which Charlie decided to quit school. While walking through Taylor Hall, an engineering student asked Larry Fuess, "What do you think of Charlie dropping out of school?" Disturbed at the question, Larry got into his car and drove to the Shelley Street apartment and found Charlie, who reported he had, without telling Kathy, resigned from the university and sold his books and other items. Fuess found him packing bags, determined to leave everything, including Kathy. "She'll be o.k.; she has a job now. She'll be better off." He wanted to become a bum; he did not know why, he just had to do it. He also spoke of the separation of his parents, and how he had "something personal to settle." Not surprisingly, when she returned from a day of work at Lanier High School, Kathy was shocked and bewildered. Charlie told her he was leaving her. Later that evening they visited Larry and his wife, Elaine. No one could get him to open up. "But Charlie, why, why?" pleaded Kathy. He said nothing, but just shook his head.[9]

In an attempt to help his friend, Fuess called their instructor, Barton Riley. Although late, Riley intervened, but this time he had run out of patience. "This is ridiculous, you are not going to do it!" Riley, himself an ex-marine, using a stern voice, ordered Charlie to skip his (Riley's) classes, focus on other classes and do make-ups later. Stunned, Charlie replied, "Yes, sir." When he saw Riley the next day he said, "Thank you, sir."[10] Giving orders may have been the best way to deal with Charlie; the kindness and patience initially exhibited by his teacher, and always used by his wife and good friends, did not work.

II

The phone calls from C. A. Whitman kept coming; Charlie estimated an average of one every forty-eight hours. Relentlessly, C. A. pleaded with him to intercede with his mother and try to get her to return to Lake Worth. C. A. believed that was the only source of conflict between him and his son: "The only animosity was that I fought like the devil to get her back." C. A. did not believe that Charlie had anything to do with Margaret's departure, but he surely believed that he could use Charlie to get her to return.[11] Charlie never had any intention of trying to convince his mother to return to Florida, but still, the phone calls kept coming.

"He was at the point of hypertension, even in his everyday life," observed Elaine Fuess.[12] While he may have shown all the other signs of hypertension, he did not suffer from high blood pressure. In an effort to help Kathy's uncle, Frank E. Holloway, who had been hospitalized in Houston and had required a transfusion, he donated blood to the Travis County Medical Society Blood Bank six times within a ten-month period. On all but one occasion his blood pressure was measured, and none of the measurements was high.[13]

With frequent calls from C. A. constantly reminding him of how much he hated his father, and at the same time how much he was *like* him, Charlie successfully maintained the nice facade through, as the *National Observer* later wrote, his "fierce will power to suppress his strains and vices."[14] Kathy must have been encouraged when he finally succumbed to her pleas and sought professional help at the University of Texas Health Center. On 29 March 1966, about three weeks after Charlie had moved his mother from Florida to Texas, he saw Dr. Jan D. Cochrum, a general practitioner who had been on staff for only a year and a half. Dr. Cochrum prescribed Valium, a mild sedative, and referred him to a staff psychiatrist. Cochrum described the visit as routine and unremarkable. He remembered treating Charlie only after seeing a picture of him four months later, when he commented that Charlie was "every bit as nice a guy as he looked in the picture."[15]

Dr. Maurice Dean Heatly, the staff psychiatrist at the University Student Health Center, was generally well-regarded. He came from a prominent family; his brother served as the Chairman of the House Appropriations Committee in the state legislature. Dr. Heatly engaged in a number of volunteer and part-time activities.[16] However, Heatly's style and manner did not impress all of his patients. One former student, Bill Helmer, wrote of visiting Heatly for marital problems and depression. Helmer described how he sat and listened to the doctor talk on the telephone to a driller engaged in the installation of a well on the Heatly ranch. Heatly's treatment reportedly consisted of a prescription for Librium.[17]

Before seeing Dr. Heatly, Charlie completed an information sheet. He neatly printed his curt answers. When asked about his chief problem, he answered, "That's why I'm here." When asked if college work was hard, he replied, "Some of it." He also replied to a question about hobbies and interests by listing hunting, karate, and scuba diving, but he also added, "Main interest [is] how to make money."[18]

Heatly's first impression was that Charlie was a "massive, muscular youth" who "seemed to be oozing with hostility." He later characterized Charlie in a way that would haunt him and the University of Texas for decades: "There was something about him that suggested and expressed the all-American boy." For approximately one hour Charlie opened up and became as candid as he would ever be about his own state of mind and true feelings. He did refer to several commendable achievements as a marine, but he tended to dwell on his lack of achievement and what he saw as impediments to reaching his goals. Heatly noted a self-centered and egocentric patient, but one who made clear he wanted to improve himself. Charlie became emphatic; something was happening to him and he didn't seem to be himself.[19]

Heatly surmised that the real reason for the visit was Charlie's distress over the separation of his parents. Charlie described the "gross disharmony" of the Whitman household and his summons to Florida to retrieve his mother. He then related how C. A. Whitman phoned frequently and relentlessly in vain attempts to convince Charlie to intercede with his mother. The invectives against C. A. Whitman continued. Charlie included a clear enunciation that he was just like his father, especially in the manner in which he treated his wife. Charlie admitted to assaulting Kathy on two occasions, though he added that she feared him less now because of his greater efforts to control his violent behavior. He described his father as a semi-literate but demanding near-perfectionist who had achieved a great deal. Therein lay a significant difference between the father and son, and a source of much turmoil. C. A. Whitman had achieved much; Charlie had not. He dwelt on his childhood and his relationship with his father. Charlie readily admitted that he lived for the day when he could consider himself his father's superior in society and in all other fields of human endeavor.[20]

Charlie's lack of real accomplishment and achievement became a mental cancer. Making Bs when he knew he could make As disconcerted him. With Heatly, he talked rapidly for long periods and demonstrated overt hostility. Then he would slow down and come very close to tears. Heatly made numerous, but largely unsuccessful attempts through inquiry to get Charlie to become more specific about his experiences. Charlie did share one fantasy with Heatly— he often thought "about going up on the Tower with a deer rifle and shooting people." Heatly was nonplussed. He had heard many references to the Tower by students over the years. The Tower spawned many sick jokes such as "I feel like jumping off the old Tower!" To

Heatly the Tower was a "mystic symbol" of the university and the frustrations of college life. Since its construction it had become impossible for many to think of UT without thinking specifically of the Tower. The doctor interpreted Charlie's Tower reference as a "transient feeling" or an expression of depression common among students.[21] Heatly concluded that Charlie was not dangerous, but asked him to return at the same time one week later and/or to call at any time he needed help. Further treatment depended completely on Charlie's initiative. Dr. Maurice Heatly would never see Charlie again. Minutes after Charlie Whitman left his office, Dr. Maurice Dean Heatly recorded his notes on the session. He had no idea that the document, numbered 8009, would become the most scrutinized document of his career and that it would change his life forever.

As the university would later correctly argue, Dr. Heatly had three courses of action available to him after his session with Charlie on 29 March 1966. First, he could have determined that Charlie was not a psychiatric case. Second, he could have scheduled a series of visits for further observation, which was what he attempted to do. Serial visits, however, are voluntary and must be agreed to by the patient. Third, he could have diagnosed Charlie as psychotic and committed him involuntarily.

Commonly, references to harming individuals, e.g., "I am going to kill my wife tonight," tend to be taken more seriously than references like "I'd like to blow up the whole damn school," or in this case, "going up the Tower with a deer rifle and shooting people." Many perfectly sane individuals, especially college students, make sick jokes and have fantasies about killing their teachers, boyfriends, girlfriends, parents or spouses. Moreover, Charlie never demonstrated a behavior pattern that could justify a hard commitment. He had been making such statements for years. Five years earlier fellow Goodall-Wooten dorm residents summarily dismissed the idea as facetious. To most people he was "nice." Only minutes before the Heatly session, Dr. Cochrum still thought of Charlie in those terms.

During the next four months there would be no significant demonstrations of dangerous behavior witnessed by anyone which would justify an involuntary commitment. No one appreciated how volatile Charlie was becoming—not even Kathy. Francis Schuck, Jr., while on a visit to the Whitmans shortly after Kathy began her teaching career, observed that Kathy's job gave the young couple more financial security than they had ever before enjoyed. The faculty member closest to Charlie, Barton Riley, who had him in two classes and two labs during the semester of the Heatly session, reflected only five months later, "Surprisingly, this dang guy, I thought, had high values."[22]

III

He took drugs. Charlie had convinced himself that chemicals could give him energy to do more, and to do better. Of course the drugs made things worse. They very likely caused one of his more painful frustrations—headaches. Dexedrine, an amphetamine capable of inducing insomnia, became his drug of choice. It also caused mood swings and extreme nervousness. Often used for weight loss, that was not a side effect Charlie suffered. According to Larry Fuess, "[H]e had a weight problem as long as I've known him. He was always going on a diet." Another of his friends claimed Charlie took the pills "like popcorn" and in March 1966, he stayed awake for three days and two nights—going home only for food and a shower. During the same semester, Nelson Leissner visited his sister Kathy. They fixed food and brought it to Charlie, who did not return home from campus during his brother-in-law's two-day visit. Nelson's visit was most likely sometime between 23 May and 3 June, a period Charlie's friends deduced he got no sleep at all. It became a Leissner family joke that Charlie visited Needville to catch up on his sleep. The family knew he took something to stay awake, but they claimed he showed no signs of serious drug abuse.[23]

Others claimed he gave pills to friends who studied with him. Clearly, he had a steady supply of an illicit substance he knew to be illegal. He cited his source as "a friend," someone off campus. During periods of extreme stress, Charlie used Dexedrine to stay awake for very long periods of time. During "finals week" in June of 1966, he allegedly stayed awake for a period of five days and nights, and two days later he repeated that miraculous feat. If true, he would have endured a two-week period with very little sleep.[24]

Clearly, Charlie considered the possession of the pills only a minor violation of the law. He did not believe that the drugs changed his behavior. It was, Charlie asserted, "no big deal, they won't hurt you." But the drugs did hurt him. Their use affected his work, his relationships, and his reasoning. The greatest single effect on him was a loss of efficiency, which racked his mind and caused him to doubt his self-worth. During the fall of 1965, after a long period without sleep, Charlie decided to take a one-hour nap. A classmate had great difficulty waking him. Other classmates witnessed Charlie struggling for three to four hours over calculations that should have taken fifteen minutes. At times he visibly shook and could not hear the volume of a normal spoken voice. He drifted, and sometimes had to be shaken in order to gain his attention.

He simply did not know what he was doing with the drugs and denied their effects. He once indicated to a friend his preference for Dexamyl because it was better than Dexedrine and did not give him headaches as often. In truth, Dexamyl contained Dexedrine and small amounts of amobarbital, a barbiturate. Fewer headaches resulted from the fact that when Charlie took Dexamyl he was taking less Dexedrine and counteracting those reduced dosages with a "downer." He also took Librium to go to sleep.[25] In addition to illicit drugs, the medicine cabinet in the Whitman home on Jewell Street contained thirteen bottles of prescription drugs from seven physicians.[26]

There is considerable debate over the extent of Charlie's drug use and how much it altered his behavior. An investigation by the Texas Pharmacy Board, for purposes of providing testimony for the Texas Legislature, would later conclude that he was a serious abuser. The testimony clearly implied that drugs played a major role in Whitman's psychological problems. The conclusions were based on affidavits of students who witnessed his drug use.[27] Other acquaintances have a more moderate view. Leonardt Kreisle, an engineering professor and Charlie's former academic advisor, dismissed the conclusion. "I had seen him many times, and I never saw dilation of his pupils. If he did use drugs he didn't use much." In a statement to Austin police, Larry Fuess wrote: "I personally never saw Charles J. Whitman take drugs to stay awake. I was aware that he carried a bottle of medicine, but I do not know for sure what was in it."[28]

Like most other aspects of his life, the truth about Charlie's drug abuse may well lie somewhere between two extremes. In this case, however, the opposing views can be reconciled. Most likely, he seriously abused drugs on occasion, staying up for days at a time to study for final exams or other important tests. On those occasions classmates witnessed serious pill-popping and its disturbing effects on Charlie. Under normal circumstances, while interacting with family, teachers and neighbors, he probably took few or no Dexedrine tablets. Further, if his headaches were related to his Dexedrine use, they were likely caused by the drop of Dexedrine levels in his blood when he reduced his dosage, indicating an inconsistent drug intake. To combat headaches he took an over-the-counter remedy called Excedrin, which contains caffeine, a stimulant believed to assist in headache relief by dilating blood vessels. By his own account, Charlie took hundreds of Excedrin tablets in short periods of time.[29] Charlie was not a drug addict, but drugs did affect his efficiency, which is what ultimately troubled him most.

Like his use of drugs, Charlie's violent temperament has been debated. Secondary sources include various unnamed "classmates" reporting how he had physically assaulted a Saudi Arabian student who sat in Charlie's chair by mistake. Reportedly, he threw the hapless student out of the classroom altogether.[30] Larry Fuess, Charlie's closest friend at the time of the alleged incident, flatly refuses to believe the story. In any case, other than fighting while in the Marine Corps, which led to his court martial, and his admission to Dr. Heatly that he got physical with Kathy on two occasions, there are no other significant reports of violence. Most people thought he was nice. Dr. Kreisle thought that too much had been made of Charlie's temper. "He did sometimes lose his cool. He got impatient with people when they said they'd do something and didn't do it.... He knew something was wrong with his head."[31]

By 1 August of 1966 many forces had contributed to a decision by Charlie Whitman to become one of the most violent and destructive individuals in American criminal history. Those forces were demons crusading to conquer his mind, and soon they would win. But many people face similar demons and they do not fight back by becoming violent.

Dr. Heatly was right. Charlie was oozing with hostility.

[1] Lawrence A. Fuess; Connally Report, pp. 9–10.

[2] APD Files: *University of Texas Transcript*, Charles J. Whitman.

[3] FBI Files: *Cole Report*, 17 August 1966, pp. 20–21; Connally Report, p. 4.

[4] FBI Files: *Cole Report*, 17 August 1966, p. 18; Unidentified clipping in AHC dated 5 July 1973; *Austin American-Statesman*, 1 August 1986; *Time*, 12 August 1966.

[5] FBI Files: *Cole Report*, 9 August 1966, p. 3, and 17 August 1966, p. 24, Leduc Statement, p. 6; C. A. Whitman quoted in Time-Life, p. 49.

[6] FBI Files: *Cole Report*, 17 August 1966, pp. 11–12; Time-Life, p. 50; Margaret Whitman's unfinished letter is in APD Files; APD Files: *SOR* by Sgt. Rutledge, 4 August 1966.

[7] Dr. Dana Farnsworth quoted in *Austin American-Statesman*, 9 September 1966.

[8] Texas DPS Files: *Intelligence Report*, 10 August 1966; *Life*, 12 August 1966; *Texas Observer*, 19 August 1966; Time-Life, p. 49.

[9] Lawrence A. Fuess; Time-Life, p. 49; AJS.

[10] Time-Life, p. 49; Lawrence A. Fuess; Texas DPS Files: *Intelligence Report*, 10 August 1966.

[11] C. A. Whitman quoted in *Austin American-Statesman*, 7 August 1966; AJS.

[12] Elaine Fuess quoted in *Austin American-Statesman*, 7 August 1966.

[13] APD Files: Travis County Blood Bank, *History of Donations*.

[14] *National Observer*, 8 August 1966.

[15] Connally Report, p. 12; Dr. Jan D. Cochrum quoted in *Austin American-Statesman*, 3 and 7 August 1966.

[16] *Austin American-Statesman*, 3 and 7 August 1966; *Texas Observer*, 19 August 1966.

[17] *Texas Monthly*, August 1986.

[18] UT Health Center.

[19] Ibid.; Connally Report, p. 10; AJS; Dr. Heatly quoted in *Texas Observer*, 19 August 1966; *Austin American-Statesman*, 3 August 1966.

[20] UT Health Center.

[21] Ibid.; AJS; *Newsweek*, 15 August 1966; *Texas Observer*, 19 August 1966; *Austin American-Statesman*, 3 August 1966.

[22] Connally Report, p. 4; UT Health Center; Barton Riley quoted in *Texas Observer*, 19 August 1966.

[23] APD Files: *DOI*, Interview of L. A. Fuess 8 August 1966; *Affidavits*, Thomas Frank Sewell, 5 August 1966, Nelson Leissner, 12 August 1966; Texas DPS Files: *Record of Investigation*, n.d.

[24] APD Files: *Affidavit*, Richard Owen Clark, 8 August 1966.

[25] APD Files: *Affidavits*, Thomas Frank Sewell, 5 August 1966, Richard Owen Clark, Robert Don McCrary, 8 August 1966; *Austin American-Statesman*, 6 July 1986.

[26] APD Files: *SOR* by Ed Tramp, 25 August 1966.

[27] Unidentified clipping in AHC; *UTmost*, September, 1991.

[28] Professor Leonardt Kreisle quoted in *Daily Texan*, 1 August 1986; Connally Report, p. 10; APD Files: *Affidavit*, Lawrence A. Fuess, 7 August 1966; Lawrence A. Fuess.

[29] APD Files: Charles Whitman's Notes, *Affidavit*, Robert Don McCrary, 8 August 1966; *UTmost*, September 1991.

[30] Time-Life, p. 46.

[31] Leonardt Kreisle quoted in *Daily Texan*, 1 August 1986.

6

After
Much
Thought

I

During the summer of 1966 mass murder frequented the news. Truman Capote's *In Cold Blood* ushered in a "new journalism," where real events were reported with fictional techniques. Capote engaged in a prolonged investigation to detail the mass murder of the Clutter family of Holcomb, Kansas, by two wanderers on 15 November 1959. Although first serialized in *The New Yorker* magazine in 1965, *In Cold Blood* was still the year's most talked about bestseller in 1966.

Mr. Herbert Clutter, an affluent wheat farmer, employed

several farm hands. Floyd Wells, a former employee, later served time in the Kansas State Penitentiary where he became friends with a fellow prisoner named Richard E. Hickock, who made repeated efforts to learn as much about the Clutter family as possible. Specifically, Hickock was interested in finding out if the Clutters had a safe in their home. Wells either suggested or Hickock conjured up a nonexistent safe located in a wall behind Herb Clutter's office desk. Eventually, Hickock was paroled. Shortly afterwards he and a friend named Perry E. Smith headed for the Clutter home, where they expected to steal at least ten thousand dollars. They did not know that Herbert Clutter had a well-known reputation for not carrying cash; anyone in Holcomb could have told the pitiful fools that Herb Clutter paid for everything by check.

Hickock and Smith sneaked into the home through an unlocked door (most people from Holcomb saw no need to lock doors) and terrorized the family before killing Mr. Clutter, his wife Bonnie, and their two children Kenyon and Nancy. Each of the victims had been tied at the wrists. Mrs. Clutter and her children were murdered by shotgun blasts to the head from short range. Mr. Clutter's body was found in the basement of his home; he had been shot in the head and his throat had been slashed.[1]

Still in prison, Floyd Wells notified the warden of Hickock's interest in the murdered family. A manhunt ensued and shortly thereafter Hickock and Smith were arrested in Las Vegas after having traveled much of the United States and Mexico. Both men confessed and revealed that the brutal murder of the family of four netted only fifty dollars. After his arrest, Smith said of Clutter, "He was a nice gentleman [and] I thought so right up to the moment I cut his throat."[2] Hickock and Smith were hanged in April of 1965. Capote released *In Cold Blood* the next year. Hickock, and especially Smith, became infamous characters not only in American criminal history, but in literature as well. *In Cold Blood*, specifically its brilliant descriptions of two mass murderers, made Truman Capote an American icon.

In late July of 1966 America was horrified by a mass murder in Chicago. A lone drifter and abuser of alcohol and drugs named Richard Speck forced his way into a large but crowded apartment that functioned as a student nurses' dorm for the South Chicago

Community Hospital. Six of the nine young nurses who lived in the house were trapped immediately. He took their money and waited for the other three to return. Speck bound them with bedsheets he had cut into strips. For the next four hours, Speck committed some of the most heartless and brutal murders in American criminal history. He did not seem to tire of killing; he took eight of the nurses, one at a time, and murdered them with his bare hands. Although armed with a knife and a pistol, he strangled five of the young women and stabbed only three. He also sexually assaulted one, Gloria Davy, who bore a tragic resemblance to Speck's former wife. The terror-stricken student nurses could hear the last gasps of each victim as she died. After each murder, Speck paused to wash his hands, so that the young women were conditioned to expect Speck's return for another victim every time the lavatory faucet was turned on—then off. The ninth intended victim, Corazon Amurao, maneuvered herself under a bed where she hid for several terrifying hours. Speck apparently lost count of his victims and overlooked her. At 5:00 A.M. she heard the familiar ring of an alarm clock. Ms. Amurao remained hidden beneath the bed in the still and eerily quiet apartment. At 7:00 A.M. after managing to free herself of the strips of bedding that Speck had used to tie her, she crawled out to find three of her dead friends in the next room; she pushed out a window screen and stepped out onto a second floor ledge, where her screams alerted the neighborhood to the grisly tragedy.[3]

Chicago officials called the murder of the young women the "Crime of the Century." It paralyzed the city. Unlike the victims of Chicago's other notorious mass murder, the St. Valentine's Day Massacre, these victims were beautiful young women, innocent students engaged in the laudable work of easing the pain of others. One of the most intense manhunts in American history ensued, and Richard Speck was arrested a few days later in a cheap hotel after he attempted to commit suicide by slashing his wrists.

The *In Cold Blood* murderers, Richard E. Hickock and Perry E. Smith, and Chicago's Richard Speck reinforced a neat, albeit erroneous, stereotype many Americans had of murderers as creepy-looking drifters, the kind who could be seen and avoided because they *looked* like murderers. They were brutal animals with no conscience who relished the terror they induced in their victims. Their sick and sadistic crimes could never happen in public places where civilization takes the form of righteous witnesses and law enforcement. Hickock, Smith and Speck were seen as fugitives who valued their lives. They were melodramatic movie-like demons interested in surviving; they were not normal-looking people living and working among us. And they were ugly and probably stupid, too. Capote's vivid depiction of Richard Hickock's tattoos reinforced the commonly-accepted image of mass murderers in America:

> The tattooed face of a cat, blue and grinning, covered his right hand; on one shoulder a blue rose blossomed. More markings, self-designed and self-executed, ornamented his arms and torso: the head of a dragon with a human skull between its open jaws; bosomy nudes; a gremlin brandishing a pitchfork; the word PEACE accompanied by a cross radiating, in the form of crude strokes, rays of holy light; and two sentimental concoctions—one a bouquet of flowers dedicated to MOTHER—DAD, the other a heart that celebrated the romance of DICK and CAROL, the girl whom he had married when he was nineteen, and from whom he had separated six years later in order to "do the right thing" by another young lady, the mother of his youngest child.[4]

Perry E. Smith's tattoos received less attention:

> While he had fewer tattoos than his companion, they were more elaborate—not the self-inflicted work of an amateur but epics of the art contrived by Honolulu and Yokahama masters. COOKIE, the name of a nurse who had been friendly to him when he was hospitalized, was tattooed on his right biceps. Blue-furred, orange-eyed, red-fanged, a tiger snarled upon his left biceps; a spitting snake, coiled around a dagger, slithered down his arm; and elsewhere skulls gleamed, a tombstone loomed, a chrysanthemum flourished.[5]

Richard Speck had an acne-scarred face, and he, too, chose to adorn his body with tacky permanent ink. One of his many tattoos held an accurate and direct description of himself—BORN TO RAISE HELL.

In an odd sort of way, Speck, Hickock and Smith sustained America. Reinforced stereotypes wrapped comfort into a neat little package which held the evil of the crimes together with the ugliness and utter wickedness of the men who carried them out. No room existed in such a package for handsome, bright, nice killers, especially mass murderers.

During the same week that the mass media informed America of the horror Richard Speck had wrought in Chicago, Charlie Whitman, young John Whitman, and his friend visited the observation deck of the Tower. The power of mass murder to capture the attention of, to shock, and to break the heart of a nation could not have escaped Charlie. He had to have been impressed with the new notoriety of the demonic drifter. During that awful week, the infamous label "Crime of the Century" was repeatedly attached to the Speck murders. No one knew that the dubious distinction would last only nineteen days.

II

On 5 April 1966, when Charlie should have been seeing Dr. Heatly for his follow-up session, he instead entered the Main Building of the University of Texas and boarded the passenger elevator to the twenty-seventh floor of the Tower. From there he ascended three steep half-flights of stairs and a short hallway leading to the twenty-eighth floor and a reception area for visitors interested in stepping onto an outside observation deck. A receptionist, whose duties included inviting visitors to sign the guest book and answering questions about the university, was stationed in the area.[6]

Three receptionists staffed the station in shifts. Each had a nameplate to put on a single desk that faced a glass-paneled door which opened onto the deck. A beige vinyl couch for visitors, especially those winded by the stairs, was located next to and east of the desk. Hanging on the east wall next to the couch was a telephone. One of the three receptionists, Mrs. Lydia Gest, later recalled that Charlie visited the deck many times and frequently sat on the couch for brief conversations, a common practice for many UT students.[7]

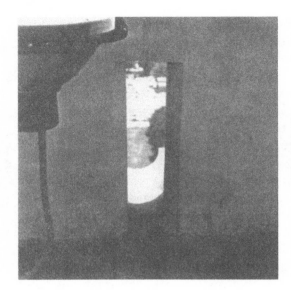

Looking at the ground through one of the rain spouts on the floor of the Tower deck (1966). *Austin Police Department Files.*

Located 231 feet above ground level, the observation deck circles the twenty-eighth floor just below the massive clock at the base of the Tower's columned crown. A limestone parapet borders the deck. Four feet tall and approximately eighteen inches thick, the wall's size and strength made visitors comfortable, but also invited foolishness from reckless college students who straddled, sat, or walked around the top of the parapet. The deck receptionists sternly enforced the rules.

Three large rain spouts for draining water from the floor of the deck descend from each side of the parapet. The spouts jut out from the lower end so that water does not drain down the side of the building. Trying to see into the deck through the spouts from the ground was nearly impossible, but looking at the ground through the spouts from the deck was effortless. The occupants of the Tower's "high ground" could walk right up to the spouts, peer through them and see a wide-angled view of the grounds below. Military experts could hardly have designed better gunports.[8] The strength and thickness of the parapet provided an impenetrable cover. Because of his marine background and fondness for guns, Charlie Whitman instantly recognized the value of the observation deck as a fortress.

East of the campus, but visible from the Tower lay flat, rich, grassy farmlands, along with some of the poorer sections of Austin. To the west rose the panoramic Texas Hill Country—the land of Lyndon B. Johnson, then President of the United States. The hilly northwest section of Austin crept closer to small towns like Jollyville and Cedar Park. Immediately visible from the west side of the Tower, one of the better-known streets of Austin, Guadalupe Street, formed the western border of the campus. Just before the 21st Street inter-section stood the Goodall-Wooten Dorm, where, on a balcony outside of room 706, Charlie first spoke of shooting people with a deer rifle. From the Tower, the West Mall opened to the Drag where the Stu-dent Union and the Academic Center were located. To the north, one might glimpse the old Lanier High School off Burnet Road and the new school under construction on Peyton Gin Road. In that direction Austin crept towards Pflugerville and Round Rock. To the south, only nine blocks away from the Littlefield Fountain and the entrance to the South Mall, stood the majestic Texas capitol, and twelve blocks south of that flowed the Colorado River, which Austinites insisted on calling Town Lake. The University of Texas encircled the Tower on all sides with a host of Spanish-style build-ings sporting red terra cotta-tiled roofs. On any school day, thousands of teachers, students, workers, tourists, and motorists walked or trav-eled within a 500-yard radius of the Tower.

View from the Tower looking east (1966). *Austin Police Department Files.*

View from the Tower looking west (1966). The Hemphill's store at center left is located on Guadalupe Street, the Drag. *Austin Police Department Files.*

View from the Tower looking north (1966). *Austin Police Department Files.*

View from the Tower looking south (1966). *Austin Police Department Files.*

Charlie made another recorded visit to the Tower's observation deck on 22 July 1966, accompanied by his troubled younger brother, John. Though still a teenager, John, along with a friend named Jim Poland, had driven to Austin from Lake Worth to visit Margaret. The boys had embarked on a near-nationwide excursion, part of a summer odyssey that would be cut short in little more than one week. Charlie took them to the Tower to see the campus and the countryside.[9] On the same day he drove to the Travis County Blood Bank and donated a pint of blood, but this time he asked for five dollars. Ten days later he would visit the Tower one last time.

On Sunday morning, 24 July, Charlie, Kathy, Margaret, John and his friend joined one of Margaret's colleagues, Goldie Harris, at her home for breakfast. Afterwards the Whitman family in Texas, except for Margaret, journeyed to San Antonio to see the Alamo and other historic sites. Smiling, each with an arm around the other, Charlie and Kathy posed for their last picture together in front of a stone arch near the Alamo. Other shots show Johnnie Mike and Charlie climbing monuments and engaging in other horseplay. Goldie Harris would later state that she never saw any hint of trouble between Charlie and Kathy. She did believe that Charlie hated his father because of the way his mother was treated.[10]

John Michael "Johnnie Mike" Whitman was a favorite of his older brother Charlie. Shown here in the living room of 906 Jewell Street, Johnnie Mike visited Austin only two weeks before the Tower tragedy. *Austin Police Department Files, from film left in one of Whitman's cameras.*

(left) Johnnie Mike, an unidentified relative, and Charlie Whitman during Johnnie's visit to Austin. *Austin Police Department Files, from film left in one of Whitman's cameras.*

(right) Whitman's friends would not have been surprised to see him do juvenile things—even at the age of twenty-five. Pictured here atop the Alamo Monument in San Antonio. *Austin Police Department Files, from film left in one of Whitman's cameras.*

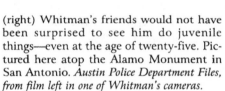

Charlie and Kathy Whitman posed for this picture during their visit to the historic Alamo in San Antonio, Texas. Two weeks later he murdered her as she slept. *Austin Police Department Files, from film left in one of Whitman's cameras.*

III

Still believing that Charlie could and would be willing to influence Margaret into returning to Lake Worth, Florida, C. A. Whitman persisted in his phone calls. The last occurred on Monday, 18 June 1966. According to the elder Whitman: "I told him he was working too hard and he ought to slow down. He was trying to do the impossible, but he didn't hear me. At times Charles did get angry with me for telling him he was working too hard."[11]

Charlie's friend, Larry Fuess, agreed. Larry could not understand why Charlie insisted on such heavy loads of very difficult classes, especially since he was not much of an engineer. Fuess, a gifted student, stood ready to help, especially since Charlie was enrolled in courses Fuess had already taken. But Charlie never asked for any help.[12] Clearly, he was trying to do too much. Fourteen semester hours for a summer session, in addition to a job, were more than he could handle. Why he insisted on such a heavy schedule while dealing with such turbulent personal problems can only be explained through his convoluted definitions of achievement and success: money and influence. The reality of Kathy being the major provider in their household genuinely galled Charlie.

In late July, 1966, Charlie resurrected a "poem" he had written two years earlier while in the brig at Camp Lejeune. In a neat print, in all capital letters, he wrote:

To maintain sensibility is the greatest effort required.
To slip would be so easy. It would be accomplished with
little effort.
Yet, to maintain is necessary in order to benefit from the
future.
Of what benefit?
Will benefit be derived from the future?

To burden others with your problems—are they problems—
is not right.
However, to carry them is akin to carrying a fused bomb.
I wonder if the fuse can be doused.
If it is doused, what will be gained?
Will the gain be worth the effort put forth?

But should one who considers himself strong surrender to
enemies so trivial and despicable?

When is tomorrow, tomorrow is when, when is the future,
the future is tomorrow—is when, tomorrow? Is tomorrow, when? Is the future, tomorrow—Is tomorrow
worth it?

What is worth? What is it?—It is worth, worth is value, value
is effort, effort is worth—effort is work, is work . . .[13]

Paralleling his life, the theme of his writings became more hopeless
and pathetic. Metaphorically, he had been "dousing the fuse" for the
past few years; no longer strong, he would soon surrender to "enemies."

Charlie's penmanship usually mirrored his mood. He neatly
printed thoughtful and happy or indifferent musings, while anger
and frustrations usually produced a scripted scrawl or were typed.
Nearly all of his writings took the form of lists, pathetic attempts at
self-help:

Whitman

1. Grow up (Think—don't be so ready with an excuse)
2. Conduct with superiors (Time and place for everything)
3. Know your status and position and conduct yourself
   accordingly
4. Courtesy (Generally show respect for seniors but lets
   personal feeling towd. indiv. show) [sic]
5. Organize yourself and your work so that the insignifi-
   cant is not a major crisis
6. When time permits exhaust all effort to find answers
   before asking the simplest of questions[14]

IV

Meanwhile, Austin was hot. "It's damn hot! Hotter than a two-
dollar pistol," could be heard during the last week in July when
temperatures were right at or above 100 degrees. The relentless heat

radiated from streets, sidewalks, and cars. Drivers burned their hands on steering wheels; occasionally, windshields of sealed, parked cars shattered. Drivers were warned that the heat inside cars could quickly kill children and pets locked inside. Searing car doors or seats often burned the arms or thighs of occupants wearing skimpy summer clothing. Walking on pavement without shoes was just plain stupid. It meant burns and blisters. Exposure to direct sunlight, even for short periods, could result in sunstrokes or heat exhaustion.

Charlie's little house on Jewell Street lacked air conditioning. Without an occasional breeze the stagnant air made the home an insufferable oven. Occasionally Charlie sat on the front porch hoping for relief. Sometimes he studied and worked at Margaret's air-conditioned apartment. At night he and Kathy slept nude in a bed positioned near a window.

In an attempt to mentally battle the heat, the City of Austin prepared for the Fifth Annual Aqua Fest, a ten-day carnival celebrating water, to be held during the first week of August. A beautiful young actress named Melody Patterson, best known as "Wrangler Jane" on the hit comedy television series *F Troop*, would serve as the Grand Marshall of the parade down Congress Avenue. Austinites anxiously awaited her arrival. Other guests for the event included actor Fess Parker, star of the series *Davy Crockett*. In the next few days Austin would see a number of celebrities. At the Paramount Theater, Adam West and Burt Ward, stars of the hugely popular *Batman* television series, would soon make a special appearance.[15]

The week of 25 July 1966 was uneventful for Charlie. He attended classes as usual and dutifully tended to his job as a research assistant. On Thursday, 28 July, he asked a classmate, Tom Brightman, to return some class notes he had lent to him. Brightman remembered Charlie as kind and gracious, explaining that he needed the notes to study them himself. On the same day he placed a payment on a class ring he had ordered from Zales Jewelry in Austin. Clearly, on 28 July his studies were still a source of concern and he had notions of completing his studies at the University of Texas.[16] The next day, Friday, 29 July, would be Charlie's last day of classes. It would also be his last day of work. His supervisor, Dr. Clyde Lee, observed, "[Charlie] was prompt and asked real mature questions. Other students said he was in good spirits on Thursday and Friday and appeared to have no real reason to be depressed." Charlie's performance on the job had always been satisfactory. On Friday, he made a routine visit to a Gulf Mart convenience store and asked an employee, Roy Hester, if the store stocked distilled water in plastic bottles. When told they did not, Charlie thanked Hester and left without incident. Hester thought Charlie seemed "perfectly normal."[17] No one suspected that he was within two days of a complete and violent breakdown.

On Saturday, 30 July, Charlie relaxed. He took an afternoon nap on the living room couch. Someone, probably Kathy, snapped a picture of him as he slept with Schocie curled contentedly at his feet.[18] It is the last known picture of Charlie Whitman alive.

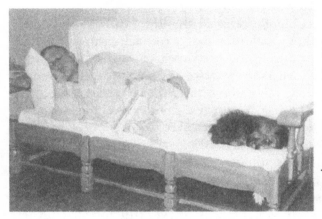

It was probably Kathy Whitman who took this photo of a sleeping Charles Whitman and their little dog Schocie only two days before he climbed the tower. *Austin Police Department Files, from film left in one of Whitman's cameras.*

V

On Sunday, 31 July 1966, it was hot. Kathy Whitman reported to work at Southwestern Bell Telephone in downtown Austin. Charlie drove her there just before 8:30 A.M., when she began a split shift that lasted until 1:00 P.M. Sometime after 11:00 A.M. he stopped by a 7-11 store on Barton Springs Road and purchased canned meat and other food items. He handed the cashier, Jessie Alvarez, a check for $10.00 to pay the $6.65 bill. He also went to Academy Surplus where he purchased a Bowie knife for $5.44 and a pair of binoculars for $18.98. The cashier did not ask for an ID because Charlie looked like "such a nice young man."[19] The Barton Springs 7-11 was located very near the Whitman's Jewell Street home, and $6.65 of groceries hardly suggests anything more than a routine trip for household supplies. But the Bowie knife and the binoculars would figure prominently in his plans for the next twenty-four hours. It was the first indication of a decision to become a murderer.

At 1:00 P.M. Charlie drove back to Southwestern Bell and picked up Kathy. They went first to a movie and then to Wyatt's Cafeteria in the Hancock Shopping Center, where they joined his mother, Margaret, for a late lunch.[20] Their arrival during her break indicates that the three had arranged to meet. By all accounts they had a pleasant meal, and Charlie and Kathy seemed to enjoy each other's company on their last afternoon together. No one suspected that he was within three hours of a breakdown.

After lunch with Margaret, Charlie and Kathy drove to north Austin where they surprised their friends John and Fran Morgan. The Morgans afterward remembered that Charlie acted strangely; he was unusually quiet. Afterwards they may have gone home, or Charlie may have taken Kathy directly to work to complete her split shift. No evidence of any unusual happenings exists. Kathy reported back to work at 6:00 P.M. and no one at Southwestern Bell remembered anything in her behavior to indicate trouble. On the contrary, all remembered a happy, upbeat employee. Charlie returned to his perfectly ordered home on Jewell Street. Kathy had always been neat. If Charlie went straight home from the telephone company (and there is no evidence to suggest otherwise), he must have gotten home at approximately 6:15 P.M. Within the next half hour, whatever doubts he may have had were gone. He made a firm decision to become a mass murderer. From that moment on he became extraordinarily and uncharacteristically focused—on killing.

VI

Later, people who saw Charlie on the evening of 31 July 1966, would describe him as unusually calm. For once Charles Whitman had no doubts, no insecurities; he was uniquely qualified for what he intended to do. He had the background and training, and he knew the terrain.

Making lists and writing in his diary brought Charlie some measure of tranquility. On Sunday, 31 July 1966, at 6:45 P.M., he made a pathetic attempt to make sense of what he was planning. He placed a small typewriter with a worn ribbon on the coffee table in the front living room and began a rambling farewell.

> Sunday
> July 31, 1966
> 6:45 P.M.
> I don't quite understand what it is that compels me to type this letter. Perhaps it is to leave some vague reason for the actions I have recently performed.[21]

In reality, Whitman had done nothing; he had not even prepared to do anything. Hauntingly, he wrote as if speaking from the grave. He knew these troubled and confused notes would be read after his death. He continued:

> I don't really understand myself these days. I am supposed to be an average reasonable and intelligent young man. However, lately (I can't recall when it started) I have been a victim of many unusual and irrational thoughts. These thoughts constantly recur, and it requires a tremendous mental effort to concentrate on useful and progressive tasks. In March when my parents made a physical break I noticed a great deal of stress. I consulted Dr. Cochrum at the University Health Center and asked him to recommend someone that I could consult with about some psychiatric disorders I felt I had.

He believed, or wanted to believe, that he had severe psychiatric problems. Interestingly, he remembered and referred to Dr. Cochrum but never mentioned Dr. Heatly by name. He clearly understood the immorality of what he planned to do, but considered himself a "victim" of his own thoughts.

> I talked with a Doctor once for about two hours and tried to convey to him my fears that I felt come [sic] overwhelm-

ing violent impulses. After one session I never saw the Doctor again, and since then I have been fighting my mental turmoil alone, and seemingly to no avail.

Up to this point, Whitman had managed to suppress the violent impulses he described.

> After my death I wish that an autopsy would be performed on me to see if there is any visible physical disorder. I have had some tremendous headaches in the past and have consumed two large bottles of Excedrin in the past three months.

Significantly, he did not indicate that he had also taken Dexedrine and Dexamyl or that they could have been the source of his headaches, a possibility he readily shared with others. Instead, he focused on Excedrin, a perfectly legal over-the-counter substance. Here Whitman paused to return the typewriter carriage twice in order to start a new paragraph. He had decided he wanted to die, but he did not choose suicide.

> It was after much thought that I decided to kill my wife, Kathy, tonight after I pick her up from work at the telephone company. I love her dearly, and she has been as fine a wife to me as any man could ever hope to have. I cannot rationaly [sic] pinpoint any specific reason for doing this. I don't know whether it is selfishness, or if I don't want her to have to face the embarrassment my actions would surely cause her. At this time, though, the prominent reason in my mind is that I truly do not consider this world worth living in, and am prepared to die, and I do not want to leave her to suffer alone in it. I intend to kill her as painlessly as possible.

In the most revealing portion of his note, he found "this world" unacceptable, largely because he did not function well in it. His peculiar acceptance of an afterlife, and his notion that life on earth was actually hell, contributed to a twisted logic in which he was actually liberating Kathy. He wished the same for his mother: "Similar reasons provoked me to take my mother's life also." In fact, he had done no such thing—yet. But he continued to type: "I don't think the poor woman has ever enjoyed life as she is entitled to. She was a simple young woman who married a very possessive and dominating man." He had reached a frightening mental state. Going beyond the familiar absurdity of mixing love and brutality, he saw murder as an act of love and protection. Charlie's mind then took another turn. "All my life as a boy until I ran away from home to join the Marine Corps," he typed, but did not complete the thought.

He heard a noise and stopped in mid-sentence. Larry and Elaine Fuess had knocked at the door. Larry had become Whitman's close friend, and the Fuess couple considered Charles and Kathy Whitman fun to be with. A number of pictures show the two couples having a delightful time. Larry, like Charlie, was an architectural engineering major and considered by some to be one of the brightest students in the College of Engineering. Elaine Fuess worked in the capitol in the computer section of the State Comptroller's office.

Whitman greeted Larry and Elaine and stated, "I was writing to a friend in Washington whom I haven't seen in five years." Both noticed that Charlie was unusually calm and in good spirits. He recounted hilarious stories of living in Goody Woo. The Fuess couple had fun listening to Charlie's stories. Some accounts of the visit claim that the three friends discussed heavy topics like the Vietnam War, that Larry asked Charlie about having to face two exams on Monday, and that he gently teased Charlie by pointing out that he had stopped biting his fingernails. Larry Fuess does not recall any such deep discussions. "I would not have teased him about biting his fingernails. I wouldn't have wanted to hurt his feelings," he maintains. Fuess also claims that they never discussed Vietnam very much on any occasion. And finally, since Fuess did not have any classes with Charlie during that semester, he could not have known if Charlie had any tests.

Larry Fuess described the conversation with Whitman as "very normal." Whitman spoke of a $750 contract he had supposedly signed to buy land along the shores of Canyon Lake. He said he had to do it. When their conversation turned to the absent Kathy, the content of the remarks stunned Elaine:

> Charlie was in high spirits. Otherwise he was quite nor-
> mal, except he seemed relieved. . . . He was talking about
> Kathy with much more sentimentality than usual. You
> don't sit in front of your best friends and just moon over
> your wife. He was unusually tender.[22]

While speaking of Kathy, he betrayed his innermost thoughts. "It's a shame that she should have to work all day and then come home to. . . ." He said it twice and finished the sentence neither time. Otherwise, Charlie had been in as good a mood as they had ever seen him, but the Fuess couple drove away believing something did not add up. The pleasant visit lasted about an hour, interrupted only by a decision to buy ice cream from a Blue Bonnet vendor cruising Jewell Street.[23] It was a good day for ice cream. It was hot.

Whitman bade farewell to his two best friends around 8:30 P.M. He took his notes and most likely placed them in a black attaché. It was almost time to go to Southwestern Bell to get Kathy.

VII

At work, Kathy spoke often of things she and her husband did together. During the last week of July, for instance, she had been preparing for a picnic at a nearby lake with a number of Lanier High School students. She made arrangements to switch shifts with her friend and fellow operator, Patricia Barber, so that she could attend. She made it clear that Charlie would be there as well. Kathy could hardly have planned to bring her husband to a function involving her students if she feared his violence. Kathy had many friends at the company. Her supervisors and co-workers unanimously asserted that if problems existed with her marriage, she covered them up extraordinarily well. Margaret Winn, a Southwestern Bell Supervisor stated, "There was never a hint of difficulty between her and Charles."[24]

Shortly before 7:00 P.M. the shift supervisor, Ruth Perry, conducted a "spot check" of Kathy's performance. Kathy explained that very soon she would return to her teaching position, but the check was done anyway. As usual, she performed in an exemplary fashion, and Mrs. Perry encouraged her to "keep up the good work." At 7:00

P.M. she took a break with another friend and fellow operator named Linda Damereau. Kathy and Linda sat and talked in the lounge. Since Kathy and Charlie had already been to a movie and had eaten with Margaret Whitman at 3:30 P.M., Kathy did not eat. On a table near the sofa, Kathy noticed the previous week's edition of *Life* magazine, featuring controversial pictures of a live birth. She could not imagine what it would be like to give birth, she said, but as a biologist she was intrigued by the pictures. During her conversation she said that she and Charlie would become parents someday.[25] Within minutes of Kathy's wholesome thought, Whitman, back at Jewell Street, typed a paragraph that began with the sentence "It was after much thought that I decided to kill my wife Kathy, tonight after I pick her up from work at the telephone company."

For Kathy Whitman, 31 July 1966 was a long workday that had started at 8:30 A.M. At 9:30 P.M. she was free to go. She walked with her good friend Kay Pearce to the area where headsets were stored; they dropped theirs off, and went on to the third-floor elevator. On the way out of the building, Kathy remarked that she hoped her husband would not stop at a new Dunkin' Donuts that had opened only three weeks earlier on the 600 block of Congress Avenue. "They are ruining my diet," she said. Although she often substituted a popular diet drink called Sego for meals, Kathy was probably more concerned about her husband's diet than her own. She had once mildly complained that he ate too many sweets and snacks at his mother's apartment and that he was getting out of shape.

Kathy and Kay Pearce exited the building through an employee entrance on 9th Street, a one-way thoroughfare going east. Whitman, as usual, was waiting for her. At street level Pearce said, "Bye. I'll see you tomorrow." She remembered Kathy getting into a large dark car. She could not see the driver, but would have thought nothing of seeing Whitman drive the new, black Chevrolet Impala. Pearce watched the car turn right and head south on Congress Avenue. The Whitmans were going home to their neat little house.[26]

---

[1] Carl Sifakis, *The Encyclopedia of American Crime* (New York: Facts on File, Inc., 1982) pp. 154–55; *Time*, 12 August 1966.

[2] Perry E. Smith quoted in Sifakis, *The Encyclopedia of American Crime*, p. 155.

[3] By far the best account of the Speck Murders is Dennis L. Breo and William J. Martin, *The Crime of the Century* (New York, Bantam Books, 1993); see also Time-Life, pp. 6–29.

[4] Truman Capote, *In Cold Blood* (New York: The Modern Library, 1965) pp. 35–36.

[5] Ibid., p. 37.

[6] Connally Report, p. 4.

[7] *Time*, 12 August 1966; *Newsweek*, 15 August 1966; *Austin American-Statesman*, 3 and 7 August 1966.

[8] Time-Life, p. 35.

[9] Ibid.; Connally Report, p. 4; APD Files: *The Daily Record of C. J. Whitman*, entry of 1 March 1964, *SOR* by John Pope, 5 August 1966; *Austin American-Statesman*, 4 and 7 August 1966.

[10] Texas DPS Files: *Series of Events of Charles Joseph Whitman*, n.d.; APD Files: *SOR* by Sgt. Rutledge, 4 August 1966. The pictures referred to in the text are in the APD File and will hereafter be cited as "Whitman Pictures."

[11] C. A. Whitman quoted in *Austin American-Statesman*, 7 August 1966.

[12] Lawrence A. Fuess.

[13] APD Files: *Charles Whitman's Notes.*

[14] Ibid.

[15] *Austin American-Statesman*, 5 August 1966.

[16] *Life*, 12 August 1966; Texas DPS Files: *Intelligence Report*, 3 August 1966.

[17] APD Files: *SOR* by unnamed officer, 2 August 1966; *Austin American-Statesman*, 2 and 7 August 1966; University Health Center.

[18] AJS; APD Files: Whitman Pictures.

[19] APD Files: *SOR* by R. Wisian, 3 August 1966; Texas DPS Files: *Intelligence Report*, 10 August 1966.

[20] *Austin American-Statesman*, 7 August 1966.

[21] APD Files: *SOR* by D. Kidd and B. Gregory, 1 August 1966, *DOI*, Interview of Lawrence A. Fuess, 8 August 1966, and *Charles Whitman's Notes* (subsequent quotes of Charles Whitman's writings are from this source); Lawrence A. Fuess. During my interview with Mr. Fuess on 6 June 1996, he recalled that Whitman had placed the typewriter on the dining room table. The APD *SOR* cited above clearly quoted Fuess as saying that the typewriter was on the living room coffee table. I have given preference to the *SOR* because it is a contemporaneous account.

[22] *Texas Observer*, 19 August 1966; *Austin American-Statesman*, 2 August 1966; Charles Whitman quoted in Time-Life, p. 51; Elaine Fuess quoted in *Austin American-Statesman*, 7 August 1966; AJS; APD Files: *SOR* by D. Kidd and B. Gregory, 1 August 1966, *DOI*, Interview of Lawrence A. Fuess, 8 August 1966; Lawrence A. Fuess.

[23] Charles Whitman quoted in Time-Life, p. 51; Lawrence A. Fuess.

[24] Margaret Winn quoted in *Austin American-Statesman*, 7 August 1966.

[25] *Austin American-Statesman*, 7 August 1966.

[26] Ibid.

7

The Neat Little House and the Swank Apartment

I

On the front lawn of 906 Jewell Street, a single sapling struggled to reach the heights of the older trees in the neighboring yards. The front yard faced south, and from the street a narrow concrete sidewalk connected the curb to two steps leading to a small porch. From the edges, thick grass struggled to grow over the sidewalk. A screen door kept flying pests outside during suffocating summers when the front door was left open. Various shades of tan brick covered all exterior walls of the house. Inside were five small rooms; the front door led to a living room,

In April of 1966 Charlie and Kathy Whitman moved to 906 Jewell Street in south Austin. At the time, the tree in the front yard was a struggling sapling. Directly behind the tree is the front bedroom used by the Whitmans, where Charles murdered Kathy on 1 August 1966. The garage to the right and behind the house is where Charlie stored "a whole lot of military stuff." *Gary Lavergne.*

which led to a small dining room and finally to a kitchen facing the back yard. On the east side of the house were two small bedrooms and a bath. The back bedroom served as Charlie's study, and on its wall Charlie hung a sign: "Strength Has No Quarter." Charlie and Kathy used the front bedroom.[1]

The neat little house did not hold many possessions. As Whitman's father-in-law later recalled, "there wasn't much; they were just kids."[2] Resources went to pay for their college educations.

Much like everything else about Kathy Whitman, her home was orderly. The Whitmans universally impressed their neighbors, who considered them a model couple: smart, beautiful, and hardworking. Kathy portrayed an innocent, small-town disposition and was both physically feminine and intellectually tough. She combined the best of two very different places: Needville and Austin. After her graduation and entrance into the teaching profession it became obvious that she supported the household. Whitman, a "massive muscular youth," worked hard, but towards nothing specific. Casual acquaintances considered him articulate and impressive, never seeing his lack of direction. More-than-casual friends knew of his ineptitude in dealing with personal and other pressures, some of which he placed on himself. Most people thought him uncomplicated and nice. No one remotely believed him to be dangerous—not even Kathy.

And so, on 31 July 1966, shortly after her shift ended at 9:30 P.M., Kathy stood at an "employees only" entrance to the Southwestern Bell Telephone Company Building at 120 9th Street, turned to Kay Pearce, smiled and said, "Bye." Then she walked along a sloping sidewalk towards a new black Chevrolet Impala parked nearby. She entered the car and made herself comfortable for a drive home with her husband.

Charles and Kathy arrived home around 9:45 P.M. Kathy had spread a full day's work over a thirteen-hour period and was scheduled to report back at 8:30 the next morning. But she was still awake at about 10:15 P.M. when her close friend and colleague from Lanier High School, a typing teacher named Eva Bayne, called to invite her to a party later in the week. Bayne remembered having a pleasant conversation with Kathy, who seemed in good spirits. Kathy accepted the invitation and the conversation ended between 10:30 and 10:45 P.M. It was Bayne's second attempt to reach Kathy that evening. She had called earlier at about 9:30 P.M. and caught Whitman just before he left to pick up his wife. When Bayne suggested that she would call back in the morning, Whitman insisted that she call again later in the evening because Kathy would be at work the next morning. Bayne detected nothing unusual in Whitman's voice. Shortly before (or after) Bayne's call, Charlie and Kathy called the Leissners in Needville.[3]

At 9:15 P.M., Margaret Whitman's shift at Wyatt's Cafeteria ended, and she accepted an invitation to the home of Goldie Harris. At the Harris home Margaret enjoyed the company of a new friend as they sat, talked, and ate ice cream. During the afternoon Austin had reached a record high temperature for all of 1966—101 degrees. About 10:30 P.M. Margaret called her son at home to let him know her whereabouts. Whitman asked if he and Kathy could go to her air-conditioned apartment to study and "cool off before going to bed." Margaret then rushed home to meet him.[4]

Shortly after separating from her husband and moving to Austin, Margaret had moved into Apartment 505 of the "Penthouse."

Known in Austin as "swank" apartments, they were located at 1212 Guadalupe Street, on the corner of 13th, about ten blocks south of the section of Guadalupe called the Drag. Due east, the state capitol dominated the urban scenery. Shortly after sunrise on clear days, its shadow nearly reached The Penthouse. Not surprisingly, the eldest Whitman son spent a lot of time with his mother. Margaret designated him as next of kin on her new resident information sheet. She doted on him enough to hurt the feelings of her other son Patrick, making him feel neglected. She stocked an unhealthy supply of junk food that attracted Charles, and he ate enough of it to concern Kathy.

Whitman left his Jewell Street home for the Penthouse at or slightly before midnight. Kathy took off her wedding band and placed it with her gold watch and a dinner ring on her bedroom dresser. Her purse contained her driver's license and $2.08. She took off her clothes and went to bed nude; it was hot. She was probably asleep when her husband left.[5]

The Penthouse Apartments, located on the corner of 13th and Guadalupe Street, just south of the "Drag" and within the shadow of the Texas State Capitol. Margaret Whitman moved into apartment 505 here shortly after separating from C. A. Whitman in March of 1966. *Gary Lavergne.*

II

The midnight hour arrived, and only a couple of minutes into 1 August 1966, Margaret Whitman, dressed in pajamas and a robe, walked down to the lobby of the Penthouse and waited for her son to arrive. She walked over to the door and greeted Charles only a few minutes later and introduced him to the night watchman, a UT student named Richard "Dick" Thommassen. The observant guard noticed that Whitman carried a black attaché. Earlier, Margaret had told Thommassen that her son intended to study, so his having an attaché did not seem unusual. "This is my Charlie," she said to the watchman, and then mother and son went up to her apartment.[6]

Margaret and her son reached the door of Apartment 505 between 12:15 and 12:25 A.M. He wasted no time. He followed her into the south bedroom, and in front and to the left of one of her twin beds he attacked his mother. Exactly how he killed her, i.e., what he did first, will never be known. On the next day a five-foot rubber hose was found in the black attaché. Most likely, he used the hose to strangle her from behind until she collapsed, unconscious, which would explain why no one heard any screams or sounds of a struggle. Given their relative size and strength, Whitman could easily have kept his mother still until she died.

Whitman also did something to the back of her head. Due to his fondness for and mastery of firearms, the massive damage to her skull was commonly interpreted to be a gunshot wound. But no autopsy was performed on Margaret and those reports cannot be positively confirmed. Compelling reasons to question whether Whitman shot her also exist. Neighbors directly below Margaret claimed they could easily hear virtually anything dropped on the floor above. The walls of apartments such as the Penthouse were relatively thin. If Whitman had shot his mother, or if a significant struggle had occurred, someone in the Penthouse should have heard something. Rather than shooting her, Whitman quite possibly bashed in her head with a heavy object.

He also hit her left hand so viciously that her fingers were nearly crushed, the diamond in her engagement ring popped out, and the wedding band was deeply embedded in her flesh. The wound on her fingers had a straight edge, leading to a popular explanation that she suspected danger, tried to escape the attack of her predator-son, and got her hand caught in a door. Again, it is inconceivable that Margaret would have had time to acknowledge danger and have her hand crushed during a life-and-death struggle without anyone hearing anything. Surely she would have screamed loudly enough for neighbors to hear, if not in fear then in pain, as her fingers were being crushed. During the investigation into Margaret's death the Austin

Police Department did not know of allegations that C. A. Whitman had tried unsuccessfully to remove Margaret's rings before she left him. If Charles Whitman knew of such a struggle, the destruction of her rings would almost certainly represent a determination not to let his father retrieve them. The wounds on her left hand were almost certainly inflicted post-mortem.[7]

Whitman inflicted one more wound on his mother; he used a large hunting knife to stab her in the chest. In all probability, Margaret Whitman never actually saw her son strike the fatal blow. He did it quickly and in a way that did not allow her to make any noise. He avoided attracting attention. He had more killing to do.

While Charles Whitman was still in his mother's apartment, two men named Steven Foster and Scott Smith stepped off the elevator on the fifth floor and headed towards apartment 511. They later reported hearing what they described as a child crying and whimpering. Charles Whitman had just killed his mother.[8]

Given the nature of his mother's fatal wounds, he probably washed his hands and the hunting knife before he sat down with a blue ink pen and a lined, yellow legal pad to write.

> Monday, 8-1-66, 12:30 A.M.
> To Whom It May Concern:
> I have just taken my mother's life. I am very upset over having done it. However, I feel that if there is a heaven she is definitely there now. And if there is no life after, I have relieved her of her suffering here on Earth. The intense hatred I feel for my father is beyond description. My mother gave that man the 25 best years of her life and because she finally took enough of his beatings, humiliation, degradation, and tribulations that I am sure no one but she will ever know—to leave him. He has chosen to treat her like a slut that you would bed down with, accept her favors and then throw a pittance in return. I am truly sorry that this is the only way I could see to relieve her suffering but I think it was best. Let there be no doubt in your mind that I loved the woman with all my heart. If there exists a God, let him understand my actions and judge me accordingly.[9]

M-96815

Monday
8-1-66
12:30 A.M.

To WHOM IT MAY Concern,

I have just taken my mothers life. I am
very upset over having done it. However I feel
that if there is a heaven she is definitely
there now. And if there is no life after,
I have relieved her of her suffering here on
earth. The intense hatred I feel for
my father is beyond description. My mother
gave that man the 25 best years of her life
and because she finally took enough of his
beatings, humiliation and degredation and
tribulations that I am sure no one but
she and he will ever know — to leave
him. He has chosen to treat her like
a slut that you would bed down with, accept
her favors and then Throw a pitance in
return.
    I am truly sorry that this is the only
way I could see to relieve her sufferings
but I think it was best.
    Let there be no doubt in your mind I
loved that woman with all my heart.
    If there exists A God let him understand
my actions and judge me accordingly.

                    Charles J. Whitman

The note Charles Whitman left on the yellow legal pad he placed on his mother's body. *Austin Police Department Files.*

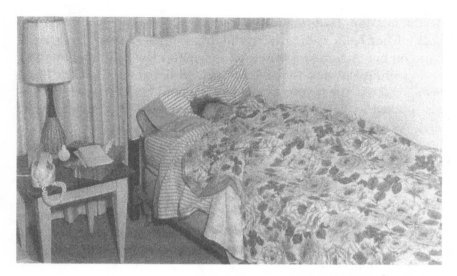

Shortly after midnight on 1 August 1966 Charles Whitman committed his first murder when he killed his mother at the foot of one of the twin beds in her bedroom in the Penthouse Apartments. He then lifted her body and covered her with the floral bedspread. Top photo, *Texas Department of Public Safety Files*. Bottom photo, *Austin Police Department Files*.

Through this tirade, Whitman clearly intended to hurt his father by identifying the Whitman patriarch as the motivation for what he had done and was about to do. Whitman knew that if his plans came to fruition the mass media would descend upon the Whitman home in Lake Worth, Florida. His revengeful mind probably envisioned a righteous nation seeking retaliation and taking out its hatred on his despised father. The reference to C. A. Whitman giving "pittances" to Margaret was simply untrue, and calls into question everything else he writes about his father. Hatred and spite had joined the demons that now ruled Charles Whitman's mind.

Near 1:00 A.M., Whitman secured Margaret's body in such a way as to delay its discovery long enough for him to complete his deadly mission. He lifted her onto the bed. With the wound on the back of her head hidden in her pillow, he placed Margaret's right hand on her abdomen, positioned the yellow legal pad on her body, and carefully covered the stab wounds in her chest with her floral bedspread. As the Justice of the Peace would later observe, "If you just looked in you would think she was asleep."[10] Near the front right corner of her twin-sized bed, Whitman used rugs to cover the blood on the floor that marked the spot of his mother's brutal murder. To further delay the discovery, he wrote a note to The Penthouse houseman and posted it on her door.

> Roy,
> I don't have to be to work today and I was up late last night. I would like to get some rest. Please do not disturb me. Thank you.
> Mrs. Whitman

Whitman left the apartment at approximately 1:30 A.M., but instead of entering his car and going home, he returned to the lobby at about 1:45 A.M. Dick Thommassen had been relieved only forty-five minutes earlier by his roommate Charles Bert Hardy. Thommassen had not mentioned Whitman to Hardy. Whitman explained that his mother had fallen asleep and that he had accidentally locked himself out of the apartment. He had promised to fill a prescription for her but had forgotten to bring the bottle with him. After checking the Penthouse register to determine that Margaret did live in apartment 505, Hardy accompanied Whitman and let him in with his pass key. Whitman asked Hardy to be quiet, because Margaret was probably asleep. Hardy did not enter the apartment but waited in the hallway for a few minutes, where he noticed the note to Roy posted on the door. It was a small note torn from a pad. He did not read it but returned to the lobby. Only about five minutes later Whitman returned grinning and shaking an amber-colored medicine bottle.[11]

Exactly why Whitman chose to return to the apartment with a security guard is a mystery. Two reasonable explanations exist. First and most probable is that he may have decided that his cover-up would be strengthened if he could establish with a Penthouse em-

Roy,

I don't have to be to work today, And I was up late last night. I would like to get some rest. Please do not disturb me.

Thank You.

Mrs Whitman

The note Whitman posted to the door of his mother's apartment. *Austin Police Department Files.*

ployee that Margaret did not want to be disturbed. He wanted Hardy to see the note on the door. Another explanation would be that Whitman realized that he had forgotten a bottle of Dexedrine in the apartment after he had locked himself out. He had gone without sleep for some time, and if all went according to plan, he would need to be awake for quite a while longer. He left the Penthouse and headed home sometime between 2:00 and 2:15 A.M.

III

Whitman returned to 906 Jewell Street between 2:15 and 2:30 A.M. He must have made some effort to enter his home quietly as Kathy slumbered peacefully; he did not want to wake her. He planned to kill her "as painlessly as possible." Quietly, he approached the bed where his wife lay. Removing the bedding to expose her nude body, he used the hunting knife and his considerable strength to make five vicious thrusts through the center of her chest and slightly below her left breast.[12] Given the size of the knife and the location of her wounds, Whitman probably hit her heart, the target for which he aimed. Without struggle, Kathy died instantly. As he watched life leave his wife's body, blood flowed over the bed's white fitted sheet along her outstretched left arm. Her head, sunken into a large white fluffy pillow, was tilted slightly towards the left. Only five hours earlier she had fallen asleep without fear. She most likely went from sleep to death without ever seeing her murderer. It was just as well. Whitman was right: she was as good a wife as anyone could hope for. Her loyalty never wavered, even after physical assaults and mental anguish. She stayed with him to the very end. He replaced the bedding over her. Kathy was gone.

Again, given the nature of the fatal wounds he had inflicted, he must have had to wash his hands and the murder weapon before he retrieved the incomplete letter he had been typing only a few hours earlier when Larry and Elaine Fuess visited. Using a blue ballpoint pen he wrote in the left margin:

> friends interrupted
> 8-1-66
> Mon.
> 3:00 A.M.
> <u>Both Dead</u>

Then, after the typewritten portion, "All my life as a boy until I ran away from home to join the Marine Corps," he scrawled the rest of the sentence: "I was witness to her being beat at least one [sic] a month. Then when she took enough my father wanted to fight to keep her below her usual standard of living."

In an attempt to trivialize the area of life in which his father was clearly superior, Whitman again focused on what his father allegedly failed to provide for his mother. C. A. Whitman actually provided quite a good standard of living for his entire family, even after Margaret left Florida. There were allegations from Margaret's brothers, however, that C. A. Whitman had cut off all financial support for Margaret and Charles on 30 July, only the day before he decided to become a mass murderer.

Having placed the blame on his father, Charlie then returned to his own actions.

I imagine it appears that I bruttaly [sic] kill [sic] both of my loved ones. I was only trying to do a quick through [sic] job.

If my life insurance policy is valid please see that all the worthless checks I wrote this weekend are made good. Please pay off all my debts. I am 25 years old and have never been financially independent. Donate the rest anonymously to a mental health foundation. Maybe research can prevent further tragedies of this type.
Charles J. Whitman

In Whitman's hateful mind, it only "appeared" that he brutally murdered his mother and his wife. His twisted benevolence required a quick and thorough job to relieve them of the burden of having to live in this world. That he gave them no choice but to die seems to have escaped him. He made no mention of the people he planned to kill and seemed to be more concerned for the recipients of bad checks he had not yet written. (His bank balance at the time was $13.87.)

Even at this moment, he obsessed over money. The fact that he had never been financially independent bothered him more than the murders he had committed. It seemed to trouble him that he could not pay for the tools of his crime. The final and most heartless of his insults took the form of a post-script below his signature.

Give our dog to my in-laws please.
Tell them Kathy loved "Schocie" very much.
R. W. Leissner
Needville, Texas[13]

He did not seem to appreciate that they loved Kathy very much. Nor did he comprehend what he had just done to the Leissner family, and to a lesser extent what he had done to all of Needville. He wrote not of what he intended to do to a premier university, a city, and more innocent people. Instead, he saw to the adoption of a dog. And finally: "If you can find in yourself to grant my last wish cremate me after the autopsy." He placed the note in an envelope and addressed it and the note "to whom it may concern" and placed it on the bed with Kathy's body. Austin Police Chief Bob Miles later observed, "Considering the situation, he was quite rational in his notes."[14] To others the notes are the most compelling *prima facie* evidence of Whitman's insanity and irresponsibility. Actually, they were neither. They were further attempts to have questions and guilt directed at C. A. Whitman of Lake Worth, Florida.

Just before 3:00 A.M. on 1 August 1966, Whitman killed his wife, Kathy, as she slept. Five vicious thrusts to her chest with a large hunting knife probably meant that she went from sleep to death without ever knowing who killed her. Only a few hours earlier she had pleasant telephone conversations with a teaching colleague and her family in Needville, Texas. *Texas Department of Public Safety Files.*

After killing Kathy, he had to have spent a considerable amount of time reviewing his diary entries about her over the years. His entry of 23 February 1964 had been devoted almost entirely to her. He gushed about her versatility, physical features and his life with her. It was to last forever. Above the top line of the entry he wrote in large letters, "I still mean it. CJW 8-1-66." He used the same light blue ballpoint pen he had used to write "Both Dead" on the note entitled "To whom it may concern."

On 23 February 1964 he had closed his comments about her: "My Darling Kathleen, I love you very much. That statement is so simple but maybe someday I'll be able to convince you of all the emotions and feelings that it encases. My wife, you are wonderful." Shortly after he killed her he added: "Only time has shown me how right I was in these thoughts over 2-1/2 years ago. My wife was a true person. CJW"

Whitman wrote four more notes. On a slip of paper he used a green felt-tipped pen to write: "Have the film developed in these cameras." He placed the two cameras and the note next to Kathy's

I don't quite understand what it is that compels me to type this
letter. Perhaps it is to leave some vague reason for the actions I
have recently performed. I don't really understand myself these days.
I am supposed to be an average reasonable and intelligent young man.
However, lately (I can't recall when it started) I have been a victim
of many unusual and irrational thoughts. These thoughts constantly
recur, and it requires a tremendous mental effort to concentrate on
useful and progressive tasks. In March when my parents made a physical
break I noticed a great deal of stress. I consulted a Dr. Cochrun
at the University Health Center and asked him to recommend someone
that I could consult with about some psychiatric disorders I felt
I had. I talked with a Doctor once for about two hours and tried to
convey to him my fears that I felt come overwhelming violent impulses.
After one session I never saw the Doctor again, and since then I have
been fighting my mental turmoil alone, and seemingly to no avail.
After my death I wish that an autopsy would be performed on me to
see if there is any visible physical disorder. I have had some tremendous
headaches in the past and have consumed two large bottles of Excedrin
in the past three months.

It was after much thought that I decided to kill my wife, Kathy, tonight
after I pick her up from work at the telephone company. I love her
dearly, and she has been as fine a wife to me as any man could ever hope
to have. I cannot rationaly pinpoint any specific reason for doing this.
I don't know whether it is selfishness, or if I don't want her to have
to face the embrassment my actions would surely cause her. At this time,
though, the prominent reason in my mind is that I truly do not consider
this world worth living in, and an prepared to die, and I do not want
to leave her to suffer alone in it. I intend to kill her as painlessly
as possible.

Similar reasons provoked me to take my mother's life also. I don't think
the poor woman has ever enjoyed life as she is entitled to. She was a
simple young woman who married a very possessive and dominating man.
All my life as a boy until I ran away from home to join the Marine Corps

*friends
interrupted
8-1-66
Mon
3:00 A.M.
Both Dead*

*I was a witness to her being beat at least
one a month. Then when she took enough
my father wanted to fight to keep her because
her usual standard of living.*

*I imagine it appears that I brutaly
kill both of my loved ones. I was only
trying to do a quick thorough job.*

The half-typed, half-handwritten letter that Whitman left on his wife's body. His
notation, "Both Dead," indicates that he had already killed his mother by this time,
too. *Austin Police Department Files.*

Then a person without a degree

I STILL MEAN IT. APD 81-66
888 DTDIC   23 FEB '64

I started to talk about her last night but I decided not to. However I would like to write down some of my thoughts about my wife, so that I can compare them with the ideas and thoughts I have in the years to come. My wife Kathy is one of the most versatile young women I have ever known. In fact due to the closeness of our relationship I can honestly say that she is the *most* versatile woman I have ever known. I don't think there is anything that she cannot do if she puts her mind to it. By professional standards she is not beautiful, she is too short. And she does not have a versatile figure. But to me, she is everything I want in a wife. To me as her husband, she is beautiful, her only physical fault in my opinion is that her knees and thighs are heavier than they should be. Other than that she is gorgeous, her face and hair are just perfect. Her eyes are like twinkling stars, they are what fascinated me on our first meeting. Her breasts are more than ample and in the nude they are just fabulous. Perfectly shaped. I am constantly amazed at her tiny waist, and I just adore her hips. In high heel shoes I would match her lower legs against any recognized bathing beauty. To me the overall package is just perfect. She fulfills my every smallest desire as for as her physical being goes. Since our marriage I have never looked at another woman and made a preference for her over Kathy, except for her upper legs.

The 23 February 1966 diary entry on which Whitman wrote, "I still mean it," after killing his wife that he claimed to love and admire so much. *Austin Police Department Files.*

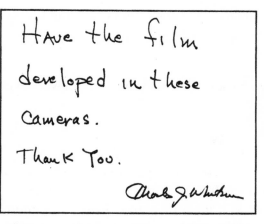

Have the film
developed in these
Cameras.
Thank You.
Charles J. Whitman

It is still not entirely clear why Whitman wanted the film in his cameras developed. *Austin Police Department Files.*

wedding band on the dresser. The photos depicted a livestock show and carnival held the previous March and other happier occasions in San Antonio and Town Lake. To his brother John, whom he had seen only a few days earlier, he wrote a short letter.

> 8-1-66
> Monday
> 3:00 A.M.
> Dear Johnnie,
> Kathy and I enjoyed your visit. I am terribly sorry to have let you down. Please try to do better than I have. It won't be hard. John, Mom loved you very much.
> Your brother,
> Charlie

The letter he wrote to his brother Patrick hints at deep and bitter divisions within the Whitman family:

> 8-1-66
> Monday
> 3:00 A.M.
> Pat,
> You are so so wrong about Mom. Maybe some day you will understand why she left Daddy. Pat, Mom didn't have any desire to harm Daddy whatsoever. She just wanted what she had worked for. She really needed that $40.00.

Thanks for sending it. She'll never know about that Grandmother or not.

Charlie[15]

Whitman's final letter to his father, C. A. Whitman, has never been
made public.[16]

IV

Whitman's grandiose schemes for mass murder required meticulous planning. For the next seven hours Whitman remained focused
to an extent he had seldom, if ever, demonstrated on other, more
wholesome pursuits. First, he retrieved from the small garage a green
footlocker in which he would store his arsenal and other supplies. A
forwarding address was stenciled in white letters on the marine locker:
"C. A. Whitman, P.O. Box 1065, Lake Worth, Fla., USA" along with
"Lance Cpl. C. J. Whitman" followed by a fleet marine address. He
packed as though remembering his assertion that "an army could be
held off" from the Tower. The Austin Police Department later cata-
logued an amazing array of supplies including but not limited to:

Channel Master 14 Transistor AM-FM Radio (portable)
 with brown case
Robinson Reminder (note book, no writing)
white 3-1/2 gallon plastic water jug (full of water)
red 3-1/2 gallon plastic gas jug (full of gasoline)
sales slip from Davis Hardware for 1 August 1966
four "C" cell flashlight batteries
several lengths of cotton and nylon ropes (different lengths)
plastic Wonda-scope compass
paperMate black ball point pen
one Gun Tector, green rifle scabbard
hatchet
Nesco machette with green scabbard
Hercules hammer
green ammunition box with gun cleaning equipment
Gene brand alarm clock
cigarette lighter

canteen with water
green Sears rifle scabbard
Camallus hunting knife with brown scabbard and whitt
    stone
large Randall knife with bone handle with the name of
    Charles J. Whitman on the blade with brown scab-
    bard with whitt stone
large pocket knife with a lock blade
10-inch pipe wrench
eye glasses and a brown case
box of kitchen matches
12 assorted cans of food and a jar of honey
two cans of Sego
can of charcoal starter
white and green 6-volt flashlight
set of ear plugs
two rolls of white adhesive tape
solid steel bar (approximately one foot long)
Army green rubber duffle bag
green extension cord
lengths of clothes line wire and yellow electric wire
bread and sweet rolls
gray gloves
deer bag[17]

Amazingly, room for guns and ammunition (which the above list does not include) still remained. Whitman's elaborate preparation may have been motivated by a genuine belief that he really could hold off an army from the Tower deck and would be able to stay there as long as he liked; he had enough supplies for several days.

Without question Whitman thought clearly enough to hide effectively the murders he had already committed. He had to explain why Kathy would not show up for work at 8:30 A.M. Knowing that Southwestern Bell switchboards are manned twenty-four hours a day, he called the on-duty shift supervisor at 5:45 A.M. and told her that Kathy suffered from diarrhea and vomiting and could not report for work. He concluded by apologizing to the supervisor.[18]

Whitman's loaded trunk, showing some of the contents. The radio he kept with him to hear the broadcasts about himself is on the floor in front of the trunk. *Austin Police Department Files.*

Once the weapons and his supplies were inside, Whitman had trouble moving the heavy footlocker. At about 7:00 A.M. he left 906 Jewell Street and drove west of downtown to Austin Rental Company at 900 West 10th Street. Arriving around 7:15 A.M., he rented a two-wheeled dolly for the twenty-four-hour rate of $2.04. On his way back home he stopped by Austin National Bank, on the corner of 5th Street and Congress Avenue, and cashed two $125.00 checks, one from his account and the other from an account he shared with Margaret.[19]

Whitman selected his weapons carefully from the many available at his Jewell Street home. After taking inventory of what he had and what he "needed," he decided to buy more weapons. Between 9:00 and 9:30 A.M. Whitman traveled farther north than his other preparations had taken him. Many accounts of his movements have made much of his excursion northward to the small Charles Davis Hardware at 4900 Burnet Road. But Davis Hardware was not that far from Whitman's area of activity and getting there took only a few minutes. At Davis Hardware he bought a 30-caliber Carbine, 3 boxes of shells, two boxes of 35-caliber Remington shells, and one box of 9mm Luger bullets. The attending salesman, Ted Beard, remembered that Whitman "knew exactly what he wanted." They had a brief conversation in which Whitman indicated plans for a trip to Florida to shoot wild hogs. He purchased about $100 worth of merchandise. About fifteen minutes later, however, he returned to Davis Hardware to return a clip that was bent.[20]

From Davis Hardware, Whitman drove to what was probably his favorite gun shop, Chuck's Gun Shop, located at 3707 East Avenue—now Interstate Highway 35 (IH 35). Any central Texan who knew guns knew Chuck's Gun Shop. During the previous year Whitman and his father had made purchases at the shop. Frequently during the past year Whitman had returned to make payments on those earlier purchases. On 1 August 1966, he entered the establishment through the right front double doors. He bought four more boxes of carbine shells, two boxes of 6mm shells, and a can of Hoppe's #9 cleaning solvent. The owner's wife waited on him. The bill

Whitman's arsenal included (from left to right) a 35mm Remington, an illegally customized Sears 12-gauge shotgun, a 6mm Remington bolt action, and a 30-caliber M-1 carbine. The carbine enabled Whitman to fire rapidly, but by far the most accurate and deadliest was the scoped 6mm Remington. *Austin Police Department Files.*

totaled $48.63. Whitman wrote a check and in jest asked the sales-woman not to contact the bank to make sure it was good.[21] (Later in the week the check bounced.)

Less than a mile across IH 35 from Chuck's is the Hancock Shopping Center. When Whitman arrived at about 9:40 A.M. he went straight to the sporting goods section of the Sears store to survey the rifles. He told a clerk named James D. Morehead he wanted to see the 12-gauge automatics. Morehead opened the gun cabinet and Whitman lifted a shotgun to his shoulder and told the clerk that it felt "light compared to the twenty-one pound gun I carried in the service." He bought the gun after asking if there was "mechanism" inside the wooden stock. He also asked if any carbine clips were in stock, but there were none. Here, too, he talked of going to Florida to shoot hogs. He charged his purchases with his Sears credit card after Morehead called for approval to charge $137.95.[22] The entire transaction took about ten minutes.

During his visit to Sears, he must have been reminded of Margaret; the Wyatt's Cafeteria where she worked was a prominent part of the Hancock Center and clearly visible from the route he would have taken from Chuck's Guns. He had not yet explained why Margaret would not be at work by 11:00 A.M. He went straight home to do so. From the Hancock Shopping Center Whitman could have driven south towards home in any number of ways. The University of Texas Tower, like an overbearing chaperon observing the movements of people going about their business, would have overlooked all possible routes. If he thought about what he was going to do, he had to have fixed his eyes upon the deck and the rain spouts on each side of the parapet.

V

It did not seem unusual to Mrs. Johnny Whitaker, a next-door neighbor, when she saw Whitman get out of his car with two rifles; even the neighborhood children, like young Mark Nowotny, knew "he just had a whole bunch of army stuff" in the garage. Everyone knew he spent an inordinate amount of time at firing ranges, and no one in the neighborhood had heard anything unusual or disturbing the previous evening.

Whitman went directly to the door at the rear of the garage and deposited the guns. He had arrived at 906 Jewell Street slightly before 10:30 A.M. He entered the house and called D. W. Quinney, the manager of Wyatt's Cafeteria, and manufactured an illness for Margaret. His fabrication mirrored the one he had used to explain Kathy's absence. Margaret had diarrhea and vomiting and would not be able to report to work.[23] Much would be made of Whitman's selection of those specific bogus symptoms. Attempts would be made to connect diarrhea and vomiting with his use of drugs. The insinuation was that he used symptoms with which he suffered as a drug abuser. That connection is possible, but weak. Today, patient information leaflets for Whitman's drug of choice, Dexedrine (dextroamphetamine), do not list diarrhea but rather constipation as a possible side effect.[24]

Minutes later Whitman returned to the garage and placed the shotgun in a vise. Using a hacksaw, he cut off much of the barrel and stock. As Whitman sawed, the neighborhood postal carrier, Chester Arrington, noticed him in the garage and walked over to the back yard for a chat. Startled, Arrington reminded Whitman of the illegality of his alterations of the shotgun. Charlie responded, "It's my gun, and I can do what I want with it." They spoke for a total of about twenty-five minutes, mostly about guns. According to Arrington, "It was about an hour and forty-five minutes before the killings. He was very, very, very calm." The postman went about his rounds. Shortly afterwards, a very young neighborhood kid walked into the garage; Whitman gave him a new "toy"—the barrel he sawed off the new Sears shotgun.[25]

Whitman continued to prepare his arsenal, the last step in his elaborate arrangements for mass murder. He cleaned the guns, presumably with the fluid he purchased at Chuck's Gun Shop. He then packed a 6mm Remington with a 4-power scope, a 35-caliber Remington rifle, a 30-caliber Carbine, the new Sears (now customized) 12-gauge shotgun, a 357 Magnum Smith/Wesson revolver, a 9mm Luger pistol, a Galesi-Brescia pistol, the large hunting knife he had used to kill Kathy and Margaret, and about 700 rounds of ammunition. Some of the longer guns were rolled into a blanket and would later be tied to the front of the dolly and footlocker.

The 35-caliber Remington and the 30-caliber Carbine were accurate to about 100 yards; the ranges of the pistols were even more limited. Whitman's alteration of the 12-gauge shotgun made it even less accurate over long distances. By far the deadliest weapon in Whitman's arsenal was the 6mm Remington, a powerful rifle, very popular in Texas with deer hunters, and designed for long-range accuracy. The rifle expels a very slim, high-velocity missile over a long distance on a nearly flat plane. The bullets Whitman used were designed to kill by shock; they flattened into a mushroom shape upon impact. Because of its shape, power and speed, the Remington is very resistant to atmospheric interference. Without a scope, targets 300 yards away are reasonable. Even an average shot should be able to hit a target at that distance within six and one half inches, and Whitman was no average shot.[26]

Whitman left behind other guns at 906 Jewell Street: a 410 shotgun, a 25-20 Winchester rifle, and two matched Colt Derringers.[27] He would use almost all of the weapons in his arsenal, but the 6-mm Remington pierced the heart of Austin. From the top of the Tower, all of the other weapons, even in the hands of a trained sharpshooter like Charles Whitman, were of little use. He bought the 12-gauge shotgun for the purpose of short-range battle, apparently anticipating some sort of shootout inside the building, maybe in narrow hallways or staircases. He would use it to secure the twenty-eighth floor and its exterior deck.

In Austin at 11:00 A.M. on 1 August 1966, it was hot. The official temperature at the municipal airport measured 96 degrees, but Austin's concrete and asphalt jungle shot the sun's rays upward as if to take revenge on people. Whitman was wearing sneakers and a red plaid shirt and jeans. To look like a janitor or a repairman in order to haul a large footlocker to the top of the Tower without attracting suspicion, he went back into the house to put blue nylon coveralls over the clothes he already had on. In the 96-degree heat the outfit must have been insufferable.

Kathy's body had lain in the neat little house for over eight hours. No one will ever know if Whitman looked at her one last time. Elsewhere in the house Whitman located one of the many lists he had written or typed over the past few years. He often typed action

verbs and clichés in capital letters. What he called his "Thoughts to
Start the Day" included:

READ AND THINK ABOUT, EVERY DAY
STOP procrastinating (Grasp the nettle)
CONTROL your anger (Don't let it prove you a fool)
SMILE—Its [sic] contagious
DON'T be belligerent
STOP cursing, improve your vocabulary
APPROACH a pot of gold with exceptional caution (Look
    it over—twice)
PAY that compliment
LISTEN more than you speak, THINK before you speak
CONTROL your passion; DON'T LET IT lead YOU—
    Don't let your desire make you regret your present
    actions later (Remember the lad and the man)
If you want to be better than average, YOU HAVE TO
    WORK MUCH HARDER THAN THE AVERAGE
NEVER FORGET; when the going gets rough, the ROUGH
    get going!!!!!
YESTERDAY IS NOT MINE TO RECOVER,
BUT TOMORROW IS MINE TO WIN OR TO
LOSE. I AM RESOLVED THAT I SHALL
WIN THE TOMORROWS BEFORE ME!!!

At the top of his "Thoughts to Start the Day" Whitman scribbled
"8-1-66. I never could quite make it. These thoughts are too much
for me."[28]

Note found at 906 Jewell Street. *Austin Police Department Files.*

Shortly after 11:00 A.M., Whitman left the neat little house at 906 Jewell Street for the last time. With a tightly-packed footlocker on the back seat of his new black Chevrolet Impala and the small blue two-wheeled dolly in the trunk, Whitman drove to the University of Texas at Austin.

---

[1] The description of the interior of 906 Jewell Street is from information provided by Lawrence A. Fuess.

[2] Raymond W. Leissner quoted in *Austin American-Statesman*, 1 August 1986.

[3] APD Files: *SOR* by R. Kelton, 7 August 1966; Texas DPS Files: *Series of Events of Charles Joseph Whitman*, n.d.

[4] *Austin American-Statesman*, 7 August 1966, 6 July 1986; APD Files: *SOR* by Sgt. Rutledge, 4 August 1966; Time-Life, p. 51; *Dallas Morning News*, 1 August 1986.

[5] APD Files: *SOR* by D. Kidd and B. Gregory, 1 August 1966.

[6] APD Files: *SOR* by D. L. Moody, 1 August 1966; *Austin American-Statesman*, 7 August 1966.

[7] The allegation that C. A. Whitman tried to remove Margaret's rings is in FBI Files: *Cole Report*, 9 August 1966, p. 3 and 17 August 1966, p. 24.

[8] APD Files: *SOR* by D. L. Moody, 4 August 1966; *Playboy*, October, 1970.

[9] As in previous chapters, Charles Whitman's notes are quoted from APD Files: Whitman Notes.

[10] APD Files: *Hospitalization Offense Report (HOR)* by D. L. Moody, 1 August 1966; *Austin American-Statesman*, 2 August 1996, Justice of the Peace Dellana quoted in 4 August 1966, 7 August 1966; Connally Report, p. 5; *Dallas Morning News*, 1 August 1986.

[11] APD Files: *Affidavit*, Charles Bert Hardy, 1 August 1966, *SOR* by D. L. Moody, 1 August 1966; Time-Life, p. 53 and *Dallas Morning News*, 1 August 1986 both erroneously reported that Whitman returned to the Penthouse at about 5:30 A.M. The story originated from an error, possibly typographical, in a document which served as a summary/sequence of events in the Texas DPS Files. The reports in the same file do not support Whitman's returning at 5:30 A.M., and neither does the APD File.

[12] Reports of the number of stab wounds in Kathy Whitman's chest vary from two to five. An on-site inquest of Justice of the Peace Frank W. McBee clearly stated that there were five stab wounds. A copy of the inquest is in AHC and will hereafter be referred to as "McBee Inquest"; Connally Report, p. 5; Time-Life, p. 53; *Austin American-Statesman*, 2 August 1966, 1 August 1986; *Time*, 12 August 1966.

[13] The allegation that C. A. Whitman cut off all financial support to Margaret and Charles Whitman came from a voluntary statement of Margaret's brother, Walter Hodges. It is in FBI Files: *Cole Report*, 17 August 1966, p. 13; APD Files: Charles J. Whitman's Notes, *SOR* by John Pope, 4 August 1966.

[14] Austin Police Chief Bob Miles quoted in *Austin American-Statesman*, 7 August 1966; APD Files: Charles J. Whitman Notes.

[15] APD Files: *The Daily Record of C. J. Whitman*, entry of 23 February 1964 with notations added 1 August 1966, Charles Whitman letters to John Whitman and

Patrick Whitman, 1 August 1966, *SOR* by K. R. Herbert, 4 August 1966; *Texas Observer*, 19 August 1966.

[16] *Austin American-Statesman*, 1 August 1976; Time-Life, p. 53.

[17] APD Files: *SOR* by Officer Ligon, 1 August 1966.

[18] *Austin American-Statesman*, 2 and 7 August 1966.

[19] Ibid., 7 August 1966 and 6 July 1986; *Newsweek*, 15 August 1966; APD Files: *Austin Rental Company*, receipt, 1 August 1966, *SOR* by J. Pope, 4 August 1966.

[20] Texas DPS Files: *Series of Events of Charles Joseph Whitman*, n.d.; *Austin American-Statesman*, 7 August 1966; Time-Life, p. 32.

[21] Texas DPS Files: *Series of Events of Charles Joseph Whitman*, n.d.; APD Files: *SOR* by J. Pope, 4 August 1966.

[22] Texas DPS and APD Files: *DPS Voluntary Statement*, James D. Morehead, 2 August 1966, *Sears*, receipt and credit card slip, 1 August 1966; *Austin American-Statesman*, 2 and 7 August 1966; Time-Life, p. 32.

[23] APD Files: *SORs* by D. Kidd and B. Gregory, 1 August 1966, and by B. Gregory, 2 August 1966; Time-Life, p. 32; *Texas Observer*, 19 August 1966; Mark Nowotny quoted in *Austin American-Statesman*, 7 August 1966.

[24] For a discussion of the relationship between Whitman's fabricated symptoms and his drug abuse see AHC, unidentified clipping in AF Murders—Mass, M8960 (1). Constipation as a side effect of Dexedrine is taken from Database Edition 94.4, copyright 1994 by Medi-Span, Inc., used by many pharmacies throughout the country to generate Patient Information Leaflets on prescriptions. A Patient Information Leaflet on Dexedrine was kindly provided by Jim Davies of Cedar Park Pharmacy, Cedar Park, Texas.

[25] Chester Arrington's quote of Charles Whitman is in *Daily Texan*, 1 August 1989 and *Austin American-Statesman*, 27 July 1989; Time-Life, p. 32; Phillip Conner, interviewed by the author on 18 August 1995. Hereafter cited by name only.

[26] *Austin American-Statesman*, 2 August 1966. For an excellent analysis of Whitman's arsenal see Russell Tinsley in *Austin American-Statesman*, 4 August 1966.

[27] APD Files: *SORs* by B. Gregory, 2 August 1966, George Phifer, 9 August 1966, Carl Booth, Jr., Treasury Department, Dallas, Texas, n.d.

[28] APD Files: Whitman Notes; *Austin American-Statesman*, 7 August 1966.

8

The Glass-Paneled Door

On 1 August 1966 beneath a cloudless sky, Charles Whitman drove from the neat little house on Jewell Street to the University of Texas at Austin. Weather forecasters predicted warm, humid nights and hot sunny days. Experienced Austinites knew the pattern: cumulus clouds greeted early morning commuters with spectacular golden formations, but soon intolerant and relentless sunshine melted them away. It would be hot, and if any humidity dared linger, an afternoon thermal thundershower would pelt the area until the sun returned with a vengeance to turn the fallen rain into steam rising from the streets and sidewalks. A light southerly wind, not strong enough to bring relief, accompanied the heat and humidity. When Whitman left his home for the last time, at or slightly after 11:00 A.M., the temperature had climbed to the upper nineties. Vacationers and students on semester break flocked to Barton Creek, where cold spring-fed water supplied bathers with a momentary refuge from the heat. But most Austinites could afford no such luxury and instead wearily prepared for another one of "those" days. It was hot—damn hot.[1]

The drive to the university would not have taken more than twenty to twenty-five minutes. Whitman entered the UT campus through a security checkpoint on 21st Street near the corner of Speedway Avenue, the northern extension of Congress Avenue, between 11:25 and 11:30 A.M. He approached the little white outpost manned by Jack O. Rodman, a UT Security Officer there to relieve the regular security guard during a lunch break. Whitman retrieved his wallet, holding ninety-six dollars remaining from the checks he had cashed earlier in the morning, and presented a Carrier Identification Card to gain admission to the campus. The guard would have been familiar with the ID which was issued to individuals with a frequent need to transport heavy or bulky materials onto the campus. Whitman had been issued such a card as part of his lab assistant duties in Dr. Clyde Lee's highway research project. Whitman explained that he had to unload equipment at the Experimental Science Building and that he needed a loading zone permit for longer than the usual twenty-minute time limit.

Rodman peered through a back window of the car and saw an "Army" issue footlocker covered with a quilt. He also noticed a black attaché. As Rodman looked at the items in the back seat, Whitman, probably to divert the guard's attention, volunteered that other items were in the trunk. Most likely, he wanted Rodman to look into the trunk at the innocent looking two-wheeled dolly instead of poking his head into the car, where he very likely would have noticed the stench of the Hoppe's #9 Gun Cleaning Solvent. The circumstances were normal enough, and the incident quite unremarkable; Rodman began to scribble out a loading zone permit. "I told him that since he had this [the footlocker] to unload that I would give him a while longer." Throughout the encounter Whitman held his ID card so that it could be seen plainly; he wanted Rodman to remember the name Whitman. Rodman did not date the permit but gave Whitman a window of forty minutes—from 11:30 a.m. to 12:10 P.M. Only a few minutes after the brief encounter, Rodman returned to security headquarters for his lunch.[2]

Whitman drove directly to a parking lot adjacent to and north of the Tower where he parked in an area reserved for university administration officials. He opened the trunk and retrieved the dolly, then unloaded the footlocker and other items from the back seat of the car. For some reason, he left the black attaché behind. With his considerable strength he had little trouble taking the cargo up a few cement steps to the entrance of the building. Between 11:30 and 11:35 A.M. Charles Whitman entered the Tower.

Once inside, his plan to pass as a janitor worked well. No one asked any questions or barred his way as he proceeded directly to the elevators. Twenty-seven floors above, Dr. Antone G. Jacobson, an associate professor in the biology department, his young son and daughter, ages two and six, and Dr. J. G. Duncan had just heard the 11:30 A.M. chimes and were descending the stairs connecting the observation deck to the twenty-seventh floor. Jacobson distinctly remembered leaving only the receptionist and a young couple on the deck. When they reached the first floor, the Jacobson party nearly stumbled over the loaded dolly Whitman was waiting to wheel onto the elevator. Like everyone else, Jacobson presumed Whitman to be a "workman with dolly and equipment." Almost immediately Jacobson and Duncan noticed a smell. "It was very hard to identify, but I remember thinking of guns at the time," Jacobson would recall. The professor would also recall that the dolly held more than just a footlocker. A long bundle about eight to ten inches in diameter had been tied to the front of the footlocker, and the load had been capped by several parcels.[3]

Once Dr. Jacobson and his party maneuvered around Whitman and his gear, Whitman entered the elevator, but it did nothing. He then asked Vera Palmer, the elevator attendant and one of the three deck receptionists, for help. She assumed him to be a repairman. "Your elevator is turned off," she said, then reached for a switch and made elevator #2 functional. Whitman smiled and in a barely audible mumble said, "Thank you, ma'am. You don't know how happy that makes me."[4] There are no accounts of anyone else being in the elevator with Whitman during what was probably an uninterrupted thirty-second trip to the twenty-seventh floor, which ended at or just before 11:40 A.M. The schedule called for Vera Palmer to assume her duties on the deck within the next half hour.

On the twenty-seventh floor signs with arrows directed visitors to the observation deck, but Whitman had been there many times. He knew precisely where to go and what to do. Tragically, the signs also gave him an exact measure of altitude; he knew precisely how to set the four-power scope on his 6mm Remington for maximum accuracy. He lugged the heavily laden dolly, one step at a time, up three half-flights of stairs and a short, narrow hallway to a landing. As he ascended the stairs the wheels of the dolly rolled over each step, to be abruptly stopped by the face of the next step. The procedure produced a series of hollow-sounding "thuds." On the twenty-seventh floor librarian Jules Emig heard noises which sounded to him like someone was moving something heavy up the steps to the reception area.

Whitman reached the twenty-eighth floor, and when he walked from the landing through the door into the reception area, he came face-to-face with the receptionist, Edna Elizabeth Townsley.

II

Edna Townsley, Vera Palmer, and Lydia Gest, the three receptionists who supervised the observation deck, had worked out an intricate shift schedule to staff the popular attraction seven days a week. They also kept watch over the elevators. The vacationing Lydia Gest would normally have been on the deck at 11:40 A.M. on 1 August 1966; Edna Townsley would normally have had the day off.[5]

Townsley was a forty-seven-year-old divorced mother of two sons named Terry and Danny. Her sons were a source of pride for Edna, who made sure they were meticulously cared for. "I'm not going to send my boys off to school without their starch," she would say as she ironed their blue jeans.[6] She and her boys lived in north Austin. She had a reputation for being direct and even brusque. Her friends called her "one hell of a scrapper." It was Edna who became infamous among students for insisting that every visitor sign the guest register. She did not allow sick jokes about jumping off the deck and could be stern and quick to turn away children who attempted to sneak onto the deck without their parents. But Edna had a quick sense of humor and was remembered by many for her loud, unique laugh. Tower employees frequently heard her guffaw. Many just shook their heads and said, "Oh! That's Edna." She had joined the UT staff in 1954 and was transferred to the Tower four years later as an elevator operator. On 1 August 1966 she reported to her desk in the reception area on the twenty-eighth floor at 8:00 A.M.; she expected to be relieved at noon by Vera Palmer.[7]

Edna Townsley and Charles Whitman were alone in the reception area on the twenty-eighth floor. It is quite possible that she knew Whitman from his previous visits. She might have been the first to recognize him and demand an explanation for the dolly and the gear. Many of her friends, knowing of her temperament, conjectured that she probably struggled with Whitman, but that is not likely. She may have been a scrapper, but the six-foot, 198-pound ex-marine would easily have overpowered her slim, five-foot-four-inch frame. Additionally, the known sequence of events permitted little time for a struggle. Whitman attacked her immediately. He probably struck her as soon as she turned her back on him, in the same manner in which he had killed his mother Margaret. Near the center of the south wall, close to the entrance to the stairs, he hit Edna on

Scene near desk on the twenty-eighth floor of the Tower. *Austin Police Department Files.*

the back of the head, probably with the butt of a rifle. The vicious blow shattered the posterior of her cranium; parts of bone were ripped away. Her glasses flew from her face as she hit the floor. He hit her again above the left eye and broke her skull again.[8] As she lay bleeding, a ghastly pool surrounded her head. Whitman grabbed her legs and dragged her across the room towards the beige couch, creating a dark, thick streak across the room. He moved the beige couch away from the wall and placed her behind it and out of sight. There Edna Townsley lay, still alive, but critically injured and bleeding profusely.

Whitman was still bending over the couch when a young couple, Don Walden and Cheryl Botts, stepped into the reception area from the outer deck. They were the same couple Dr. Jacobson had seen only a few minutes earlier. Don Walden was a twenty-two-year-old senior English major from San Antonio who worked at Austin's Continental Trailways bus station to pay his way through college. His guest was nineteen-year-old Cheryl Botts of Rockdale, Texas, in Austin visiting her grandmother. She planned to enter Howard Payne College in the fall and major in elementary education. They had been on the deck for almost forty-five minutes and had intended to stay until noon to hear the chimes. Walden showed Botts the countryside and the campus and pointed out a number of sites they would visit later in the afternoon. By 11:50 A.M. they had had enough of the deck and decided to leave. They entered the reception area and noticed the unattended receptionist's desk. Whitman stood silently erect and looked directly at them. He held two rifles, one in each hand. Cheryl would remember seeing a "good-looking young blonde man holding guns." Don thought the presence of the guns unusual and started to ask Whitman if he was there to shoot pigeons; his silence probably saved their lives. Oblivious to the danger they were in, they smiled and said, "Hello." Their greeting seemed to disarm Whitman, who returned the smile and said, "Hi, how are you?" As they walked towards the exit to the stairway, Cheryl looked down and noticed what she would later describe as a "dark stain" which "appeared as if someone had taken a mop and drug it across the floor." Whitman stood silently near Edna's desk "half facing" the couple as Cheryl warned Don not to step in the "stuff"—Edna Townsley's blood. On a landing at the top of the stairs the couple walked around a chair lying on its side; they thought nothing of it and headed for the elevator on the twenty-seventh floor.[9]

Why did Whitman let Don Walden and Cheryl Botts live? There are a number of possible explanations. First, he had committed three murders by the time he encountered Walden and Botts. In each of the killings he probably did not face his victims directly. He may have had an aversion to doing so. Second, he may have been disarmed by the innocence and cordial manner of the young couple. They smiled and said "Hi," so he may have found it difficult to kill them. That is possible, but not likely. He had already killed three innocent people and would soon kill and maim many more, some of whom were children. In a few minutes he would shoot a newspaper boy off his bicycle. Third, and most likely, is that he simply was not prepared to begin his murderous spree. Securing the twenty-eighth floor and deck made killing Edna Townsley a necessity. From the deck, he had a radius of several hundred yards of a densely populated university for a target. Whitman wanted to kill a lot of people, but could care less whom he killed. The window of survival for Walden and Botts could not have been more than a minute, but they made it. Austin Police Chief Bob Miles would later describe them as "the luckiest people in Austin." By the end of the day, they would know that to be an understatement.

III

They were on their first vacation in two years, and the M. J. Gabour family of Texarkana, Texas, was having a ball. They were touring Texas, heading for Austin, to visit M. J.'s sister Marguerite; San Antonio, to visit Mike's good friend Jack Rogers; Houston, to catch a couple of baseball games in the new Astrodome; and Galveston, to spend time on the beach. Mr. Gabour owned and operated a Gulf service station in Texarkana and everyone was surprised when he announced that he would lock it up for a week's vacation. His wife, Mary, who was active in the Altar Society and the Catholic Youth Organization in their church parish, had not intended to make the long trip, planning to stay home instead with their daughter Mary Jane, a recent high school graduate. Mary Jane had just landed a new job at a drugstore and did not want to ask for time off. The mother and daughter looked forward to time together, as Mary would later write, sort of "a holiday for the girls." But Mary's sixteen-year-old son Martin (called Mark) pleaded with her to go along. He apparently felt that in his mother he had a powerful ally; he wanted to make sure his father followed through on the entire trip. M. J. Gabour, a hard worker, was not very good at "loafing." Apparently, Mark's fears were well-founded. M. J. began talking of a shorter trip, leaving on Wednesday instead of Sunday. Mary intervened and agreed to go. They would leave on Sunday, 31 July, after 6:00 A.M. Mass, and were to return the following Sunday, 7 August 1966.[10]

Mark Gabour was within one month of beginning his junior year of high school. His older brother, Mike, had just completed his first year in the United States Air Force Academy. Mike had arrived from the academy during the last week of July. His grades were good; the family had much to celebrate. Mr. Gabour's sister, Marguerite, lived at 2606 Cascade Street. She and her husband, William A. Lamport, served as hosts for the joyous family affair, using the occasion to show off their hometown. While there was much to see, no visit to Austin would be complete without viewing the city and its surrounding countryside from the observation deck of the landmark UT Tower. It was their first stop.[11]

Don Walden and Cheryl Botts, the "luckiest people in Austin," were in an elevator descending toward the ground floor while the Gabours and the Lamports followed the twenty-seventh floor signs and arrows pointing to the stairs to the twenty-eighth floor reception area. If anyone had noticed the Gabours and Lamports walking towards the stairs, they had been dismissed as just another family of tourists, talking and laughing and happy to be together. Mark and Mike, in their youthful exuberance, led the pack and ascended the stairs first. Mary and Marguerite followed closely behind; farther back by at least one flight came the men.[12]

At the top of the stairs Mike noticed that the doorway had been barricaded by a desk that had been turned on its side. Two chairs had been placed above that. He and Mark were delayed long enough for Mary and Marguerite to reach the landing adjacent to the door. They did not know exactly what to do. Mary thought that a janitor was still cleaning. "I don't think they've finished cleaning yet. We'll have to come back later," she said as she turned and looked at Marguerite. Mary would later write that Marguerite looked back with a stern look that suggested, "They can't do this to us!"[13]

"Well, I'll see what's going on," Mike said as the boys pushed the desk and leaned for a look inside the room. Mike started to squeeze past the desk. They saw Whitman to their left gazing out of one of the windows. Mike, too, thought the young man was a janitor cleaning the room. Whitman then turned to his right and ran towards the doorway. Using the sawed-off 12-gauge shotgun illegally customized for just such a situation, he leveled the weapon and sprayed Mike and Mark with deadly pellets as they retreated from the doorway. It could have been the only face-to-face murders Whitman committed. He wanted no more interruptions; he wanted to step outside.

Mike let out a loud scream. Apparently, for a split second, Mark saw what was happening and lowered his head as if to duck. He was shot fatally through the top of the head. They both tumbled backwards and down the stairs as Whitman ran to the doorway and continued to fire at the family rolling down the narrow steel and concrete steps. He fired repeatedly, at least three times, sending dozens of pellets after the helpless victims. In her autobiography Mary would later write:

> I never heard a sound from Mark or Marguerite, so I assumed they were all right. I could see Mike writhing up on his shoulder in pain and then coming down, and each time he came down I thought he was hitting me in the face with his feet. I seemed to be falling just ahead of him. The pain was terrific, and I kept thinking, "I can't say anything to him, and he can't help it, but I do wish he would lose his shoes." Then I thought he did lose them as the blows grew lighter. I really don't know if the pain was from his shoes, the stairs as I hit them, or a bullet. He did lose his shoes and so did I.[14]

The wounds covered their bodies, especially their backs. Mary, although critically injured, thought of Mike's scream and assumed correctly that he had been hurt very badly. She heard nothing from Mark and her sister-in-law Marguerite and assumed they were all right; in reality, they were dead. Marguerite died instantly from a wound in her right chest. Whitman spent no time watching the dying family fall. He immediately restored the barricade.[15]

Whitman never saw the men below. Nearly deafened by the tremendous noise, they recovered in time to see their families rolling down the stairs. Mr. Gabour turned Mark over and knew immediately that the head wound was fatal. Mark's eyes were open and his face frozen in terror. It was equally clear that his sister Marguerite had been killed. In shock, William Lamport picked up Marguerite's purse. M. J. Gabour grabbed Mary's white shoes and together the men ran around the twenty-seventh floor searching for help.[16]

Mike Gabour had been knocked unconscious, but he regained consciousness about forty-five minutes later. He had four head wounds, a shoulder wound and another in the left leg. He saw blood

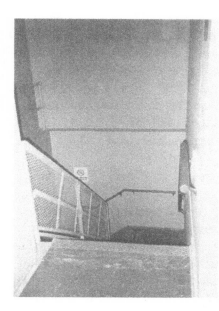

(left) Charles Whitman placed the receptionist's desk at the top of the last flight of stairs leading from the 27th floor to the reception area. Here he fired upon Marguerite Lamport and Mike, Mary and Mark Gabour. Whitman then stood at the top of the stairs and fired at least two more shotgun blasts as the helpless family tumbled down the stairs. *Gary Lavergne.*

(right) Whitman murdered Mark Gabour and Marguerite Lamport on the stairway at the end and to the left of this little hallway between the 27th and 28th floors of the Tower. Mary and Mike Gabour were critically injured and had to endure for over an hour before being rescued by Austin Policemen. *Austin Police Department Files.*

everywhere; it had splattered the walls and covered the steps until it dripped in a gruesome flow to the bottom of the stairs. He worried that Whitman would return to finish off the survivors so he tried desperately to pull himself to safety. He could not. "There was too much blood; I could get no friction."[17]

<h1 style="text-align:center">IV</h1>

The meticulous plans unfolded. The battle lines were drawn. Whitman had established control of the twenty-eighth floor and access to the observation deck. The shots he fired to annihilate Marguerite Lamport and Mark Gabour and critically injure Mary and Mike Gabour rang through the upper floors of the Tower. On the twenty-sixth floor, the Classics Department had been alerted to something unusual. The first loud noise was "like a heavy cabinet falling." Others thought scaffolding had collapsed. Leoda Anderson, a secretary, phoned maintenance to see if there had been an elevator accident. Studying the Greek classics at the time were two Catholic nuns from San Antonio's Incarnate Word High School, Sisters Aloysius Nugent and Miriam Garana. Sister Aloysius would later recall, "We were sitting in class when we heard this noise, like knocking out a wall. Then this terrifically loud man's voice yelling, 'Help! Help!'"[18]

Two men, Fred Mench, an instructor in the Classics Department, and his assistant Herbert Ritchie, proceeded up the stairway to investigate. David Latz, an assistant to the director of admissions, and James Zinn, the husband of a receptionist on the twenty-fourth floor, joined them on the stairway. They found Mr. Gabour calling for help and in a state of confusion. Farther up, by one flight of stairs, they saw the bodies lying in pools of blood. Mench quickly instructed Ritchie to call the police, but Ritchie did not know how to operate the campus PBX, so Mench called. Ritchie looked out the window and began to see pedestrians falling everywhere.

Mench and Ritchie cried, "Get back. There are bodies all over." Margaret Arnold, another secretary on the twenty-sixth floor, phoned her husband, William, located in another campus building, telling him to stay put. The group retreated to room 2608 and huddled together on the west side as far away from the stairs as possible.

They could not have known it, but they inadvertently located themselves near what eventually became the most violent side of the Tower. After locking and bolting the door, they barricaded the room with filing cabinets, chairs, and a blackboard. "It was like being in a battle. Bullets were hitting all around, and we didn't know what to expect." The eight-member group huddled together: Sister Aloysius Nugent, Sister Miriam Garana, Leoda Anderson, James Hynd, Florence Haywood, Margaret Arnold, Herb Ritchie, and Elaine Anderson. Fred Mench ran down the stairs warning people on every floor to stay out of the halls. On the twenty-fourth floor David Latz and nine other people barricaded themselves in rooms 2404 and 2405. For the next hour and a half, they stayed close to the floor, away from the windows, and prayed.[19]

The schedule called for Vera Palmer to go to the twenty-eighth floor to relieve Edna Townsley at noon, and as usual she boarded the elevator for the trip to the twenty-seventh floor. As the doors slid open at about 11:55 A.M., a dazed William Lamport, holding Marguerite's purse and shoes, stated emphatically, "Lady, don't you dare get off this elevator; go on down!"[20] Without hesitation, Palmer complied.

In the reception room, Whitman placed his sawed-off 12-gauge shotgun back into the footlocker. Edna Townsley, the Gabours and the Lamports had slowed his progress long enough for him to miss a change of classes that usually found the West and South Malls teeming with hundreds of students and faculty. Probably while still in the reception area he tied a white bandanna around his head to keep perspiration from falling into his eyes and draped the binoculars he had purchased only the day before around his neck. He knew that what he had done and was about to do would be considered an atrocity. Carrying a knapsack filled with ammunition, he let himself become a killing machine, but unlike most mass murderers, he had prepared everything meticulously. Although he probably thought he was a little late, he was there nonetheless. He had secured the reception area and it would be some time before anyone would head for the twenty-eighth floor. Between the shooting of the Gabours and his exit to the observation deck, he shot an already critically wounded Edna Townsley on the top and left side of her head. But the "scrapper" was not dead yet, and there is little satisfaction in knowing that Whitman would die first.

As the shadow of the Texas state capitol retreated from its daily reach for the swank apartment on Guadalupe Street, the mother of Charles Whitman lay dead, and in the neat little house on Jewell Street the body of his wife was also yet to be discovered. Behind a beige couch on the twenty-eighth floor of the Tower lay a dying receptionist, and on the landing in the stairway one flight below were two dead and two wounded. Still it was not enough. Employees and students of the Classics Department on the twenty-sixth floor huddled and prayed as the patriarchs of the Lamport and Gabour families ran throughout the Tower in a desperate attempt to help their families. Meanwhile, Whitman's terrorist mission unfolded. He reloaded the footlocker onto the dolly and wheeled it towards the south exit. As he opened the door to the deck a flush of hot Austin air engulfed him. The view to the south was familiar. There stood the other symbol of Austin—the dome of the Texas capitol.

And then he walked through the glass-paneled door.

And then he walked through the glass-paneled door. *Gary Lavergne.*

[1] *Newsweek*, 15 August 1966; *Austin American-Statesman*, 1 and 7 August 1966; Time-Life, p. 31.

[2] APD Files: *SORs* by B. Landis, D. Kidd, 1 August 1966, and by A. Whitsel, 4 August 1966.

[3] APD Files: *SOR* by George Phifer, 4 August 1966; *Austin American-Statesman*, 2, 6, and 7 August 1966; Time-Life, p. 31.

[4] Texas DPS Files: *Intelligence Report*, n.d.

[5] APD Files: *SOR* by John Pope, 4 August 1966; *Austin American-Statesman*, 3 August 1966.

[6] Edna Townsley quoted in *Austin American-Statesman*, 3 August 1966.

[7] Ibid., 3 and 7 August 1966; *Texas Monthly*, August 1986.

[8] In the Texas DPS File there are drawings of the layout of the deck and reception area which includes the position of many things, including the location of Whitman's murder of Edna Townsley. The drawings are hereafter cited as "Drawings." APD Files: *SOR* by B. Landis, 1 August 1966; *Time*, 12 August 1966; *Austin American-Statesman*, 2, 3, and 7 August 1966.

[9] APD Files: *Affidavits*, Cheryl Botts, 4 August 1966, and Donald W. Walden, 4 August 1966; Time-Life, pp. 32–34; *Austin American-Statesman*, 5 August 1966.

[10] Mary Gabour Lamport, *The Impossible Tree*, (Austin: Ginny Copying Service, Inc., 1972), pp. 105–109; *San Antonio Daily Express*, 17 March 1967; *Austin Citizen*, 1 August 1977.

[11] Lamport, *The Impossible Tree*, pp. 105–109.

[12] Ibid.

[13] Mary Gabour quoted in *The Impossible Tree*, p. 109.

[14] Texas DPS Files: *Intelligence Report*, 17 August 1966; Lamport, *The Impossible Tree*, p. 109.

[15] Texas DPS Files: *Intelligence Report*, 17 August 1966; Lamport, *The Impossible Tree*, p. 109; APD Files: *SORs* by E. Tramp, 1 August 1966, *Crimes Against Persons Offense Report (CAPOR)* by D. Kidd, 1 and 2 August 1966; *Time*, 12 August 1966; Time-Life, p. 34; Transcript of an interview with Mary Gabour Lamport, dated 2 August 1972, by Art Young of KRMH-FM Radio, in AHC Mass Murder File (hereafter cited as Lamport Interview). A few years after the Tower Incident M. J. and Mary Gabour divorced. Mary later married her former brother-in-law, William Lamport. Hence, Mary Gabour and Mary Lamport are the same person; *Texas Monthly*, August, 1986.

[16] Texas DPS Files: *Intelligence Report*, 22 August 1966; APD Files: *SOR* by H. Moe, 2 August 1966; *Austin American-Statesman*, 1 August 1976; Ramiro Martinez, in an interview with the author on 3 April 1995; Phillip Conner. Interviews will hereafter be cited by name only.

[17] *San Antonio Daily Express*, 17 March 1967; *Austin American-Statesman*, 2 and 7 August 1966; APD Files: *SOR* by H. F. Moore, 5 August 1966.

[18] Sister Aloysius Nugent quoted in *Summer Texan*, 1 August 1986; *Austin American-Statesman*, 2 August 1966.

[19] Sister Aloysius Nugent quoted in *Summer Texan*, 1 August 1986; *Austin American-Statesman*, 2 August 1966; APD Files: *SOR* by H. F. Moore, 5 August 1966; Time-Life, p. 34.

[20] Vera Palmer remembered seeing a "man in a white shirt with tennis shoes in his hand," as the elevator door opened onto the twenty-seventh floor. The *Austin American-Statesman*, 2 August 1966, reported, and it has been widely assumed, that the man was Whitman. It could not have been. By that time Whitman was already

shooting from the deck. Whitman wore blue nylon coveralls; it was why so many presumed him to be a janitor. Additionally, in order for Vera Palmer to have seen Whitman on the twenty-seventh floor she would have had to follow him nearly immediately after making the elevator functional for him on the ground floor. Why would she not recognize a man she assisted only seconds earlier? In which case, she would also have had to decide to relieve Edna Townsley at least twenty minutes earlier than their scheduled shift change. In a statement to the Texas DPS, Palmer indicated that the time of her arrival on the twenty-seventh floor was at or near 11:55 A.M., or about five minutes before their scheduled shift change. (See Texas DPS Files: *Intelligence Report*, n.d.) Moreover, if Whitman held his tennis shoes in his hands when Palmer "saw" him, he would have had to change his shoes (and clothes) on the deck. Charles Whitman would never have taken the time to do such a thing. Anyway, the known sequence of events does not allow for such a change, and even if it did his shoes and clothes would have had to disappear; the Austin Police Department made a detailed inventory of what Whitman brought to the Tower and shoes and clothes were not on the list. (See APD Files: *SOR* by Officer Ligon, 2 August 1966). Finally, in his statement to the Texas DPS William Lamport recounted telling a woman to stay on an elevator and going on down. (See Texas DPS Files: *Intelligence Report*, 22 August 1966.)

9

Strange Noises

I

Once outside on the observation deck Charles Whitman began to spread out his arsenal. He placed the footlocker on the west side, approximately halfway between the northwest and southwest corners. Each side of the deck measured about fifty feet in length, forming a 200-foot perimeter from which he could shoot. Large lamps, which on special occasions cast an orange glow on the crown of the building, were bolted into the walls of the parapet. The lamps never seemed to get in the way of visitors, and unfortunately they did not get in Whitman's way either. Center portions of the interior walls of the parapet, directly below the huge clocks, jutted out slightly, creating protrusions ideally suited for a dangerous game of hide-and-seek. Except for a few ornate carvings and the faces of the huge clocks, the walls were made of smooth, pale limestone. When Don Walden and Cheryl Botts left the deck, they surrendered it to Whitman's exclusive use; only a dying Edna Townsley occupied the interior of the twenty-eighth floor. Because Whitman had successfully secured the Tower's upper floor and deck, storming the fortress would require a serious and incredibly courageous effort. In order to delay further unwelcomed visitors, he wedged the Austin Rental Service dolly against the glass-paneled door on the south side.

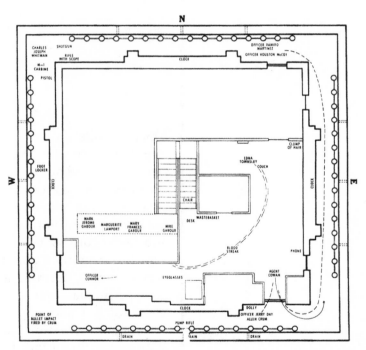

The structure and design of the 28th floor reception area and observation deck made for a dangerous game of hide and seek. Whitman attempted to obstruct access to the area by placing Edna Townsley's desk and a chair at the top of the stairs. The large blank areas on the west and north sides were used for storage, and visitors had no access to the carillon and clock. As a result the only way to confront Whitman on the deck was through the south door. *Texas Department of Public Safety Files.*

Whitman's white bandanna kept perspiration from affecting his vision. Later, as the citizens of Austin fought back, the bandanna served as a headband to keep dust and bits of limestone from getting into his eyes. He did not spend much time moving his arsenal and supplies about the deck, but he did manage to scatter "a lot of stuff everywhere," according to Ramiro Martinez. After setting out his guns, Whitman reached for his 6mm Remington with a four-power scope. He would have the luxury of aiming for the first dozen or so shots, but shortly afterwards he would be forced to rush. Positioning himself below the huge gilded clock on the south side, which read 11:48 A.M., he leaned over the wall, worked the bolt action, visually placed the cross hairs of the scope, and chose his first target.[1]

The glass-paneled door, located on the south side of the Tower, against which Whitman wedged the dolly to keep others from following him. *Austin Police Department Files.*

She was described as "a child of the 60s." Eighteen-year-old Claire Wilson had just finished a nine-week anthropology test and was walking with her eighteen-year-old boyfriend and roommate, Thomas F. Eckman. He was a child of the 60s, too. Reportedly, both were members of the highly controversial Students for a Democratic Society (SDS). She was also eight months pregnant and due for a normal delivery of a baby boy in a few short weeks. Thomas was from Toledo, Ohio, where he had just graduated from high school, but he knew Austin because his father, Professor F. W. Eckman, had taught English at the University of Texas during the 1950s before joining the faculty of Bowling Green University. The *Austin American-Statesman* later reported that Thomas and Claire lived at 806 East 23rd Street, just a few blocks east of the campus. At about 11:45 A.M. they met near Benedict Hall and headed north and then west.

As Claire and Thomas emerged from the protection provided by the shade of the large, mature trees on the east side of the quadrangle on the South Mall, they strolled into the sunshine within the cemented open area between the steps at the curb on Inner Campus Drive and the Main Building and Tower. The area is called the "upper terrace" of the South Mall. The heat of the day was especially brutal to anyone in an advanced state of pregnancy like Claire Wilson. The hard surface of the upper terrace emitted energy as the sun neared its high-noon position. Looking down on her from a fortress 231 feet above, Whitman pulled the trigger. With his four-power scope he would have clearly seen her advanced state of pregnancy. As if to define the monster he had become, he chose the youngest life as his first victim from the deck. Given his marksmanship, the magnification of a four-power scope, an unobstructed view, his elevation, and no interference from the ground, it can only be concluded that he aimed for the baby in Claire Wilson's womb.

Other people in the area were to tell of hearing a strange noise. It was unlike the usual sounds of construction: the clinking and clanging of metal against metal or the falling of wooden studs or planks. It was not hammering either—everyone knew what that sounded like—nor was it the steady screeching of power tools drilling or cutting. It was a popping sound. The terror on the South Mall had started.

"Help me! Somebody help me!" screamed Claire Wilson as she fell to the searing concrete heated by ninety-eight degrees of relentless sunshine. A decade later Claire remembered, "I thought I'd stepped on an electric wire. It never hurt. It was something giant. It went beyond pain."

The missile from Whitman's 6mm Remington, designed to kill by shock, ripped a rather large hole in her hip and, according to hospital and police reports, traveled through her stomach, colon, and uterus, fracturing the skull of the once-healthy son she carried. Her baby died instantly. Immediately, Thomas Eckman knelt, reached out and asked her what was wrong. Before she could answer, a 6mm round entered his back left shoulder just below the neck. Given the trajectory, the bullet entered and fatally damaged the internal thoracic area. Eckman died instantly and fell on his critically injured girlfriend. Many of his friends knew Thomas Eckman to be a "gentle and affectionate boy" and were convinced that he died trying to shield Claire.[2]

In the English building just south and west of the upper terrace where Claire Wilson and Thomas Eckman had fallen, James Ayres had been teaching a Shakespeare class since 11:30 A.M. The class had reviewed *Henry IV* and in particular the character Falstaff. After the strange noise rang through the buildings bordering the South Mall, Ayers hesitated, glanced at the window, then continued. The strange noises repeated and echoed, so the students moved to the window facing the upper terrace, where they saw bodies falling. In the meantime, another English professor walked into the room and announced that someone was shooting people from the Tower.

Opposite the English building, north of the upper terrace, in the Main Building on the fourth floor's Stark Library, Norma Barger heard the same strange noises and looked outside. In a very short time she saw six bodies lying in grotesque positions all over the South Mall. On a university campus pranks are common. "I expected the six to get up and walk away laughing," Barger said. That was until she saw the blood, and more people beginning to fall.[3]

Only a few feet west of Claire Wilson and Thomas Eckman, near the top of the steps connecting Inner Campus Drive to the upper terrace, stood a physics professor named Dr. Robert Hamilton Boyer. Boyer had completed a year as a visiting professor in applied mathematics at the University of Texas in 1965 and was familiar with his surroundings. During his brief teaching career at UT he made many close friends among faculty members and was considered by his colleagues to be a brilliant mathematician and physicist. His impressive academic career included a Rhodes Scholarship; at age thirty-three he had accomplished much and had a bright future in academe. An example of his work included "a search for a rigorous solution of Einstein's equations which would give the complete gravitational field of a rotating body like the Sun or a galaxy." Another close friend, Alfred Schild, an Ashbel Smith Professor of Physics, described Dr.

Boyer as a potential insider of the U. S. establishment, but a "free spirit by choice and inclination." Boyer, according to Schild, did not believe Americans were gentle enough, and that they were far too competitive, aggressive and easily swayed towards war and killing.

Boyer had just completed a one-month teaching assignment in Mexico, and in a letter to a close friend, he had written, "I shall probably be passing there the first week in August." On 1 August 1966, he had been in Austin for less than a full day and had been staying at the home of a friend, a UT philosophy professor named Robert Palter. He planned to leave on Tuesday (the next day) for Pittsburgh and continue to Liverpool, England, to join his family, but his plans were complicated by a nationwide airline strike, forcing him to purchase a train ticket and to telegraph his parents informing them of changes in his itinerary. Dr. Boyer was ready to travel: he had $200 in American travelers checks, another $150 in Bank of America travelers checks, a University of Liverpool ID card, a passport to England, and only $1.75 in change on his person.[4]

Robert Palter drove Boyer to the campus at approximately 11:40 A.M. Boyer proceeded directly to the Main Building, where he took care of personal business. It is possible that he was on the first floor of the building as Charles Whitman wheeled his footlocker to the elevator. In any case, Boyer was to meet Palter in the faculty lounge at 12:30 P.M. for lunch. A few minutes before noon, however, Robert Boyer looked to the east and saw Claire Wilson and Thomas Eckman fall to the hot pavement. He may have decided to descend the steps to take cover behind the wall that separates the grassy lower terrace of the South Mall from the concreted upper terrace, but he never made it. Just before he could reach the top step, Whitman shot a round from the 6mm Remington into his lower left back, destroying his kidney and sending him sprawling across the steps near the statue of Jefferson Davis. He fell hard, severely bruising his chin, lacerating his face and cutting the left eyebrow area on the cement steps. But his fall quite likely caused no pain; almost immediately Dr. Robert Hamilton Boyer was dead.[5]

Judith Parsons and Leland Ammons were more fortunate. They were able to reach the wall separating the upper and lower terraces. Huddled just below the statue of Jefferson Davis, they began shouting at others, telling them to get down. They also pleaded to others to call for an ambulance and notify the police. After witnessing Whitman shoot several others, Parsons and Ammons wisely decided to stay behind the wall and close to the ground.[6]

UT's Computation Center, located directly east of the Tower, was built into the side of a hill so that steps cradle the sides of the building and its roof is actually a pedestrian walkway. In that area a twenty-two-year-old native of Redlands, California, named Thomas Ashton strolled towards the Tower. After earning a B.A. degree in business administration from the University of California system the previous June, and before entering the business world, he was attracted to the Peace Corps because of its opportunities to travel and provide goodwill for America. He had arrived in Austin along with seventy-six other Peace Corps trainees on 20 June 1966. He was among several trainees assigned to teach English in Iran, all of whom were scheduled to leave on 14 September. Ashton had just finished a class and was to meet several of his friends, other Peace Corps trainees, in the Student Union for lunch. Undoubtedly, Ashton noticed the strange noises, saw bodies fall, and looked towards the Tower to ascertain what was going on. As he gazed directly towards the west, Whitman aimed and shot him in the left chest. Ashton would die at Brackenridge Hospital at 1:35 P.M.[7]

On the upper terrace David Gunby, a twenty-three-year-old electrical engineering major from Dallas, was walking. He had enrolled in summer school to earn credits in engineering and physics. With his wife, who worked in one of the university's libraries, Gunby lived in the Brackenridge Apartments. By 11:55 A.M. Gunby knew it was going to be one of "those" days—damn hot. Reportedly, he was dressed in a sport shirt and bermuda shorts. The Tower deck, twenty-eight floors above, placed Gunby at a steep angle to Whitman, but not steep enough to escape the sniper's attention. The missile Whitman fired tore through Gunby's upper left arm and entered his abdominal cavity.[8] Like Claire Wilson, he lay critically injured on an extremely hot sidewalk in full view of Charles Whitman, who, at any time, could decide to shoot again.

Claire Wilson, David Gunby, and many others wounded during Whitman's reign of terror could only endure the fear—and the heat. For some, it lasted over an hour. "We got a lot of people with second degree burns lying on that hot pavement," said Dr. Robert Pape, the

Director of Medical Education at Brackenridge Hospital. The deck had no shade and the sun beat down directly on the top of Charles Whitman's head, but if there had been shade Whitman would probably not have made use of it. He did not even bother to take off the coveralls he had on top of his clothes, and the white headband kept sweat out of his eyes. He wanted to kill as many people as possible as quickly as possible. As the morning turned into afternoon the white headband soaked up more and more sweat.

"Devereau" is an unusual first name in Texas; nearly everyone called him Matlin (pronounced "MATE-lin"), his middle name. Devereau M. Huffman was near the completion of his doctoral program in psychology, specializing in business administration. He taught classes at the university as well. Incredibly, at age thirty-one, he would be one of the older victims. He, too, happened to be strolling the South Mall after having left the psychology building. Whitman sent a round through his right arm. Huffman, like the other wounded, could only endure. As he lay face down near the bushes encircling the upper terrace, he did his best to "play dead."[9]

An attractive young brunette named Charlotte Darenshori had been working in the office of the Dean of the Graduate School for only a month. She was the wife of a salesman named Sherman and the mother of a three-year-old daughter. When she reported to work on 1 August 1966 she wore a sleeveless blue shift. The air conditioning of her office building made closing the windows and exits necessary, which made hearing noises outside extremely difficult, if not impossible. The occupants of the offices never heard the strange noises, but a full view of the South Mall was visible through the closed windows. As she looked outside Charlotte saw three people fall on the pavement. Instinctively, she ran out of the office, through a hallway, and out of the building onto the upper terrace to help. She headed directly to the nearest body, and upon reaching the young man, bent over. Then, for the first time, Charlotte heard the strange noises. After looking up, she immediately realized what was going on. Shots were landing all around her. She does not recall what went through her mind, but she headed straight for the nearest cover— the concrete base of one of a pair of very large stainless steel flagpoles in the center of a grassy area adjoining the quadrangle. The base measured five feet in diameter and was only about two feet tall.

Above the base, a decorative metal structure engraved with symbols of the Southwest—mostly cacti—tapered upwards, forming a cone from which rose the flagpole. The concrete and metal barely provided enough cover to shield the petite secretary, but she could not move without exposing herself to Whitman's deadly fire. The flagpole's central location in the open grassy area would have made any attempt to leave the area extraordinarily dangerous. Since Charlotte had not been wounded, and as such needed no help, her best option was to just stay still. And she would—for the next one and a half hours—in indescribable heat.

Charlotte Darenshori became as much a symbol of the unfolding tragedy as the Tower or Charles Whitman himself. Pictures and newsreel footage of a helpless young woman frozen in terror with her head pressed against the base of a hot flagpole and her legs tightly folded beneath her were immediately beamed around the world. While Charles Whitman became a symbol of evil, Charlotte Darenshori epitomized innocence and reassuring heroism in the midst of terror. From her hiding place behind the flagpole, she could see the man she had sought to help:

Charlotte Darenshori hiding behind a flagpole as a wounded man lies on the grass nearby. UPI staffer Tom Lankes took the photo while the sniper's bullets were still flying in the area. It was one of the first news pictures taken at the scene and the most widely published on the story. *UPI/Corbis-Bettmann.*

He could see me when I was behind the flagpole. He kept trying to get my attention to come help him, but there was absolutely no way I could have done that. And he kept moving. I told him: "Just keep still."[10]

Still, large numbers of people in the area failed to recognize the danger. Many did not know what rifle fire sounded like; to them it was just a series of strange noises. Others, like a student named William "Bill" Helmer, who knew gunfire when they heard it, and even saw the gun barrel, thought "some fool was going to get himself into a lot of trouble." Still others saw bodies lying on the pavement and in the grass. They saw Charlotte desperately hugging a flagpole and wondered what could possibly be going on. It had to be some kind of stunt, a frat prank, or maybe the drama department had sent out a bunch of flaky actors to do weird things—who knows? There was not a whole lot that could surprise a seasoned Austinite— except mass murder. But the bodies kept falling, the blood was real, and the man on the deck, a consummate actor for a number of years, was no longer acting.

Only about seven minutes earlier Don Walden and Cheryl Botts had stepped off the elevator onto the first floor of the Tower. They had been on the deck and spoken to Charles Whitman. After reaching the first floor, they went to the registrar's office and completed forms for Don to receive a registration packet. Then they walked down the hallway of the Main Building, exited through the west doorway, crossed a driveway, and entered the Academic Center which formed a portion of the northern border of the West Mall. They noticed that flags strung up the tall stainless steel poles on the South Mall were waving at half mast, and they turned east to see if a notice at one of the flagpoles might explain why. When they reached the southwest corner of the Main Building, Cheryl stopped in mid-sentence when a strange noise rang out and a man fell to the ground. The noises were not strange to Don; he knew gunfire when he heard it. Don started to run to the man as Charlotte Darenshori fled to the safety of the base of the flagpole, then he grabbed Cheryl's hand and ran quickly into the history building. Once safely inside, Don asked someone to call the police. A woman said she already had.

Cheryl used the phone to call her grandmother to tell her what was happening and not to worry.[11] For the second time in about fifteen minutes Don Walden and Cheryl Botts were the "luckiest couple in Austin."

II

The Chief of the University of Texas Traffic Control and Security, Allen R. Hamilton, first heard of trouble at the Tower at 11:48 A.M. Calls came in from a number of persons in the Tower after Whitman opened fire on the Gabours and Marguerite Lamport. Immediately he arranged for two men to go to the Tower, including L. W. Gebert, a UT Policeman who had been preparing to leave the office. He took a motorcycle to the north and east side of the building and heard shooting. From there he went over to the west side and heard two more shots. The other officer, Jack O. Rodman, had just left the Speedway checkpoint where, only twenty-five minutes earlier, he had issued a forty-minute parking permit to Charles Whitman to unload supplies at the Experimental Science Building. From the Speedway checkpoint, Rodman had motored to the security office for lunch, but before he could begin eating, Captain J. E. Shuberg told him to go to the Main Building as soon as possible. Rodman motored to the west side of the building where he met Gebert and entered the building. When they reached the elevator doors, Vera Palmer told the officers to be extremely careful because others had already been killed. Rodman and Gebert entered the elevator and ascended to the twenty-seventh floor at 11:55 A.M. Neither of the men was armed.

As UT Security policemen entered the Main Building, two young employees named Nancy Harvey and Ellen Evganides were leaving for a lunch break. Nancy majored in education and worked part time on the second floor of the Tower. She was also about four to five months pregnant. Her husband had taken on the task of building a crib for the expected arrival. As Nancy and Ellen exited the Main Building, Nancy heard three shots, but they seemed to stop. They asked a security guard if it was safe to go outside. Apparently believing the shots were being fired inside the Tower, the guard answered, "Sure." The young women then proceeded west towards the Drag. After walking about 100 yards down the West Mall, someone called out, "Hey, you shouldn't be out there!" Nancy and Ellen did not know why. They were out in the open, in public, in full view of hundreds of people. And then they heard another shot. Nancy felt a pain in her thigh; she had been hit in the hip. Her wound was frighteningly similar to that of the sniper's other pregnant victim, Claire Wilson. Whitman could very well have aimed for another unborn child. But Nancy was far more fortunate. She and Ellen, who had been wounded in the left leg and thigh by a ricochet, dashed to the safety of an area between the Academic Center and the Student Union. He did not know it at the time, but Charles Whitman had something in common with the pregnant coed he had just shot; Nancy Harvey was also from Lake Worth, Florida.[12]

When the elevator doors opened and Gebert and Rodman entered the twenty-seventh floor, M. J. Gabour staggered towards the two men. His blue overalls were splattered with blood, and he was still clutching Mary's white shoes. "Give me a gun, he has killed my wife and family." The officers then ran to the stairs and discovered the pitiful family members lying in their own blood. They could hear Whitman shooting, and at times it sounded like it came from inside the building. They wisely decided to go downstairs to secure as much of the building as they could. Once back on the ground floor, they instructed Vera Palmer to shut off the elevators. Then they secured the exits. Shortly afterwards a rumor ran through the ground floor that the sniper was on the second floor; quickly the officers got as many people as possible behind closed doors.[13]

Whitman's constant movement and ubiquitous activity convinced many on the ground that there had to be more than one sniper. Many people decided they could "see" an army up there and were afraid it might be the beginning of some kind of revolution. Many radical groups of the 60s had begun to preach of revolution against the "Establishment." Or maybe, as one of the wounded thought, it was an attempted coup. That so much violence and evil in such a short time could be caused by one person was inconceivable to most people. Only Mike Gabour knew better, but he had not yet been discovered.[14]

UPI diagram view of University of Texas campus showing the number of victims shot at each spot. (Does not include all victims.) *UPI/Corbis-Bettmann.*

During the first fifteen minutes, very few of Whitman's shots missed, even when he moved around to shoot. And Charles Whitman moved often. No one knew at any time where he was, unless of course, they could see him as he fired and then for some it was too late. Many others could only see the barrel of a rifle. Richard Embry, an eyewitness, told of how Whitman moved: "There is this concrete and iron sort of barricade that he hides behind. Then he pops his head over to take another shot. You can see the gleam of the gun."[15]

As Whitman moved he used the parapet to conceal his movements, popping up only to shoot in an area where unknowing people felt safe. Many reports describe groups of people as far away as Memorial Stadium standing in the open to watch the tragedy unfold, telling one another they were safely out of range, only to scatter in an almost comic fashion as rifle fire landed near them. T. J. Rudolph, a witness who watched from a safe distance with a ten-power telescope, observed Whitman pop up, take aim and fire, but he also observed a sniper patient enough to pick out a target first. After shooting, Whitman always crouched and ran. As Bill Helmer would later write: "The sniper would lean out over the parapet, bring the rifle to bear on a target, fire, tip the weapon up as he worked the action, then walk quickly to another point to do the same thing."[16]

While the drama was unfolding, Whitman's movements slowed but never stopped. It was not until the very end of the event that the world knew, for sure, that there was only one sniper. At the University News and Information Service, Amy Jo Long received a call at 11:55 A.M. from university employees at the Humanities Research Center. "Someone is shooting people from the Tower. There is blood all over the place. Don't come here. We have locked ourselves in." Only three minutes earlier, at 11:52 A.M., the Austin Police Department received their first call reporting trouble at the university. The complainant identified himself as Michael Hall and his location as the history building. He reported gunshots around the main plaza (South Mall) coming from the Tower. Only one minute later, at 11:53 A.M., an officer would be assigned to the case and dispatched to the scene. His name was Houston McCoy.[17]

---

[1] Ramiro Martinez, interviewed by the author on 3 April 1995; Houston McCoy, interviewed by the author on 10 March 1995, both hereafter cited by name only; Time-Life, p. 35; *Austin American-Statesman*, 1 August 1976.

[2] APD Files: *CAPOR*s by D. Kidd, E. Tramp, 1 August 1966; *Austin American-Statesman*, 2 and 7 August 1966, 30 July 1967, Claire Wilson quoted in 1 August 1976; Fahrenthold and Rider, *Admissions*, pp. 80, 90, and 93. It is generally accepted that Whitman started his sniping on the south side of the deck and that Claire Wilson was his first victim. Her companion, Thomas Eckman, was almost certainly his second target. It is not possible to reconstruct perfectly the sequence of victims afterwards because of the rapidity of the shots and Whitman's ubiquitous tactics. The sequence I have chosen serves the purpose of logic and clarity.

[3] *Austin American-Statesman*, 1 August 1976; Norma Barger quoted in *Time*, 12 August 1966.

[4] APD Files: *HOR* by E. Tramp, 1 August 1966; *Texas Observer*, 19 August 1966; *Austin American-Statesman*, 2 and 7 August 1966.

[5] APD Files: *HOR* by E. Tramp, 1 August 1966; Time-Life, p. 36.

[6] *Austin American-Statesman*, 2 August 1966.

[7] Ibid., 7 August 1966; APD Files: *HOR* by E. Tramp, 1 August 1966; Fahrenthold and Rider, *Admissions*, p. 90.

[8] APD Files: *CAPOR* by D. Kidd, 2 August 1966; *Austin American-Statesman*, 2 August 1966; *Dallas Morning News*, 4 September 1966; Unidentified clipping in AHC.

[9] APD Files: *CAPOR* by D. Kidd, 2 August 1966; Dr. Robert Pape quoted in Fahrenthold and Rider, *Admissions*, p. 88; *Dallas Morning News*, 4 September 1966; *Austin American-Statesman*, 2 August 1966.

[10] Charlotte Darenshori quoted in *Austin American-Statesman*, 1 August 1986.

[11] APD Files: *SOR* by Lt. Phifer, *Affidavits* of Donald W. Walden and Cheryl Botts, 4 August 1966; William J. Helmer quoted in *Texas Monthly*, August 1986.

[12] APD Files: *SORs* by A. Whitsel and S. Schulle, 4 August 1966, Sgt. Pilgrim, 5 August 1996, *CAPORs* by G. Blomstrom, 1 August 1966 and D. Kidd, 2 August 1966, *Persons Injured and Admitted to Brackenridge Hospital*, 2 August 1966; *Daily Texan*, 1 August 1991; *Dallas Morning News*, 4 September 1966; *Austin American-Statesman*, 2 and 4 August 1966, 30 July 1967.

[13] APD Files; *SOR* by S. Schulle, 4 August 1966; *Austin American-Statesman*, 7 August 1966.

[14] *Texas Observer*, 19 August 1966.

[15] Richard Embry quoted in *Austin American-Statesman*, 2 August 1966; *Dallas Morning News*, 2 August 1966.

[16] William J. Helmer quoted in *Texas Monthly*, August 1986.

[17] APD Files: *Radio Dispatch*, 1 August 1966; *Austin American-Statesman*, 2 and 7 August 1966.

10

Houston

I

"I am just a West Texas Cowboy." Indeed!

Houston McCoy embodied the Texas stereotype: a slow West Texas drawl, an elliptically-shaped face, piercing frontier eyes that look beyond bodies into souls, selective use of soft-spoken brutally honest words, often hiding a toughness no one should mess with. A more Texan name could hardly be conjured. McCoy stood well over six feet tall, with a thin, almost boyish frame West Texans described as a "long drink of water." His elongated musculature sug-

Only seconds before confronting Charles Whitman, Houston McCoy had to dodge friendly fire from police and civilians, but he still had flashing thoughts of his wife Ruth and sons Stefan and Kristofer. Ruth would not find out about Houston's heroics until he got home late in the afternoon of 1 August 1966. *Photos courtesy of Ruth McCoy.*

gested agrarian roots and hard work as a boy and young man.

McCoy hailed from Menard, Texas, a hamlet about 150 miles west of Austin near no large or even mid-size city. "If you find yourself in Menard, it's probably 'cause you want to come here," mused one resident. In 1958, Houston graduated from Menard High School, home of the Yellow Jackets, and was named "Best All-Around Boy." He spent his young adulthood attempting to leave his hometown. He enrolled in Lamar Tech (now Lamar University) in Beaumont and attended classes there for a short time before serving a three-year hitch in the United States Army which included an assignment to Germany, where he met and then married a native German girl named Ruth. In the early 1960s Houston, like many young Texans, was attracted to Austin's cultural offerings. His introduction to law enforcement was routine and unromantic. He was in need of a job when he saw an ad for police recruits in the *Austin American-Statesman*.[1]

By August, 1966, Officer McCoy had been with the Austin Police Department for nearly three years, but he still considered himself a rookie. He and Ruth had two baby boys whose names reflected their proud German heritage: Kristofer, age two, and Stefan, age one. The pay for an Austin policeman was not very good, but McCoy was proud to be with the APD; he and Ruth got by.[2]

For the Austin Police Department, 1 August 1966 had started as a normal day. Nine traffic units reported for work at 6:00 A.M. and were to serve until 2:00 P.M., ten patrol units reported at 7:00 A.M. and were to serve until 3:00 P.M., and six motorcycle units reported at 7:00 A.M. and were to serve until 5:30 P.M. McCoy reported for duty at 6:45 A.M., and less than fifteen minutes later he was on the road in Unit #219. He had been assigned to patrol midtown, the east section and Lake Austin. As in most growing cities, motorcycle, patrol and traffic units stayed busy during rush hours. After the traffic died down, in the time-honored tradition of police officers everywhere, McCoy took a few minutes for coffee. Afterwards, as the morning moved slowly and the heat began to build, Houston began looking for something to do.

Near IH 35, at the bottom of the hill where the French Legation overlooked downtown Austin, McCoy and his good friend and fellow officer Billy Paul Speed, who had been assigned traffic Unit #353, pulled up to each other and had a short conversation. At the site of Austin's infamous "Pig Wars" the two young men spoke of their futures.[3]

Billy Speed, like Houston McCoy, was a young man and a new father. He and his wife, Beverly Jean, had celebrated the arrival of their daughter only slightly more than one year earlier. Like Houston, Billy had served a hitch in the military, training as a paratrooper. He had been with APD only thirteen months, receiving his commission on 2 July 1965, and so was still a rookie. He was a well-built officer, but at five-feet-eight inches tall, weighing 159 pounds, he looked rather small, especially next to someone like McCoy. Together the two young officers talked. Billy had begun to think seriously about quitting the police force. He made only $360 a month and thought there had to be a better way to make a living. Fifty cents in change is all the money he had on his person on 1 August 1966. At age twenty-three, he told Houston of plans to go to college.[4]

Billy and Houston did not spend much time talking; both continued their patrols. Houston drove south towards Lake Austin where he parked beneath the Interregional Highway Bridge that spanned the lake. Breezes funnelled over the river and the shade cast by the bridge helped the area stay relatively cool, making it what Houston thought was an ideal place to "hide." He was wrong. Shortly after his arrival, a city worker walked to the car and told him of a Social Security card wedged in the branches of a newly planted tree. He walked over to the tree, retrieved the card and noticed a pair of pants and shoes lying near the bank of the river, but saw no one bathing nearby. Houston then placed the card in his shirt pocket and the clothes and shoes on the back floorboard of the police car. Further east, he spotted three Hispanic youths swimming in the river in clear violation of an Austin city ordinance. Officer McCoy made himself visible, hoping the kids would take the hint, get out of the water and run away. He preferred to give people a good scare and let them get away. His supervisors often pointed out to him that he did not make many arrests or write out many tickets. Unfortunately, these young boys did not take advantage of Houston's window of opportunity. He was forced to go down to the river and deliver a vintage West Texas tongue-lashing. After the incident Houston returned to his car. It was 11:53 A.M.[5]

Poor reception on the radio made the dispatcher's voice impossible to understand. Houston thought there must have been interference of some type, or maybe being beneath a bridge screwed up the radio waves. The voice of the dispatcher, what little could be heard, was shrill and excited. Houston knew something was wrong. He quickly moved to an open area on Holly Street and positioned his unit in such a way as to be able to respond in any direction. He called out over the radio attempting to locate anyone who could understand the transmission and relay it to him; at first no one answered. Frustrated, McCoy tried again, "Can you at least tell me where to go? Slow down!" After the dispatcher repeated the whole message, Officer McCoy was able to decipher "University Tower."[6] So began what is arguably one of the most incredible two-hour ordeals ever experienced by a law enforcement officer.

Located at 12th and Rio Grande Streets, Billy Speed was engaged in an investigation of a minor traffic accident. He, too, heard the urgent calls. Subsequent transmissions called for all units to back Officer McCoy. Without finishing the accident report, Officer Speed hurried north towards the University of Texas to assist his friend.[7]

McCoy raced toward the Tower, still attempting to find out what was wrong. En route he heard the word "shooting." He raced even faster as he unlocked the shotgun in the car, a Winchester model 1200, 12-gauge pump, labeled APD #19. Seconds later a clearer message from a motorcycle unit reported that the shooting was still in progress. McCoy then turned west on 19th (now Martin Luther King Boulevard), reached Guadalupe Street just two blocks south of the Drag, and turned north to reach the University of Texas Campus at the corner of 21st and Guadalupe. Only a couple hundred yards to the east, at the confluence of 21st and University, very near the elaborate Littlefield Fountain, Billy Speed parked his car and ran northward through the South Mall with his shotgun, heading for the Tower.[8]

II

The Drag was always crowded. It represented both a business center and a cultural island. It was the kind of stretch that could only be found next to a large campus. Nothing quite equaled it in Texas—a haven for "free thinkers," a term which for most Texans meant "weird people." But the business side of the Drag was quite serious, representing substantial commercial activity. Its proximity to the university made store-front property some of the most valuable real estate in Austin.

As Whitman moved from the south to the west side of the deck, pedestrians on the Drag began to hear strange noises. But the Drag was noisier than the South Mall. The sounds of commerce and traffic muffled the popping from the Tower. Some customers in stores heard it and peered outside to see people looking around, searching for an explanation. Initial reactions were identical to those on campus. "Everyone's first impression was that it was a joke," related Diane Casey, an eighteen-year-old student. "I thought it was a cap pistol, maybe some sort of a fraternity prank," said Margaret Allen, an employee of Sheftall's Jewelers at 2268 Guadalupe Street.[9]

Across the street from the University Co-op, the largest store on the Drag, at the entrance to the West Mall leading to the Main Building and Tower, seventeen-year-old Alex Hernandez and his younger cousin were riding the same bicycle to deliver the 1 August

1966 edition of the *Austin American-Statesman*. Alex reportedly had ten brothers and sisters at home. He and his younger cousin had harnessed themselves together by slipping the newspaper bag over both of their heads as they rode the bike. They would not have been on the Drag had they not agreed to substitute for someone who was due to return from vacation the next day. Whitman quickly took advantage of a chance to shoot at a moving target. He aimed at the two boys and fired, hitting Alex. The bullet went through his hip, blowing out much of the top of his leg, smashing the femur bone, and lodging into the bicycle's seat. The boys were thrown to the sidewalk. His cousin tried to help. As Alex remembered later: "He was only ten or eleven years old and he tried to help me. I said, 'You can't help me, just go and hide.' I remember tears coming down as he tried to help me." In a short time Alex Hernandez slipped into a state of unconsciousness, but pedestrians managed to pull him to safety in a shaded area.[10]

Across the street Adrienne de Vergie stepped off a city bus at the stop in front of the Co-op. She had been downtown, where she had bought a pale blue dress at Yaring's Department Store. As the bus drove away, her attention was diverted to the group of people huddled around Alex Hernandez. She was headed towards glass doors when a man grabbed her by the arm and aggressively shoved her into the store, saying: "Don't you know what's happening?" No, she did not. Neither did most other pedestrians along the Drag. Most did not realize Whitman was shooting until they actually saw someone fall. Even then, few realized where the shooting was coming from.[11]

Seventeen-year-old Karen Griffith never recognized the danger. She was looking forward to her senior year at Austin's new Lanier High School, and probably even knew Kathy Whitman, who had contracted for her second year of teaching there. Karen was walking along the Drag in a northerly direction when Whitman shot her. The bullet entered the upper portion of her right arm, only about two inches below her shoulder. The missile entered her chest cavity and destroyed her right lung, which later at Brackenridge Hospital had to be removed "in a desperate attempt to save her life." The bullet also severely damaged her left lung. For the next week Karen suffered from Acute Respiratory Distress Syndrome, or "shock lung," a condition physicians would learn much more about during the

Vietnam War. Her remaining lung would eventually lose all function as she struggled for life. Karen died a week later, the last of Whitman's victims.[12]

Thomas Karr walked a few feet north of Karen's position on a sidewalk on the west side of the Drag. He had just finished a Spanish exam and was pleased with the results. He had earned a good grade by staying up nearly all of Sunday night to study. At age twenty-four he was older than most students. Like Charles Whitman he was an ex-serviceman with a keen interest in hunting and guns. He was probably the only one of Whitman's victims who might have been able to outshoot his murderer. Originally from the small Texas town of Spur, he had moved to Fort Worth and become an honor student at Arlington State College. He was attending UT for the summer, living in an apartment at 803 West 28th Street. After graduation, he hoped to work for the United States Department of State.

Most reports state that Karr was headed back to his apartment from Batts Hall, after having decided to cut his next class for well-deserved rest. But he was walking in a southerly direction away from 28th Street when he caught the attention of Charles Whitman. He had probably turned to render assistance to Karen Griffith. With a large sturdy frame and wide muscular shoulders, Karr was an easier target than many of Whitman's other victims. Whitman aimed and fired a round that entered the left side of Karr's back and exited the right side. The wound sent him to the sidewalk. For many people the trauma might have brought instant death, but Karr was a big, strong man. He lasted another hour before dying on an operating table at Brackenridge Hospital at 1:10 P.M.[13]

III

As a number of university students moved Alex Hernandez to the relative comfort of shade and the safety of being out of sight from the sniper on the Tower, someone removed the bag of newspapers from around Alex's neck. A small crowd began to gather around the stricken newspaper boy. Some of the more observant students immediately realized what was going on and began to cry out for pedestrians to take cover.

Across the street in the University Co-op, Allen Crum, the floor manager, had stopped next to what was cash register number one when he noticed the group huddled around Alex Hernandez. His first impression was that a fight was in progress. He started to leave the store to assist in breaking up the brawl when a boy ran across from the area screaming that shooting was in progress and that a boy (Alex) had been shot. And then Allen heard the popping sounds from the Tower. They were not strange noises to him. He had retired from the Air Force after twenty-two years and had served as a Master Sergeant and a B52F tail gunner. Now age forty, he had spent virtually all of his adult life in the military and was well-trained in firearms.[14] Crum heard more shots, and still more. He dashed across the street to the group accumulated around the wounded paper boy. Those gathered there did not know how to stop the profuse bleeding spurting from Alex's upper leg. Crum then directed efforts to move Alex into the bushy area just south of the entrance to the West Mall and gave quick instructions to a number of students as to how to stop the bleeding. In so doing, he may well have saved Alex Hernandez's life.[15]

Shots continued to ring out, the echoes deceiving Crum, who at first thought they came from the top of the Student Union. Regardless, he dashed through normal traffic across Guadalupe Street and reentered the Co-op. About ten minutes after the shooting had started on the Drag, shouts from all directions called for everyone to take cover. The traffic kept moving, but Whitman never directed his fire at vehicles; he had not gone to the Tower to shoot cars. Once inside the store Crum instructed a Mr. Magrill to get all of the customers back and away from the windows. By that time students had halted traffic from the south, but a steady stream of vehicles continued from the north. Crum then moved to 23rd and directed traffic onto that street and off the Drag. He then dashed across the Drag to a phone where he attempted to call his wife so she would not worry, but he could not reach her.

Allen Crum then proceeded in an easterly direction along the West Mall towards the Tower. He stopped to hide behind a pillar of the Academic Center, which is the first building directly west of the Tower. There Allen Crum wisely and patiently waited until Charles

Whitman directed his fire towards the South Mall. He then dashed across a small driveway and entered the Tower through an entrance on the west side.[16]

IV

Houston McCoy reached the campus at 21st and Guadalupe. Just north of that intersection a light blue Studebaker sat motionless in the middle of the street. As he drove up to the vehicle to inspect it, he heard gunshots and saw puffs of smoke coming from the deck of the Tower. According to Houston, no one was inside the car, but after a few seconds "a fellow with big eyes runs over to me and says that some people are shooting from the Tower. I say, 'Aw really! Go find cover and stay there!'"[17]

McCoy returned to his unit and zigzagged north along the Drag to 24th Street. He turned east and then into the drive directly to the north side of the Tower, where the edge of the parking lot extends to within eighteen inches of the Tower itself. Houston parked the car so close to the back wall that it would have been impossible to open the passenger-side door. Clutching his shotgun, he looked both east and west for an entrance to the building. Unfortunately, his position, angle, and the design of the exterior walls made it difficult to see the entrances, which were recessed gates within protruding sections of the north wall. Combined with the distractions of shooting, dying and death occurring all around him, McCoy could not find either of two entrances fairly close to where he had parked the unit. Windows on the first floor were barred, so he looked up—straight up. Three rain spouts jutted out at the very top. He saw hundreds of windows; he "saw" a sniper behind every one. It "scared the shit" out of him, as he later said.[18]

He was literally too close to do anything so he returned to his car and drove north past the biology and physics buildings to Mary E. Gearing Hall, where he searched for anyone who might have a high-powered rifle with a scope. (His shotgun was worthless from that distance.) A student indicated he had such a weapon at his apartment a short distance away. They got into the squad car and raced to retrieve the weapon. The student, however, had no ammunition, so they raced to Everett Hardware Company at 2820 Guadalupe and charged three boxes of 30.06 and one box of 30.30 shells. From Everett Hardware, McCoy and the student drove to 21st and University and parked near the Littlefield Fountain, only a few feet from Unit #353, parked there by Billy Speed.[19]

From the entrance to the South Mall near the fountain, Speed and McCoy, at different times, used the same route to head towards the Tower. Under the cover of oak trees they proceeded along a wide walkway past the statues of Confederate Generals Robert E. Lee and Albert Sidney Johnston. Their routes differed when they reached the English Building. Speed stayed outside and darted across Inner Campus Drive to the safety of a wall below the statue of Jefferson Davis; minutes later, McCoy and the student entered the English Building with the scoped rifle, ready to shoot at the sniper.[20]

West Texas cowboys were seldom rich enough to afford fancy rifles with scopes. So when Officer McCoy lifted the fancy scope towards his eye, he found it difficult to keep it still enough to get a good shot. He decided to return the gun to the more experienced owner. McCoy looked out the window and could clearly see Billy Speed and Officer Jerry Culp huddled under the statue of Jefferson Davis. Still hiding were Leland Ammons, Judith Parsons and an unidentified woman in a brown checkered dress. Newsman Phil Miller of KTBC-TV arrived shortly afterwards. The time was 12:08 P.M. Above the wall and on either side of the statue, fencing the upper terrace, stretched concrete balusters and a railing. The smallest gap between any two balusters was four and one-quarter inches; the widest measured about six and five-eighths inches. Culp had gotten there before Speed and asked Speed to take cover. Each of the officers had shotguns but both knew that their distance from the sniper made returning fire gratuitous. As he faced the Tower, Speed moved a little to the right and then he and some of the others huddled against the wall stood up.

From the deck, Whitman took careful aim and saved his best shot for Billy Speed. The first shot hit the concrete between two balusters, showering Speed, Culp, and the civilians with bits of concrete and dust. Billy turned to the left to protect his eyes. Whitman fired again, sending a missile between the balusters into Speed's upper

A series of balusters and steps separates the upper and lower terraces of the South Mall. Standing below the balusters near the statue of Jefferson Davis, Officer Billy Speed looked up at the Tower just as Whitman took aim and fired. From atop the Tower, Whitman fired a 6mm round through the narrow opening, mortally wounding Speed. *Gary Lavergne.*

right shoulder, from where it continued into the chest cavity. He fell flat on his face. Leland Ammons did not think Speed was seriously wounded; it looked like a shoulder wound. Judith Parsons saw that he was bleeding quite a bit. Soon, Speed's uniform would be soaked in blood from shoulders to ankles.[21]

Culp and another officer named Robert Still exposed themselves to move Billy to a shady spot out of the line of fire. Seconds later, a woman who identified herself as a registered nurse ran from the English Building over an open area to try to comfort Speed as Culp ran into a nearby building to phone in an "officer down" situation. Everyone did all they could. A young man in a yellow shirt and shorts ran through the same open area with a tin cup of water for the wounded officer. Judith Parsons pulled off her slip so that it could be soaked in water and placed on Speed's head. The registered nurse checked everyone else out and then ran back out into the open area and into the English Building to call for more help. By the time Billy Speed was moved towards the west along Inner Campus Drive to a Cook Ambulance along Guadalupe Street it was clear that the young officer, who earlier in the morning spoke of quitting police work and going back to school, was in serious trouble.[22]

Watching the drama unfold beneath the statue of Jefferson Davis, on the third floor of the English Building, Houston McCoy and the student with the high-powered scoped rifle looked at one another in amazement. The student asked McCoy, "If I see the sniper should I kill him?"

In a frighteningly cold gaze, with piercing frontier eyes that looked into the soul, Officer McCoy replied, "You shoot the shit out of him!"[23]

Houston was not scared anymore.

---

[1] Houston McCoy; *Austin American-Statesman*, 3 August 1966.

[2] Houston McCoy.

[3] The Austin Police Department Files contain a ten-page, typed statement by Houston McCoy detailing his movements during his duty shift on 1 August 1966. It is undated, but clearly not given as part of his official duties in 1966. It is apparently in response to the growth of a controversy over whose shots actually killed Charles Whitman. It is hereafter cited as "APD Files: *McCoy Statement*, n.d."; Houston McCoy; APD Files: *Duty Logs*, 1 August 1966.

[4] Houston McCoy; APD Files: *McCoy Statement*, n.d., *CAPOR* by E. Tramp, *SOR* by Sgt. Schulle, 1 August 1966; *Austin American-Statesman*, 2, 3, and 7 August 1966.

[5] Houston McCoy; APD Files: *McCoy Statement*, n.d., *Radio Dispatch*, 1 August 1966; Phillip Conner.

[6] Houston McCoy; APD Files: McCoy Statement, n.d.

[7] *Austin American-Statesman*, 7 August 1966.

[8] Houston McCoy; APD Files: *McCoy Statement*, n.d.; Ibid.

[9] Margaret Allen and Diane Casey quoted in *Austin American-Statesman*, 7 August 1966.

[10] *Austin American-Statesman*, 2 August 1966, 30 July 1967, Alex Hernandez quoted on 1 August 1986; APD Files: *CAPOR* by D. Kidd, 2 August 1966 and *SOR* by Sgt. Pilgrim, 5 August 1966.

[11] *Daily Texan*, 1 August 1991; *Playboy*, October, 1970.

[12] APD Files: *SOR* by B. Gerding and D. Kidd, 8 August 1966 and *CAPOR* by D. Kidd, 2 August 1966; Fahrenthold and Rider, *Admissions*, p. 90.

[13] APD Files: *CAPOR* by E. Tramp, 1 August 1966 and *SOR* by Sgt. Pilgrim, 5 August 1966; Fahrenthold and Rider, *Admissions*, p. 88; Time-Life, p. 36; *Austin American-Statesman*, 2 and 7 August 1966.

[14] APD Files: *Sworn Statement of Allen Crum*, 2 August 1966. Hereafter cited as APD Files: *Allen Crum*, 2 August 1966; *Daily Texan*, 1 August 1991; *Austin American-Statesman*, 3 August 1966; Allen Crum declined my request to be interviewed but did agree to provide written responses to questions submitted to him via mail. His responses are dated 7 August 1996. Hereafter cited as Allen Crum.

[15] APD Files: *Allen Crum*, 2 August 1966.

[16] Ibid.; *Newsweek*, 15 August 1966; *Austin American-Statesman*, 3 August 1966.

[17] Houston McCoy; APD Files: *McCoy Statement*, n.d.

[18] Houston McCoy; Time-Life, p. 38.

[19] Houston McCoy; APD Files: *McCoy Statement*, n.d.

[20] Ibid.

[21] APD Files: *SOR* by J. Culp and *CAPOR* by E. Tramp, 1 August 1966; *Austin American-Statesman*, 2 and 7 August 1966, 1 August 1976; As a guest on the *Paul Pryor Show*, broadcast on KLBJ-AM radio on 1 August 1995, Phil Miller related his

experiences near the statue of Jefferson Davis. The three-hour show had many guests and is hereafter cited as "KLBJ Radio, *The Paul Pryor Show*, 1 August 1995."

[22] APD Files: *SOR* by J. Culp and *CAPOR* by E. Tramp, 1 August 1966; *Austin American-Statesman*, 2 and 7 August 1966, 1 August 1976; KLBJ Radio, The *Paul Pryor Show*, 1 August 1995.

[23] Houston McCoy; APD Files: *McCoy Statement*, n.d.

11

Ramiro

Early on the morning of 1 August 1966, a handsome young Hispanic police officer named Ramiro Martinez began his day by bringing his two-year-old twin daughters, Janette and Janice, to day care. Mrs. Vernell Martinez, a native of Fredericksburg and of proud German heritage, was an employment counselor. She had already reported to work. Ramiro was scheduled to report for duty at the Austin Police Department at 3:00 P.M.

Originally from a small West Texas town called Rotan, Ramiro was the son of a share-

In July of 1966 the Ramiro Martinez family sat for their first formal portrait. Only two weeks earlier Janice and Janette celebrated their second birthday. Two weeks later Ramiro confronted Charles Whitman atop UT's Tower. *Photo courtesy of Ramiro and Vernell Martinez.*

cropper who worked on the "one third" system—one third of the harvest went to the landowner. It was a hard way to live. Cotton was king and the Martinez family was poor. While Spanish was spoken most often in the home, Ramiro and his two brothers and two sisters, like many Hispanics of the era, were encouraged to speak English. Ramiro's father and his children were bilingual. Mother Martinez, a native of Mexico, mostly spoke Spanish. At Rotan High School, Ramiro established himself as an athlete, earning all-district honorable mention as an end on the football team. Not surprisingly, the Martinez family was staunchly Catholic, and occasionally, the children had to tolerate silly jokes about their religion. The Hail Mary, the Our Father, the Rosary and other prayers like the Act of Contrition were taught at home and the children attended Catechism regularly on Sundays. The family moved from farm to farm and did not have much, but they were good, honest people.[1]

After graduation, Ramiro attended the University of Texas at Austin for a year, but dropped out to join the Army where, like Houston McCoy, he spent most of his time in Germany. While at UT, he met Vernell, who would become his bride on 30 July 1961. Seven months earlier he had received his commission with the Austin

Police Department after going through a seventeen-week training academy. That day, 21 January 1961, was a proud one. It was Ramiro's birthday, he had made it through the academy, and John F. Kennedy took the oath of office of the President of the United States.[2]

1 August 1966 was a Monday, a work day. The Saturday before, on 30 July 1966, the couple had celebrated their fifth wedding anniversary in style at a nice hotel in San Antonio. On the way home on Sunday they stopped by the famous Smokehouse Restaurant in New Braunfels. On Monday morning Ramiro was alone at home. In many reports of the day's events, his routine has been incorrectly described as a ritual of cleaning and pressing his uniform. He was proud of his uniform, but those chores had been expertly done by Vernell. The uniform had been laid out on the bed for Ramiro by the time he was ready to dress and report to work. At lunchtime, he took out what newspapers described as a pork "steak," but, in Ramiro's words, "it was more like a piece of meat." He turned on the oven to cook it as he watched television station KTBC and Joe Roddy's news broadcast. Roddy, who had been handed a slip of paper, announced that shootings were in progress at the University Tower and that people should stay away from the campus area. Ramiro called APD Headquarters and spoke to Lieutenant Kendall Thomas, who told him to report to the scene for traffic control. He turned off the oven, hurriedly put on his uniform, and sped in his 1954 Chevrolet towards the University of Texas. As he started to leave, neighbors cheered, "Go get him!"[3]

II

Meanwhile, the Drag had become a war zone. Joe Arthur, a twenty-two-year-old sophomore remembered that "everything that moved on the sidewalk seemed to get shot at." He watched from the inside of a barber shop as four people were shot down. Just south of that position, Harry Walchuk, a thirty-eight-year-old navy veteran and political science teacher from Alpena Community College in Michigan, stood in full view of the Tower on a sidewalk. Walchuk had graduated from the University of Texas twelve years earlier but had returned to begin work on his doctorate. He was the father of six children. On 1 August, he did not have a scheduled class until

7:00 P.M., but he had been on campus all morning to work in the library. By noon he was hungry and strolled out to the Drag. He browsed at the doorway of a newsstand where he asked for a certain magazine. It was not in stock. As Walchuck turned to leave, he directly faced the Tower. Whitman aimed and fired. At six feet and 185 pounds Harry Walchuk was a fairly large, well-built man. The bullet pierced his chest and sent him to the sidewalk. Witnesses remember how his white shirt slowly turned to a blood-red and how his pipe made a clinking sound as it hit the sidewalk just before he collapsed. Harry Walchuk died of massive wounds to his lungs, stomach, spleen and heart.[4]

Across the street from the entrance to the West Mall, in front of a store called Snyder-Chenards at 2338 Guadalupe, Paul Sonntag and his steady girlfriend Claudia Rutt walked together. Both eighteen-year-olds were recent graduates of Austin High School. Claudia wore her class ring and had Paul's on a chain around her neck. Paul, from a prominent Austin family, had worked three consecutive summers as a lifeguard at the city-owned Reed Pool. He had just picked up his $75.12 paycheck from the Parks and Recreation Department, where he told Josephine Bailey, a receptionist, "As far as I know, I'll be back next summer." Sonntag had thick, sun-bleached brown hair. At five feet nine inches and 140 pounds, he looked too young to already have enrolled at Colorado University for the fall semester.

Claudia, with ambitions to become a dancer, had enrolled at Texas Christian University. TCU required incoming freshmen to be inoculated against polio, but before getting the shot, Claudia and Paul had decided to go to the University Co-op to look at and possibly buy some records. After Paul parked his car on Guadalupe near the West Mall, the couple crossed the street and hit the Drag, meeting there another 1966 Austin High School graduate named Hildy Griffith. They asked her to accompany them to the Co-op, but she declined and instead went north towards the Varsity Theater and Kinsolving Dorm, where she had been staying during freshmen orientation. The couple then encountered another classmate, Carla Sue Wheeler, and as they were conversing, a strange noise interrupted them. Paul thought it was a car that had backfired; Carla thought it was a gun. Then a stranger to the three of them, probably Allen Crum, began to warn everyone to take cover. As he did so, a bullet whipped by, causing them to dive behind a construction barricade. Paul then opened the barricade's door, saying, "Carla, come look, I can see him. This is for real."

As the young lifeguard gazed at the Tower, the blazing sun had to have caused his eyes to squint. He opened his mouth slightly. Charles Whitman was looking back at him. He aimed and fired, sending a bullet through Paul's open mouth, killing him instantly. His body knocked open the door of the barricade and he fell against a parking meter. Claudia moved toward Paul as Carla tried to restrain her. Whitman saw that, too, and fired again. The bullet hit Carla's left ring, middle, and index fingers before entering the left side of Claudia's chest.[5]

The sniper appeared to be everywhere and victims seemed to be falling on both the Drag and the South Mall at the same time. There were fewer victims to the east and north, where Whitman spent less time. The return fire tended to be more accurate from the east due mostly to privately-owned guns used by policemen. For the police, and the dozens of civilians who chose to fight back, the best guns Texas had to offer in the way of deer hunting became weapons of choice. The Austin Police Department was simply not equipped to deal with a crisis of that magnitude. The violence and domestic unrest that characterized the 1960s had not yet taken root here. Something like this had never happened before.

To the east of the Tower, situated on the sixth floor of a building under construction, two off-duty patrolmen named Con Keirsey and Nolan Meinardus, along with a civilian with a telescope, focused on the east side of the deck and patiently watched the rain spouts for a shot at the sniper. The man with the telescope spotted Whitman at one of the spouts; Meinardus fired one shot from his deer rifle and came as close as anyone would come to shooting Whitman from the ground. Meinardus, Keirsey and the civilian waited for another chance, but Whitman never returned to the east side.[6]

The top of the Business and Economics Building on the corner of 21st and Speedway had also become a center of offense against the sniper. At any given time during the incident, as many as eight APD officers, Texas DPS, Travis County Deputies, and even a Secret Service Agent assigned to protect President Lyndon Johnson focused on the rain spouts on the south side of the Tower. Whenever the barrel of Whitman's rifle poked through, a volley of shots from all directions rang out. One of the officers on the roof was APD's Detective Burt Gerding. Like most other peace officers on or near the campus, he was off duty at the time. He had brought along his personal 30.06 Springfield rifle and several bandoliers of armor-piercing ammunition. With Patrolman Ferris spotting with binoculars, Gerding returned fire. During the exchange, Ferris spotted something on the ledge of the deck just below the south face of the clock. Gerding fired three times and knocked it off with the third shot. They did not know it at the time, but Officers Gerding and Ferris knocked off one of Whitman's rifles, eliminating the 35-caliber Remington from the sniper's arsenal. Unfortunately, he had much more at his disposal.

Others on the roof of the Business and Economics Building had similar firepower. Officer R. B. Laws brought along his 300 Remington model 722 with a four-power scope and fired eight rounds. Patrolman Fred Estepp fired from a 243-caliber Remington, model 700 with a four-power Weaver scope. Detectives Harvey Gann, Tommy Olsen, Lowell Morgan, and Jack Woody each returned fire as well. The return fire made it difficult and dangerous for the sniper to fire from over the top of the parapet, so he was forced to use the rain spouts. It is not surprising, then, that Whitman did most of his killing and maiming during the first twenty minutes of the drama.[7]

But Charles Whitman had been right all along. He said he could hold off an army from the top of the Tower, and that was exactly what he was doing. And the killing continued.

III

Adrian Littlefield, at nineteen years of age, had already decided to dedicate his life to God. He would soon become an evangelist for the United Pentecostal Church. At high noon he and his wife Brenda, even younger than Adrian, were about fifty feet from the base of the Tower. They had just left the Main Building where Brenda picked up her paycheck. Just before reaching a set of steps on the east side of the quadrangle, heading towards the speech building, they heard strange noises. Adrian was seriously wounded in the stomach by a missile that entered his back. Brenda was shot in the hip. And so, two more people lay wounded on the South Mall.[8]

Farther south, at the confluence of University Boulevard and 21st Street where strange bronze creatures holding "things" emerge from the waters of the Littlefield Fountain, visitors have a majestic view of the South Mall and the Tower that arises from the Main Building. The great distance, approximately 500 yards from the Tower, provides a panoramic view. There, Roy Dell Schmidt and Solon McCown, electricians employed by the City of Austin, parked their service truck after asking reporter Joe Roddy if they could have his parking space. They had been eating lunch at 12:05 P.M. at the city's electric distribution department on West Avenue when they received instructions to make a service call. As they got closer to the campus, the traffic appeared more abnormal. Heading east on 19th, they were not allowed to turn north onto Guadalupe. Not knowing why, Schmidt and McCown proceeded east on 19th to University and turned left in a northerly direction towards the Tower. Immediately, the men spotted another city service truck, a radio television mobile news unit with Neal Spelce delivering a live broadcast, and a Chevrolet blocking the street. Schmidt thought "there might be a fire." He and McCown left their truck to see if they could be of any help. Nearby, another city employee named Don Carlson told them of the sniper and warned them to take cover. The three men then crouched behind the Chevrolet for a few minutes.[9]

Roy Dell Schmidt would have been thirty years old on 18 September. He had been a city employee since 1954. At six-foot-one and 165 pounds, he had a slender build. His height probably made crouching behind the Chevrolet very uncomfortable. He stood up to say something like, "It's okay, we're out of range." It was a fatal error. From over five hundred yards away, Whitman sent a round from the deck, over the entire length of the South Mall, over the Littlefield Fountain, over Neal Spelce's mobile unit, over the hood of the Chevrolet, and into the abdomen of Roy Dell Schmidt. "I'm hit! I'm hit!" cried the electrician as he fell to the hot pavement. Those were his last words. It was 12:19 P.M. McCown raced to the truck to call an ambulance and get a first aid kit, but Roy Dell was dead on arrival at Brackenridge Hospital less than ten minutes later.[10]

At 12:20 P.M., Melvin Hees of Armored Motor Service was working in his office in the Capitol National Bank Building and was unaware of the tragedy unfolding at the university. A friend interrupted him and inquired as to whether Hees's armored cars would be useful in removing wounded victims still pinned downed by Whitman's murderous gunfire. Hees immediately located one of the cars and got it to the campus by 12:35 P.M. It was used to evacuate at least two victims, David Gunby and Adrian Littlefield. It probably saved their lives; both young men were sent to emergency surgery upon their arrival at Brackenridge Hospital.

The armored car drivers had been assisted by an off-duty APD Patrolman named Charles Baylor. Baylor had reached 21st and Guadalupe at about 12:20 P.M. and entered the campus. He moved behind several buildings towards the South Mall where he saw six people (including Charlotte Darenshori) pinned down by gunfire. Using his personal rifle he returned fire about fifty times. He then laid down the rifle, and with two unidentified men, ran across the South Mall to rescue a man lying behind a hedge on the west side. The men lifted the man (probably Devereau Huffman) over a wall and into the arms of others. It was an incredibly courageous act. Afterwards, Baylor ran to the armored car and assisted Sergeant Ernie Hinkle in loading two of the wounded. Inside the car Adrian Littlefield's head rested upon a makeshift pillow made of a money bag containing deposit slips. "My wife," he moaned. Inside the Computation Center, Detective Ed Silvange was with Brenda Littlefield, who did not want to be moved out of the building.[11]

IV

Officer Ramiro Martinez drove from his south Austin home to the campus area and parked his rather old car on the 2000 block of San Antonio Street, just one block west of Guadalupe. He had been instructed to report for traffic duty, but after parking his car and running through the grounds of Saint Austin's Catholic Church, he reached 21st and Guadalupe and saw no traffic. Two blocks south of that intersection, at 19th and Guadalupe, students had already halted traffic. Detective John Pope later replaced the students and then would be relieved by Patrolmen Albert Hersom, Jim Beck, and Al

Riley. As Hersom turned away traffic, an unidentified man gave him a bullet-proof vest for protection. Hersom would never be able to locate the man to return the vest. Pope moved closer to the campus to keep civilians out of the line of fire. Martinez crossed Guadalupe and entered the campus grounds. Like Charles Baylor, he used the cover of buildings to reach the South Mall. He, too, saw six persons lying there. Martinez decided to go to the source; he headed for the deck.[12]

Patrolman Bob Day had already made it to the Tower. Earlier in the morning while patrolling East 8th Street he had heard the calls to support Houston McCoy. He proceeded to Benedict Hall on the southeast corner of the South Mall next to the Littlefield Fountain. He worked his way up to Batts Hall and across Inner Campus Drive from the quadrangle. As he stood at the Batts Auditorium doorway, two shots landed near him. From Batts Hall he ran across Inner Campus Drive to the wall beneath the statue of Woodrow Wilson. Looking over the wall through the decorative balusters, he saw bodies on the pavement and people hiding behind trees. Day yelled to everyone within earshot to stay away from windows and doors. And then, clutching his shotgun, Bob Day made a dash through the upper terrace past Claire Wilson, Thomas Eckman, and David Gunby. He ran through Whitman's gunfire by zigzagging. Shots landed about six feet to both the right and left of the dodging policeman. Norma Barger watched from her office in Stark Library: "I saw a policeman running across the open area and you could see the sniper's gun picking up cement dust right behind him."[13]

Once inside, Day rested for a moment to catch his breath then told everyone to stay inside. He discovered that he was the first policeman to enter the Main Building. When he asked students for the best way to get to the top, they directed him to the stairway. Officer Day told the students to lock the door behind him; there was no coming back. He stopped on the third floor and entered room 316 where he asked to use a phone to call the station for further instructions. While he was waiting to get through, a woman told him that he could get a decent shot at the sniper from the office window. He looked out, saw the sniper, and emptied his revolver. Shortly, APD was on the phone. Lieutenant Charles Barnett instructed him to stay at his position and someone would try to get a rifle to him. Bob Day waited.[14]

Meanwhile, another Officer Day, a twenty-seven-year-old, two-year rookie and an Air Force veteran, Jerry Day, had parked his unit in an alley west of Guadalupe Street. He saw three men desperately trying to help Claudia Rutt. Jerry ran across Guadalupe and used the buildings on the north side of the West Mall to circle the Main Building to the south entrance. Once inside, an employee took him to the elevator where Allen Crum approached Day and insisted upon helping. There the two men spoke bluntly. Day pointed out that Crum was unarmed and could get shot. Crum insisted that they go together. Then a Department of Public Safety (DPS) Intelligence Officer named W. A. Cowan arrived with a rifle and a pistol. He handed Crum the rifle.[15]

Outside, Ramiro Martinez decided to make a run for the Main Building through the quadrangle. He, too, used a zigzag pattern to run past the dead and wounded, but he does not know if Whitman ever shot at him. "I just ran like hell!" he later reported. Once inside, Martinez tried calling the police station to get ambulances and armored vehicles to remove the dead and wounded, but by this time APD, and Austin phone lines in general, were jammed. Jerry Day, Allen Crum and W. A. Cowan had taken the elevator to the twenty-sixth floor. From there they took the stairs to the twenty-seventh floor, where they had difficulty establishing communications with Chief Hamilton of UT Security.[16]

V

Houston McCoy left the student with the fancy scoped rifle in the English Building and headed back to his squad car on 21st Street. He told the student to move from one window to another so that Whitman could not locate the source of the return fire. From 21st Street, Houston drove to Guadalupe, turned north, and sped to 24th Street where he encountered men from Criminal Investigations Division (CID). McCoy asked about any plans for getting the sniper. They did not know of any. Shortly afterwards, another student emerged with a 30.30 rifle, but he needed ammunition so McCoy took him to Everett Hardware. The instructions for this student were the same as those given to the student with the fancy rifle—"shoot to kill."

Two blocks north another officer encountered difficulty, but not from the sniper. A city bus driver foolishly insisted on proceeding with his route through the Drag. As McCoy would later say, he disregarded the rules of good public relations, and in earthy language, told the driver he had two options: stay there or turn around. Afterwards, McCoy returned to his unit and heard the APD dispatcher call for volunteers to meet other APD and UT Security officers at UT's police station off San Jacinto Boulevard.[17] He sped away from the Drag to become part of a team being assembled to storm the Tower.

The Drag continued to be a killing field. In front of Sheftall's Jewelers, on the corner of 23rd and Guadalupe, three friends named David Mattson, Roland Ehlke, and Tom Herman were walking to a luncheon for Peace Corps volunteers. It was the same luncheon Thomas Ashton was to attend. They did not know their new friend had just been murdered as he strolled the roof of the Computation Center. David Mattson was a twenty-three-year-old native of Minneapolis; Roland Ehlke a twenty-one-year-old native of Milwaukee; nothing further is known about Tom Herman. Mattson, Ehlke, and Herman were training, along with Thomas Ashton, to go to Iran in mid-September. The sequence of events is not clear, but Mattson and Ehlke were hit with the same bullet. Ehlke was wounded in the right arm and was wounded again in the other arm and in both legs as he attempted to help Mattson. Mattson's right wrist was shattered by the sniper's bullet. Inside Sheftall's, the store manager, Homer J. Kelley, witnessed the strange movements outside on the sidewalk. Sheftall employees were skeptical as they watched the three boys attempt to crawl into the store: "We [were] across the street from a big university and I wasn't about to fall for that. And then I saw blood—so much blood."

As other Sheftall employees cried for him to be careful, the kindly, sixty-four-year-old Homer Kelley helped the wounded boys into the store. As bullets flew all around him, he stayed next to one of the wounded even as more rounds crashed through the front window of the store, tearing gashes in the carpet and wounding him in the leg.

Now Mr. Kelley was one of the wounded. He would arrive at Brackenridge Hospital with the boys he had helped.[18]

Three blocks north, at the A & E Barbershop at 2535 Guadalupe, Billy Snowden, a basketball coach for the Texas School for the Deaf, sat in the barber's chair and watched the shop's TV as his hair was being cut. Snowden, the barber, and a couple of other customers walked to the doorway and looked towards the Tower. Snowden recalled: "We thought at first that we better get back inside, but then decided we were too far away to get hit. I was standing in the door and had it about half open. The barber was standing beside me." They were so far away they did not know that Charles Whitman was looking right back at them. As a bullet went through Snowden, it tore three major nerves. His shoulder went numb. One year later Billy Snowden would be hard on himself. "What a stupid mistake, being outside, since I knew they were shooting from the Tower."[19] But the distance was extraordinary. Of all the victims, Snowden was the farthest from the Tower—well beyond 500 yards.

Just south, on the northwest corner of 24th and Guadalupe, a group of as many as eight people gathered to try to get some idea of what was going on. Not surprisingly, Whitman zeroed in on them. One of the group, Lana Phillips, an attractive, freckled-faced, twenty-one-year-old senior majoring in music, was employed in Rae Ann's Dress Shop on the Drag. After the shooting started, she walked outside. She later stated:

> I wasn't scared until I got shot. I was watching the Tower and watching people get shot. I didn't think I was within range, plus, I was standing behind some other people and I thought they would get shot before I would; I was wrong.

Whitman directed a rapid succession of shots into the group, probably with the 30-caliber automatic, and before they could scatter to safety, he sent a bullet into Lana's back right shoulder. During a lull in the shooting Lana's sister, who had witnessed the shooting from the Student Union across the street, ran across the Drag to help load Lana into an ambulance. Nearby, twenty-one-year-old Sandra Wilson fell to the sidewalk, seriously wounded in the chest.[20]

In the same group on the northwest corner of 24th and Guadalupe were an engaged couple named Abdul Khashab and Janet Paulos. Abdul, a twenty-five-year-old graduate student in chemistry and a native of Iraq, and his fiancée Janet Paulos, a native of Garland, Texas, were to be married very shortly. He was on a scholarship from his government; she was a twenty-one-year-old senior majoring in English. As Whitman directed his fire on the helpless group, a round blasted through Janet's chest, fracturing four of her ribs; she fell to the sidewalk. Before Abdul could bend over to help, he was shot in the right elbow and hip. Their wedding would be delayed, but not for long. When they married on 27 August 1966, Abdul's arm was still in a sling.[21]

Houston McCoy arrived at the University Police Station to volunteer to go to the Tower. At the station UT Security Sergeant A. Y. Barr had assembled a group of men for the job: from APD, McCoy, Harold Moe, Phillip Conner, Milton Shoquist, and George Shepard; from the university, William Wilcox and Frank Holden. Their path to the Tower traveled over open ground, through tunnels, in elevators, and through stairways. Houston McCoy had already been on an odyssey. He kept asking for a plan, but there was no plan. He had had enough of watching people die. Adrenalin complimented a resolve to get the sniper—he wanted the killing to stop.

---

[1] Ramiro Martinez; *Austin American-Statesman*, 3 August 1966.

[2] Ramiro Martinez.

[3] Ibid.; APD Files: *SOR* by R. Martinez, 1 August 1966.

[4] APD Files: *CAPOR* by Sgt. Kidd, 1 August 1966; Joe Arthur quoted in *Austin American-Statesman*, 7 August 1966; Fahrenthold and Rider, *Admissions*, p. 91; Time-Life, p. 36; *Newsweek*, 15 August 1966.

[5] APD Files: *SOR* by Sgt. Pilgrim, 5 August 1966 and *CAPOR*s by E. Tramp and T. Olsen, 1 August 1966; *Time*, 12 August 1966; *Newsweek*, 15 August 1966; *Austin American-Statesman*, 2 and 7 August 1966.

[6] APD Files: *SOR*s by D. C. Keirsey and N. Meinardus, 2 August 1966.

[7] APD Files: *SOR*s by B. Gerding, 3 August 1966, R. B. Laws, 5 August 1966, J. Woody, H. Gann, L. Morgan, and T. Olsen, 2 August 1966 and F. Estepp, 4 August 1966; *Texas Monthly*, August, 1986.

[8] APD Files: *CAPOR*s by T. Olsen, 5 August 1966, D. Kidd, 2 August 1966 and *SOR*s by Sgt. Pilgrim, 5 August 1966; *Austin American-Statesman*, 2 and 23 August 1966, and 30 July 1967.

[9] Fahrenthold and Rider, *Admissions*, p. 83; *Newsweek*, 15 August 1966; *Austin American-Statesman*, 2 and 7 August 1966.

[10] Fahrenthold and Rider, p. 83; APD Files: *HOR* by E. Tramp, 1 August 1966.

[11] APD Files: *SORs* by C. Baylor, 1 August 1966, and E. Hinkle, 6 August 1966; Unidentified clipping in AHC; *Austin American-Statesman*, 2, 7, and 23 August 1966.

[12] Ramiro Martinez; APD Files: *SORs* by R. Martinez, 1 August 1966, H. Riley, A. Hersom, and J. Beck, 3 August 1966.

[13] Norma Barger quoted in *Dallas Morning News*, 2 August 1966; APD Files: *SOR* by Bob Day, 2 August 1966.

[14] APD Files: *SOR* by Bob Day, 2 August 1966.

[15] APD Files: *SOR* by Jerry Day, 1 August 1966; Fahrenthold and Rider, *Admissions*, p. 85; Texas DPS Files: *Interoffice Memorandum* by W. A. Cowan, 2 August 1966.

[16] APD Files: *SORs* by Jerry Day and R. Martinez, 1 August 1966; Texas DPS Files: *Interoffice Memorandum* by W. A. Cowan, 2 August 1966.

[17] APD Files: *McCoy Statement*, n.d.; Houston McCoy.

[18] APD Files: *CAPORs* by D. Kidd, 2 August 1966; Fahrenthold and Rider, *Admissions*, p. 87; *Summer Texan*, 2 August 1966; *Time*, 12 August 1966; unidentified Sheftall employee quoted in *Life*, 12 August 1966; *Austin American-Statesman*, 2 and 7 August 1966 and 30 July 1967.

[19] APD Files: *CAPOR* by D. Kidd, 2 August 1966; *Dallas Morning News*, 4 September 1966; *Austin American-Statesman*, 2 August 1966, Billy Snowden quoted on 4 August 1966 and 30 July 1967.

[20] Unidentified clipping in AHC; APD Files: *CAPOR* by D. Kidd, 2 August 1966; *Austin American-Statesman*, 2 August 1966, Lana Phillips quoted on 4 August 1966 and 30 July 1967; *Dallas Morning News*, 4 September 1966.

[21] APD Files: *CAPORs* by D. Kidd, 2 August 1966 and *SOR* by Sgt. Pilgrim, 5 August 1966; *Dallas Morning News*, 4 September 1966; *Time*, 12 August 1966; *Austin American-Statesman*, 2 and 4 August 1966, and 30 July 1967.

12

The General

I

The heat—they remembered the heat. Virtually all of the wounded knew that the best way to avoid another shot from Charles Whitman was to lie still and play dead, but for many the heat became unbearable. Onlookers pitied the wounded as much for the pain caused by hot pavement as for the wounds. Claire Wilson had no choice but to lie still for more than an hour as the sun beat down on her until she could be rescued. Instinctively she picked up one leg and moved it from side to side. Witnesses mentally pleaded for her to put that leg down and keep still. "We could see people moving a bit, but they never could get up and walk away." It would have been easier if they had known that Whitman never shot anyone twice.[1]

From the top of the Tower, Charles Whitman not only held off an army but he also pinned it down and stayed on the attack. After the tragedy, many police officers' written reports stated that they were unable to move from their positions. Whitman's rapid fire suggested a shift to a greater use of the 30-caliber carbine, an automatic rifle. Earlier he tended to use the scoped 6mm Remington, a far more accurate weapon over long distances, but one that required the manual use of a bolt action. Whitman pinned down Patrolman Jim Cooney as the officer made attempts to assist Roy Dell Schmidt, the electrician Whitman killed near University and 21st Streets. "I couldn't get to the man," said Cooney.[2]

Ambulances were everywhere. For much of the time the drivers and attendants exposed themselves to Whitman's field of vision. One of the first ambulances to arrive on the scene, owned by Hyltin-Manor Funeral Home, was operated by a young man named Turner Bratton and a thirty-year-old funeral director named Morris Hohmann. Hohmann was scheduled to start his vacation only two days later. The two men drove to the entrance of Garrison Hall, where the mortally wounded Dr. Robert Boyer had been taken. Boyer's necktie had been loosened in an attempt to make him more comfortable, but the wound was too massive. He was dead on arrival—the first of the victims to reach Austin's largest medical care facility—Brackenridge Hospital. The time was 12:12 P.M.[3]

"The General," Brackenridge's Emergency Room Supervisor, ran a topnotch emergency room. On 1 August 1966 Leeda Lee Bryce, who received her military title from the doctors, had been home sick, but she had overcome her malady to arrive only minutes after Morris Hohmann delivered Dr. Robert Boyer to the emergency room. Boyer's arrival time was the only one recorded for the rest of the afternoon. By 12:15 P.M. the hospital's administrator, Ben Tobias, had activated the disaster plan. The General arrived at 12:20 P.M.[4]

A routine emergency room shift at Brackenridge consisted of two registered nurses and a few students. In a matter of minutes, ten registered nurses and about twenty student nurses crowded the entrance to the hospital. Everyone knew something was wrong, even before detailed reports had reached them to make the extent of the emergency clear. Mrs. Marion Chapman, the Director of Social Services, knew something was up when she noticed the ambulance sirens blaring right up to the emergency room door; they were usually cut off once the vehicle was safely out of traffic. On 1 August 1966 the attendants hurriedly unloaded their patients, returned to their vehicles, and sped off again.[5]

Joe Roddy, a well-known Austin newsman from KTBC, had left the campus to provide live coverage at the hospital. "It seemed like the ambulances were coming in every few seconds. I . . . remember all the stretchers they had. There were two or three dozen, just piled up, waiting,"[6] Roddy remembered ten years later. Several witnesses remember him helping to unload ambulances.[7] Leeda Bryce remembered: "It was constant . . . ambulances driving up. Then all of a sudden we had half of Austin outside the emergency room. It got to the point where ambulances were parked in the middle of the street."[8]

Other patients were cleared from the hospital's clinic, which soon became a morgue. A twenty-one-bed wing that had been closed the preceding May because of a personnel shortage was quickly reopened. For the next few hours Brackenridge would have no such shortage. Within minutes, dozens of doctors from all parts of Austin arrived to tend to the wounded. The director of the Brackenridge School of Nursing arrived with a group of students who served as "runners." If anyone needed anything they called for a runner. As Bryce remembered: "There were [doctors] in the emergency room, some in the operating room, some sitting there waiting to operate, and they all came wanting to help."[9]

The situation at Brackenridge could have easily deteriorated into a state of panic, but in the eye of the storm was the "General." Everyone listened to Mrs. Bryce, whose war-time nursing experience served her well. Her split-second decisions assigned doctors and nurses to patients according to injury and space. In the face of an incredible tragedy, Brackenridge's disaster plan worked well, and undoubtedly, saved lives.

Other divisions at Brackenridge went on alert. Soon, scores of police, reporters, relatives and friends of the wounded, and others such as blood donors, descended upon the hospital. Patrolman Elton Edwards was assigned to control traffic as ambulances delivered the dead and wounded. Even then ambulances and emergency vehicles were forced to park in the middle of streets. Once waiting rooms were filled, families were sent to the cafeteria where the Director of Dietary Services, Joyce Parma Lalonde, led her staff in the preparation of sandwiches and coffee for the duration of the crisis.[10] Mrs. Lalonde's husband, Dr. Albert Lalonde, a respected Austin neurosurgeon and the hospital's Chief of Staff, had already reported to the emergency room. One of his first patients was Claudia Rutt. She still complained of troubled breathing. Dr. Lalonde, seeing little blood on her clothes, correctly deduced internal bleeding. Dr. Jim Calhoon, the only thoracic surgeon in Austin (the other, Dr. Maurice Hood, had just left town for a vacation) took over and tried to save her by draining the excess fluid from her chest cavity, but Rutt died shortly afterwards.[11]

Brackenridge had never seen anything like it. Phone lines were so jammed that periodically the operators pulled out all lines to clear the board and prevent an overload. Of the thirty-nine victims brought to the emergency room, twelve were dead or would die there. But the institution rose to the occasion, saving those who could be saved.[12]

A flood of ambulances came. "It was just a shock. It just started coming and it just didn't stop. Every time you looked up there was somebody coming in," remembered the General. Everyone worked as fast as possible. Ambulances owned by different companies ended up mixing and mismatching supplies, but no one cared. Brackenridge doctors noticed that most of the victims had chest wounds; whoever had done the shooting had aimed! Many of the arrivals were dead; many were in serious or critical condition. Some were treated and released, and still others left before they could be treated. Still the ambulances kept coming. It was so uncalled for, thought Mrs. Bryce; it was so useless. She continued to direct the wounded to doctors, nurses, and places.[13] Dr. Bud Dryden remembered:

> I don't think the emergency room had any panic in it that day. What helped more than anything else in my opinion was Mrs. Bryce directing the doctors and directing the injured and the situation in general.[14]

But after a while, even the General began to show signs of despair. As more and more dead and wounded crowded the emergency room, Bryce became angered at the pain and suffering all around her and at the senseless cruelty apparently caused by one evil individual. In frustration she asked, "Why the hell don't they kill him?"[15] Lifesavers and healers are nonetheless human. Eventually, someone in ER would shout: "Well, they've shot the guy up there killing the people." Loud cheers followed the announcement, to the dismay of Dr. Calhoon: "Like a football game. God. That thing sort of upset me because I felt so sad that we would cheer that a guy got shot. And I still feel bad that they had to kill him."[16]

In this, as in most tragedies, regular people were transformed into superhuman, authentic heroes. And so it was with Leeda Lee Bryce. She said that if the wounded had a chance to live "we could have saved them. I believe in my doctors and nurses, and I know we had the equipment. No, if they died, it was God's will."[17]

Legends were produced as well. One oft-repeated story told of a tired young nurse who at the end of the day looked down upon her blood-soaked white shoes. In tears, she could not bring herself to clean them, but instead threw them away.

II

The tragedy attracted more than just policemen and vigilantes with deer rifles. As the shooting continued, the media, armed with cameras and note pads, spread out over the campus. One of the first to arrive was a thirty-six-year-old Associated Press reporter named Robert Heard, a former marine officer and Korean War veteran. Another reporter named Jack Keever had received a call from his wife Cindy, a UT employee. In order to keep Keever on the phone with Cindy, AP's Capitol Bureau Chief Garth Jones immediately assigned Robert Heard to the story. Jack had a few parting words for Heard: "Be careful, don't get shot."[18]

Hurrying towards the capitol's north door, Heard remembered that he had taken his Volkswagen in for repairs, so he quickly hitched a ride with a *Dallas Times-Herald* reporter named Ernie Stromberger. A security agent in a guard house on the northeast side initially stopped them, then allowed the reporters to cover the shootings.

They reached a driveway 150 yards north of the Tower on 24th Street at 12:15 P.M. Stromberger drove up behind a highway patrol car coming to a stop. When Heard saw the two patrolmen step out of the car putting shotguns together, he wondered what they thought they could do with short-range weapons against a sniper high in the Tower. He later concluded that they intended to confront the sniper inside.

The patrolmen walked to a spot on the southwest side of the Home Economics Building one block north of the Tower. From there they ran across the street toward the Biological Sciences Building. Heard decided to follow. Before beginning his trek, however, he counted to five in case the sniper (or snipers) had seen the officers and was waiting for anyone who might follow. That is probably exactly what happened.

A fairly new Austinite, having moved there from Houston on 10 January 1966, Heard was assigned campus work as an AP reporter, which had taken him only to UT's football stadium and the Gregory Gym. He knew little more of the campus and did not know that the Tower had an observation deck. Before following the patrolmen, he scanned the top story windows. Limited to about eighty percent of his normal running speed because of knee-cartilage surgery the previous June, Heard's timing could not have been more tragic. He needed to cover only twenty-six yards to reach the cover of the Biological Sciences Building. Whitman must have pulled the trigger as soon as Heard began his dash.

> I tried to run across a street in the shadow of the tower. I felt and heard a shot at the same instant. Like a brick it drove back my left shoulder, shattering the arm below the shoulder joint. "He got me!" I remember yelling. There was no pain, just a numbing sensation with my left arm flapping uncontrollably at my side.

The shot pushed him a quarter turn to his left, and after three steps he fell to the hot pavement near the Biological Sciences Building. Whitman could no longer see him. Unlike many of the other wounded, he did not have to languish on the searing pavement for very long. Incredibly courageous witnesses from the Biological

Sciences Building, who could not have known that Heard had stumbled out of Whitman's line of vision, immediately ran to him and dragged him to cover behind a car. The patrolmen looked up at the Tower from some bushes nearby and they saw Charles Whitman carefully searching for the group, now safely out of his field of vision, through binoculars he had draped around his neck. As he peered through the eyepieces just below his white headband, either hoping to finish off the wounded Heard or to relish another "hit," an angered patrolman fired back. Whitman ducked and moved to a new position to shoot at someone else.[19]

A few minutes later an ambulance arrived to carry Robert Heard to Brackenridge, and yet again, the attendants exposed themselves to danger in order to retrieve the wounded. Like Billy Snowden, who chastised himself for standing at the door of a barber shop while the shooting occurred, Robert Heard later lamented, "I forgot my marine training; I should have zigged-zagged [sic], but he was a really good shot." Hours later, doctors and staff at Brackenridge marveled at Heard's determination to complete his duties as a reporter. "He was reluctant to undergo an anesthetic and surgery in order to be alert," remembered Dr. Joe Abell, who would later operate on Heard. From his hospital bed in Brackenridge, the reporter dictated his story between instances of hospital operators "clearing the lines." Before Abell left Brackenridge he would find Robert Heard propped up in his bed typing with one hand. His account would be published all over the world. "What a shot!"[20]

At the KTBC newsroom a young reporter named Neal Spelce heard reports of shooting at the Tower over a police scanner. His first thoughts were that it could be a prank, but after arriving at the campus, Spelce witnessed the horrible reality. On live radio he announced:

> This is a warning to the citizens of Austin. Stay away from the university area. There is a sniper at the University Tower firing at will. . . . It's like a battle scene. There's a shot, and another shot, and another shot. . . . It's a battle between the sniper and the police.

The KTBC television station carried live coverage as well. Correspondent Phil Miller arrived with photographer Gary Pickle and another newsman named John Thawley. At different times, each of the journalists attempted to rescue the wounded. Whitman's shots came to within four feet of Thawley, who took cover behind a tree.[21]

Later in the afternoon the station's semi-retired news director, Paul Bolton, anchored coverage from the newsroom. Well-known in news circles, Bolton was a personal friend of President Lyndon Johnson, who happened to own KTBC, Austin's premier AM radio and only VHF television station. During a live report from Brackenridge Hospital, Joe Roddy, in a departure from a KTBC policy of not reading the names of dead people before their families had been contacted, read a list of names of the confirmed dead. As Roddy listed the names, Bolton, quite uncharacteristically, frantically interrupted the reporter. "Joe, hold it a minute, this is Paul over at the newsroom. Everyone is interested in that list of names. I think you have my grandson there. Go over that list of names again, please." After Roddy read the names again, Paul Bolton slowly removed his earphones and went home to his family. Shortly afterwards, the general public would learn that Paul Sonntag's full name was Paul Bolton Sonntag. He had been named after his grandfather.[22]

A future journalist, William "Bill" Helmer, walking towards the Student Union from the journalism building north of the Tower, heard the strange noises. At first, he thought of nail-driving guns, since UT always had construction going on somewhere. Later, when writing of the incident, Helmer would tell of others who thought of wooden planks slapping concrete or more exotic explanations like ROTC members shooting blanks during some commemoration or a "goofy crowd response experiment carried out by the psych folks." Even after looking up and seeing a gun barrel jut over the northwest corner of the observation deck, Bill thought that "some fool was going to get himself into a lot of trouble." The sniper's intent became clear as Bill headed towards Hogg Auditorium, where he discovered that a girl standing in the side yard of the Biological Sciences Building had been hit.[23]

Helmer then moved around the back of the auditorium into the Student Union. While on his way to a window with an excellent view of the Tower, he saw someone run through the lobby screaming, "That man is dead! That man is dead!" The window with the view was situated adjacent to a landing between the third and fourth floors of the Student Union. To get there visitors had to walk up a winding stairway bordered by decorative metal balusters capped by a stained oak balustrade. The large window on the east wall rose from a marble ledge about four feet above the floor in a dark, almost dreary, part of the Union. At least three students were already situated near the window when Helmer reached it. Two girls, standing to the right of an eighteen-year-old freshman pharmacy student, John Scott Allen, looked outside, as if gazing at a movie screen.

The four students watched Charles Whitman move from one spot to another; he seemed to be everywhere. Helmer remembers that whenever the sniper's rifle came into view, the return fire was swift and heavy, but not constant—more like "popping corn." After about an hour, people began to grow accustomed to the gunfire. Soon more civilians would actually go to the campus to watch, giving the sniper more targets for which to aim. Helmer and the three other students watched from the window as Whitman continued firing, probably thinking they were safe inside. Without warning Whitman poked his rifle through one of the rain spouts on the west side of the deck and sent a bullet through the edge of the window. The force sent glass slivers into the faces of the girls, but they were not badly injured. After hitting the window, however, the missile veered towards John Scott Allen and Bill Helmer. All four students hit the floor quickly, but blood began to cover the landing. Most of it came from Allen's right forearm, where an artery had been severed. As Helmer remembered, the blood shot out about three inches from Allen's arm. When Bill asked for a handkerchief to place on Allen's wound, Allen used his left arm to retrieve one from his back pocket. The students moved away from the window. Helmer would later write, "I knew exactly what to do; keep my damn head down."[24]

Inside the Student Union, Helmer heard someone cry, "They've shot an ambulance driver!" Across the street at the corner of 23rd and Guadalupe, Morris Hohmann's luck had run out.

Hohmann and Turner Bratton had already delivered Dr. Robert Boyer to Brackenridge and had returned to transport more of the wounded to the hospital. Most of the ambulances had driven to an alley behind the shops on the Drag, but a few minutes before 12:30

P.M., Hohmann's ambulance stopped near the front door of Sheftall's Jewelry. Hohmann ran inside the store, where he was told to move the ambulance to a rear alley so that the wounded could be loaded away from the line of fire. By that time seven victims were waiting inside Sheftall's to be taken to the hospital. Hohmann ran along the driver's side of the ambulance as Bratton drove slowly along the Drag. Hohmann thought that the ambulance gave him cover, but at 231 feet above ground level, Whitman could have shot him at any time. The ambulance attendants moved north and the ambulance turned left onto 23rd Street to head for the alley. Once the vehicle turned, Hohmann was completely exposed, presenting a target Whitman could not pass up. He shot Hohmann in the right thigh. Hohmann fell and managed to roll himself under a parked car, where he attempted to use his belt as a tourniquet to stop the bleeding. But his leg had swollen and the belt was too small. "I laid there for about forty–forty-five minutes waiting to be rescued, and listening to two construction workers arguing about who was going to expose themselves to recover me," Hohmann remembered.[25] The workers, Bill Davis and Phil Ward, were hiding behind the construction barricades where Paul Sonntag and Claudia Rutt had been shot earlier. They eventually pulled Morris Hohmann to safety. His own ambulance transported him to Brackenridge, where he would receive eight pints of blood and his life would be saved.

Everywhere in Austin people huddled near radios and televisions to witness the unfolding drama. Even Charles Whitman tuned his fourteen-transistor Channel Master radio, with the volume as high as possible, to KTBC to listen to Neal Spelce's vivid descriptions. He had to have been pleased with what he heard.[26]

III

The continuous shooting delivered an uneasy sense of helplessness. On the twenty-fourth floor of the Tower, Dr. Charles Laughton watched people fall on the Drag and the mall area. He watched people in front of the Varsity Theater scatter as Abdul Kashab, Janet Paulos, Sandra Wilson and Lana Phillips fell to the sidewalk. "We just barricaded ourselves in and waited," Dr. Laughton remembered.[27]

As Oscar Royvela, a twenty-one-year-old native Bolivian on a good neighbor scholarship, and Irma Garcia, a twenty-one-year-old student from Harlingen, walked south of Hogg Auditorium, heading north towards the biology lab, Charles Whitman aimed and fired. Garcia was shot first. "I felt myself reeling. The bullet turned me completely around." Her wound was to the left shoulder. As Royvela instinctively tried to help her, he too was shot. The round entered his left shoulder blade and exited under and through his left arm. Nearby, Jack Stephens and Jack Pennington dashed around a corner and ran through the open area to grab the couple by the feet and drag them to safety. Their heroism was not lost on Royvela, who one year later commented: "I want to remember the kindness of many persons who in one way or another did help me during the critical time. I shall always remember with affection all that the wonderful American people did."[28]

Avelino Esparza, twenty-six, worked nearby as a carpenter at the construction site of a new post office. As he was walking back to work, Whitman fired a round into his left arm near the shoulder. It shattered the bone in his upper arm. His brother and uncle risked their lives to drag him to safety. Esparza would later be admitted to Brackenridge in serious condition.[29]

It became difficult, if not impossible, to determine exactly how many people were wounded by the rounds fired from the guns of Charles Whitman. Many dozens more were wounded by fragments and flying limestone, concrete, and glass. Included among these victims were Della and Marina Martinez, two visitors from Monterrey, Mexico, who were hit by shell fragments; Delores Ortega, a thirty-year-old student and resident of UT's Kinsolving Dorm, who was cut on the back of her head by broken glass; undoubtedly, many dozens more could be counted as wounded. There were others who suffered from related injuries like heat exhaustion and extreme sunburns. Other students fell and hurt themselves as they ran in terror. But as the shooting continued, so did the heroism.[30]

The University of Texas Chancellor Harry Ransom, trapped in his office in the Tower, found solace in the heroism of many university students. He witnessed young adults, arguably children, running through gunfire to rescue the wounded. It was, as Ransom said, "incredible and heartlifting." Newsreel footage captured young men in

white shirts (excellent targets) dashing around the corners of buildings and over grassy areas and walkways. Others reached victims,
lifted them, and walked slowly towards the safety of a tree or wall.
Witnesses prayed for the sniper to be on the other side of the deck
or to have mercy on the slow-moving heroes. In many cases arms
and legs dangled as rescuers moved lifeless bodies. Reporter Charles
Ward would later document the story of Brehan Ellison, a Vietnam
veteran who moved two people away from the deadly fire, one of
whom later died.[31]

A twenty-two-year-old UT student and pharmacy major, Clif
Drummond, and his friend Bob Higley walked along the Drag amid
the strange noises. As Drummond remembered:

> I was meandering along when I heard two shots. At first I
> thought the noise was from workmen on the Tower; they're
> always up there. Then I saw people looking up and I saw
> some running and screaming. I still didn't believe it was
> happening until puffs of smoke floated from the Tower.
> Then people began to fall and I realized I was an easy
> target.

After realizing what was going on, Drummond, President of the UT
Student Body and the 1964 state co-chairman of Young Citizens for
Lyndon Johnson, ran into the Student Union where his office was
housed and retrieved some laboratory coats for use as bandages. He
also took off his coat and tie and slipped off his shoes—the smooth
leather soles of dress shoes slipped on hot pavement, making running difficult. Then, he ran out of the building through an exit away
from the line of fire. Immediately, he and Higley spotted Paul Sonntag
leaning against a parking meter across the street. The young men
dashed across the street toward Sonntag, and as Higley recalled later:
"we got out from under the overhang of the buildings, Whitman
could pick us up. And he found us and started shooting at us."
Drummond and Higley crawled behind cars as Whitman continued
to fire. Unlike many others, the young men took into consideration
the angle from which the sniper fired and stayed low and close to
the cars. Higley continued:

Then we got down behind a car and I could reach up, and got the student and pulled him towards me. He apparently looked up at the Tower at the time and [had] been shot in the throat. There was no visible sign of injury, but when he came down, it was very apparent he was dead.

The two brave young men cradled the body of Paul Sonntag until an ambulance arrived and took him away.[32]

After removing Sonntag, Drummond and Higley pulled another man off the street and carried two wounded girls into a building. Soon they joined an ambulance crew and assisted in the loading of more victims. They continued their work as bullets ripped into nearby construction barriers and as the hot pavement began to burn and eat away at Drummond's bare feet. "I threw the lab coats on the pavement to stand on, but they were full of blood after a while and didn't do much," he remembered.[33]

Two weeks after the incident, the *Los Angeles Herald-Examiner* reported that a nineteen-year-old carpenter named Bill Davis (one of the two men who rescued Morris Hohmann), even after repeated warnings from his boss, continued to rush out into the street to save two victims. Finally, his boss warned him to stop or he'd be fired. Davis ran out again and was later fired for lack of discipline. Orville Jansen, a workman at the Texas Theater, carried a wounded girl from the Drag to an ambulance in the alley behind some stores. He was exposed to Whitman's fire. Glenn Johnson and Alfred Gallessich, both teenagers, attempted to help the wounded along the sidewalk of the Drag. They could tell if the victims were in trouble, because their fingers turned blue.[34]

At the Student Health Center, Dr. Robert C. Stokes received a call at 12:05 P.M. to go to the Tower. He and another employee, Evelyn Anderson, rode in an ambulance to the north side of Hogg Auditorium where Jack Stephens and Jack Pennington had dragged Oscar Royvela and Irma Garcia to safety. After Dr. Stokes treated them, an ambulance arrived to take the patients away. Dr. Stokes established contact with campus security and then moved to an adjacent building where he administered first aid to Ellen Evganides. From there a university employee guided the doctor through tunnels under the South Mall to the Computation Center where he examined Brenda Littlefield, who was not seriously injured. From there, Dr. Stokes proceeded to the Tower.[35]

IV

Mary, Mike, and Mark Gabour and Marguerite Lamport were still lying on the narrow stairway between the twenty-seventh floor and the reception area on the twenty-eighth floor of the Tower. Mark and Marguerite were dead; Mike and Mary were critically wounded and helpless. Shortly after the shooting, M. J. Gabour and William Lamport had tried to move them to safety. They succeeded in moving Mark down the hallway and they placed Marguerite next to him. When they tried to move Mike, his pain was unbearable and he asked to be left alone. Later Mike tried to move himself. It was then he realized that he was paralyzed along the left side of his body. As he tried to get around Mary, he kept falling and ended up on top of his mother's head. Mary had trouble breathing. At first Mike thought Mary was dead, too. He said prayers, but soon he began to get angry and to curse the man who shot him and his family. But Mary had not raised Mike that way; she gathered enough strength to admonish her son, "Mike, don't say all those bad things."

Mike now knew his mother was still alive. "Mom, are you alright?" he asked.

"Yes, darling, I'm fine," she answered. "Someone will help us soon."

Mike kept talking and encouraging his mother to keep her eyes open and talk. He figured that if either one of them stopped they would die. And then Mike warned his mother to do precisely the opposite. He heard a door opening, followed by slow, methodical footsteps. He told his mother to play dead.[36]

---

[1] *Austin American-Statesman*, 7 August 1966, 30 July 1967, 1 August 1986; Norma Barger quoted in *Dallas Morning News*, 2 August 1966.

[2] APD Files: *SOR* by J. Cooney, 3 August 1966; *Austin American-Statesman*, 7 August 1966.

[3] Fahrenthold and Rider, *Admissions*, p. 82; *Austin American-Statesman*, 2 and 3 August 1966.

[4] *Austin American-Statesman*, 2 August 1966.

[5] Ibid.

[6] *Dallas Morning News*, 1 August 1986.

[7] Fahrenthold and Rider, *Admissions*, p. 85.

[8] Leeda Lee Bryce quoted in *Austin American-Statesman*, 1 August 1986.

[9] *Austin American-Statesman*, 2 August 1966.

[10] APD Files: *SOR* by E. Edwards, 2 August 1966; Fahrenthold and Rider, *Admissions*, pp. 79, 85, 89; *Austin American-Statesman*, 1 August 1986.

[11] Fahrenthold and Rider, *Admissions*, pp. 79, 85, 89.

[12] APD Files: *SOR* by E. Edwards, 2 August 1966; Fahrenthold and Rider, *Admissions*, pp. 79, 85, 89; *Austin American-Statesman*, 1 August 1986.

[13] Leeda Lee Bryce quoted in *Dallas Morning News*, 1 August 1991; APD Files: *CAPOR* by D. Kidd and *SOR* by G. Phifer, 2 August 1966; *Austin American-Statesman*, 2 and 23 August 1966.

[14] Dr. Bud Dryden quoted in *Austin American-Statesman*, 1 August 1986.

[15] Leeda Bryce quoted in *Austin American-Statesman*, 1 August 1986.

[16] Dr. Jim Calhoon quoted in *Austin American-Statesman*; Fahrenthold and Rider, *Admissions*, p. 89.

[17] Leeda Bryce quoted in *Austin American-Statesman*, 1 August 1986.

[18] I had the pleasure of meeting Jack Keever and Robert Heard on 16 March 1996 while serving on a panel for the South By Southwest Media Conference in Austin, Texas. My conversations with these gentlemen are hereafter cited by name only. Robert Heard, a distinguished journalist in his own right, graciously agreed to review my manuscript. He summarized his experiences that day in letters to me dated 15 and 23 May 1996. All information about Keever and Heard is from the letters and the following other sources: *Daily Texan*, 1 August 1991; *Austin American-Statesman*, 2 August 1966, Robert Heard quoted in 30 July 1967; *Dallas Morning News*, 4 September 1966.

[19] APD Files: *CAPOR* by D. Kidd, 2 August 1966.

[20] Fahrenthold and Rider, *Admissions*, pp. 89–92; Robert Heard; Robert Heard to Gary M. Lavergne, 15 May 1996 and 23 May 1996; Robert Heard quoted in *Austin American-Statesman*, 30 July 1967, *Daily Texan*, 1 August 1991 and *Time*, 12 August 1966.

[21] VHS tapes of news coverage of the twenty-fifth anniversary of the Tower tragedy were kindly provided to the author by Neal Spelce (hereafter cited as "Spelce Tapes"); *Summer Texan*, 2 August 1966; KLBJ, *The Paul Pryor Show*, 1 August 1995.

[22] An audio tape of the Bolton-Roddy exchange was played on KLBJ, *The Paul Pryor Show*, 1 August 1995 and a more complete recording of the entire broadcast was generously given to me by William Helmer of Chicago, Illinois.

[23] William Helmer's accounts and quotes are taken from articles he wrote for the *Texas Observer*, 19 August 1966, *Texas Monthly*, August 1986 and *Playboy*, October, 1970.

[24] APD Files: *CAPOR* by D. Kidd, 2 August 1966; Bill Helmer quoted in *Texas Observer*, 19 August 1966.

[25] Morris Hohmann quoted in *Dallas Morning News*, 1 August 1986 and 1 August 1991.

[26] APD Files: *CAPOR* by D. Kidd, 2 August 1966 and an unidentified log; Spelce Tapes; *Summer Texan*, 2 August 1966; *Austin American-Statesman*, 2 and 23 August 1966, 30 July 1967, 1 August 1986, and 27 July 1989; *Texas Observer*, 19 August 1966; KLBJ, *The Paul Pryor Show*, 1 August 1995; Fahrenthold and Rider, *Admissions*, p. 87.

[27] Dr. Charles Laughton quoted in *Austin American-Statesman*, 7 August 1966.

[28] APD Files: *CAPOR* by D. Kidd, 2 August 1966; *Dallas Morning News*, 4 September 1966; *Summer Texan*, 2 August 1966; *Austin American-Statesman*, 2 and 7 August 1966, Oscar Royvela quoted in 30 July 1967.

[29] APD Files: *CAPOR* by D. Kidd, 2 August 1966 and *SOR* by Sgt. Pilgrim, 5 August 1966; *Austin American-Statesman*, 2 and 4 August 1966, and 30 July 1967.

[30] APD Files: *CAPOR* by D. Kidd, 2 August 1966.

[31] *Summer Texan*, 2 August 1966; *Daily Texan*, 1 August 1991.

[32] Clif Drummond quoted in *Austin American-Statesman*, 3 August 1966; Bob Higley quoted in *Dallas Morning News*, 1 August 1991.

[33] *Austin American-Statesman*, 3 August 1966.

[34] *Los Angeles Herald-Examiner*, 12 August 1966 in a clipping provided by Houston McCoy; *Austin American-Statesman*, 2 August 1966.

[35] APD Files: *Food and Drug Administration Statement*, Robert C. Stokes, MD, 5 August 1966. Dr. Stokes did not mention his patients by name. The identification was made by the author.

[36] Mary Lamport, *The Impossible Tree*, pp. 109–11; *Austin Citizen*, 1 August 1977.

13

Independent Actions

In a short time, nearly all of Austin's police force had reported for duty. Some of the officers went directly to the campus. Others, including Officers George Shepard, Phillip Conner, Harold Moe, and Milton Shoquist, went to police headquarters first. There, the team was given tear gas and a walkie talkie and told to report to the campus area. Since the officers were in possession of communications equipment and tear gas, when they reached 21st and Speedway, Sergeant Marvin Ferrell, who had been directing officers to their assignments, sent them to the UT Security Office a few blocks north of the Tower at 24th and San Jacinto. There Houston McCoy asked them if they had any additional shotguns. They did not. He also asked if they had any directions or a plan. They did not. At the office, UT's Security Chief Allen R. Hamilton directed one of his men, Sgt. A. Y. Barr, to lead the APD team to the Tower.

From the university police station, the band of officers walked through the campus to an area directly east of the Tower. From that position there appeared to be only one way to get to the Tower—a dash over an open area. McCoy wondered aloud if there was a safer way for six men to get to the Main Building. William Wilcox, a university employee, knew of a maze of tunnels connecting the buildings to allow for relative ease when maintaining the campus infrastructure—telephone, power lines and water lines. Through the tunnel connecting the Computation Center to the Main Building, Wilcox guided McCoy's team.[1]

Inside the Tower, APD officer Jerry Day, DPS intelligence officer W. A. Cowan, and the civilian Allen Crum had already taken the elevator and stairs to the twenty-seventh floor. As Day, Cowan and Crum climbed towards the top, Ramiro Martinez unsuccessfully attempted to establish contact with APD headquarters before deciding to join Day and the others on the twenty-seventh floor. He walked toward the elevator, but before he could enter it a young man holding a clipboard asked him for his name. "Why do you want my name?" Ramiro asked. The man said he really did not know, but he felt the need to do something. In any case, Ramiro gave the man his name and entered the elevator, alone. The doors closed and he heard familiar elevator sounds and felt the well-known push on his heels and the soles of his feet as the elevator began to defy gravity. Like a typical occupant, he stood quietly and watched the illuminated numbers change, going up—and up.

Ramiro's parents would have been proud. He remembered the prayers he had been taught at home and at Catechism on Sunday mornings in Rotan, Texas. Raising his right hand to his forehead to begin the Sign of the Cross, he closed his eyes, pledged his life to God and asked for forgiveness of his sins:

Oh my God, I am heartily sorry for having offended thee, and I detest all my sins because of thy just punishments, but most of all because they offend thee, my God, who art all good and deserving of all my love. I firmly resolve, with the help of thy grace, to sin no more and to avoid the near occasions of sin. Amen.

The elevator doors opened onto the twenty-seventh floor. Ramiro Martinez stepped out and joined Crum, Day, and Cowan, the latter two struggling to establish communications with UT Security Chief Allen Hamilton in order to request more shotguns. They also wanted the firing from the ground to stop.

Meanwhile, the first policeman to enter the tower, Patrolman Bob Day, still waited on the third floor for someone to bring a rifle; he had been instructed to hold his position.[2]

On the twenty-seventh floor, a librarian named Jules Emig and his wife Patricia had been closer to the shooting than anyone in the Tower, except for the Gabours and Lamports. Emig had heard three shots and seen M. J. Gabour and William Lamport running through the twenty-seventh floor crying for help. Shortly afterwards, they could hear Mike and Mary Gabour moaning. James Zinn ran in and asked them to call for help. After doing so, they locked themselves in a room with Gabour and Lamport. The group looked out of the twenty-seventh floor window directly below Charles Whitman, and like him, they could see the victims being shot. Concrete and limestone made the gunshots sound as though the firing was coming from the inside of the building. Suddenly, someone knocked on the door. The panic-stricken group was relieved to discover it was Officer Jerry Day, who had come to clear the twenty-seventh floor.[3]

II

Neal Spelce had asked them not to do it. But as the drama unfolded, hundreds of Austinites began, as Police Chief Miles would later say, to "stupidly" flock to the university. It was as if a citizen's militia had been called to the campus. Chief Miles would later deny it, but on numerous instances Austin Police officers encouraged and even supplied civilians with the weapons to shoot back at the sniper.

Houston McCoy actually made two trips to Everett Hardware to get ammunition for civilians. After hearing a radio call for officers to stop firing at the Tower below the twenty-sixth floor, Officer L. Janetzke ran down the Drag spreading the request.

In buildings, on rooftops and through windows, dozens of people, policemen and civilians side by side—with varying degrees of accuracy—fired at Whitman with pistols, shotguns and rifles. From the English Building a civilian mumbled, "I'm going to get the son-of-a-bitch." Elsewhere another civilian, this one dressed in camouflage, fired an M-14 mounted on a tripod. Husbands with wives working in the Tower went home for their deer rifles to return and join in the fray. Don Vandiver, a newspaper reporter, had been handed a forty-five-caliber pistol; he chose not to use it. Throughout the campus students claiming to be "good shots" searched for weapons and asked the police for guns. Gunmen lined the rooftops adjoining the Tower. Soon, Whitman could not peer over the parapet, take aim, and shoot. He was forced to use the rain spouts and could not stay there long. As soon as he appeared, an avalanche of ground fire hit the Tower all around him. On the floor of the deck chunks of limestone were scattered amongst an even covering of pale dust. As Whitman ran from

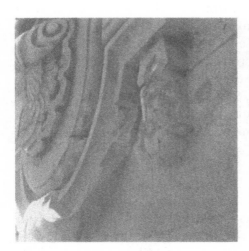

Police and civilian fire directed at Whitman hit the walls of the Tower instead, creating an even coating of pale dust and gravel-size chunks of limestone covering the red tile floor of the deck, and leaving gunfire marks on the ornate exterior. *Austin Police Department Files.*

Photo of the Tower with an arrow pointing to dust kicked up from return fire from the ground. *UPI/ Corbis-Bettmann.*

one position to another, the bits of rock crunched under his sneakers.

The police could do little. Trying to disarm dozens of civilians in the shadow of a Tower housing the deadliest sniper in American history would have been foolish. After all, the return fire was largely successful in pinning Whitman down; nearly all of the dead and wounded were hit during the first twenty minutes. Austin's response to the incident exposed evidence of Texas's fondness for deer hunting and Army surplus items. In *Texas Monthly* Bill Helmer would repeat the story of an incident in the San Jacinto Cafe, where, as customers watched coverage of the Tower massacre on television, a man carrying a deer rifle hurriedly purchased a six-pack of beer and rushed right out.[4]

Such varying degrees of qualifications with so many weapons could have been disastrous. The fact that no one was hurt as the result of "friendly fire" was miraculous. Charles Whitman probably could have posed as just another civilian wanting to help, had he decided to come down from the Tower and escape. Could he have gotten out of the building? If stopped and questioned, he could easily have produced a student identification card, a permit to be on the campus from 11:30 to 12:10 P.M., and a card showing an honorable discharge from the marines.

Ultimately, the Tower incident would reinforce the Texas tradition of bearing arms. When asked to comment on the civilians' use of firearms, Chief Miles responded:

> They did it on their own. I imagine some of them had military training. And I don't want to condemn their action because their fire did help pin him down. And most important it was not irresponsible shooting. They were shooting at the Tower.[5]

But there were other people in the Tower besides Charles Whitman.

III

Houston McCoy kept asking for a plan. That none existed bothered him immensely. Once inside the Tower he was surprised at the number of people in the hallways and rooms; the place was full. "In my mind, there was nobody in the building." He had been in the Tower only once before to take a competitive typing exam for the Texas Employment Commission. He had not stayed long. Once instructed to begin, the other test-takers, about thirty women, had filled the room with the noise of fingers assaulting keys at a rate much faster than Houston dared to dream about. He had slowly removed the paper from the typewriter's carriage and gracefully left the room.[6]

After entering the Tower, Officer McCoy's team utilized the expertise of Frank Holden, an Otis Elevator employee. McCoy asked if it were possible to take the elevator all the way to the very top of the Tower—that is, up into the crown of the building itself, even higher than the deck. His plan was to get above the "snipers" and shoot down upon them. Holden knew of a way to get there. The elevator could be taken to the twenty-seventh floor, after which a panel could be removed from the car's ceiling. Conceivably, once on top of the elevator an officer could climb through the shaft to the very top, a columned area above the clocks. The team, consisting of Officers McCoy, Conner, Moe, Shoquist, Shepard and the civilian Holden, entered the elevator and went directly to the twenty-seventh floor.

The men stood shoulder to shoulder in the crowded elevator, and as the car went up Officer McCoy took no chances. He pointed his shotgun directly at the seam created by the two sliding doors. No one knew what they were going to find when the doors opened. Earlier, while still crawling through the tunnels below the Main building, McCoy had taken his shotgun off safety and chambered one of four 00 shells. As the elevator car stopped, McCoy raised his shotgun to eye level. When the door opened, the men in the elevator gasped; they saw a gun pointed directly back at them. Jerry Day, pointing his revolver at the same seam in the door, came face-to-face with Houston McCoy. Slowly, the two men lowered the barrels of their weapons, breathed, and as McCoy would later say, "We gave each other a shit grin."[7]

First, the officers decided to clear the twenty-seventh floor and remove the wounded. They also collectively rejected the idea of using tear gas. Later McCoy would say, "You don't fire tear gas at a killer. You kill the son-of-a-bitch. No matter how much tear gas you shoot at him, he can still fire that rifle." Day introduced McCoy to a "peculiar-acting gray-haired man," M. J. Gabour, still clutching Mary's shoes. Gabour caused a stir when he demanded a gun to go after the sniper. "They've killed my family," he said. Jerry Day was forced to remove Gabour and had serious difficulty keeping him downstairs.

Officer Moe remembers seeing a much quieter William Lamport holding Marguerite's purse. Although Lamport's clothes had been splattered with blood, Moe thought he was a university employee. As Day brought Gabour and others to the ground floor, the other officers searched the twenty-seventh floor for more civilians.

Day had not told McCoy that Martinez and Crum had moved on towards the twenty-eighth floor and the deck. For a second time Crum had insisted on going. "No sir, buddy, you are not going by yourself," he told Martinez, who thought Crum was a campus security officer and had no objection. After all, Crum had a pocket liner in his shirt pocket like many policemen used, he was with two officers Martinez knew, and more importantly, he had a rifle. Why would a civilian be up there with a rifle?[8]

At this point, Mike Gabour was telling his mother to play dead. He did not know who was coming. As the officers approached, Mike peeked and saw Ramiro Martinez in his police uniform. Using his right arm, he waved Martinez and Crum over. The men reached Mike by stepping over the other family members. Martinez asked how many gunmen were there. Mike said there was only one. Martinez then asked, "Where is he?"

Mike replied, "Outside." When Martinez and Crum started to go up the stairs Mike asked them to move him out of the line of fire of a possible gunfight, but he screamed in agony as they moved him. They then moved Mary, who was facedown on the floor. Martinez saw so much blood surrounding Mary's face he actually feared she would drown in it. Mary was relieved when Mike was finally taken off her. The blood stains on Officer Martinez's white shirt later caused onlookers to mistakenly conclude he had been wounded.[9]

Martinez and Crum proceeded up the stairs, Crum suggesting that they assault the stairs "service style." Both military veterans knew what that meant; as one moved up the other watched and covered. Upon reaching the top landing, they found Edna Townsley's desk lying on its side, along with a chair and a metal trash can, blocking the doorway. They moved the heavy desk only enough to get into the room, about two feet. Then Crum asked, "Are we playing for keeps?"

"Damn right we are!" Martinez answered.

"Then you'd better deputize me."

"Ok, consider yourself deputized."

They were on the twenty-eighth floor in the reception area. Crum kicked the metal trash can across the room to see if anyone would respond. Nothing happened. They immediately saw a trail of blood streaked across the room from the southwest—the "goo" that Cheryl Botts had warned Don Walden not to step in. They also saw Edna Townsley's glasses on the floor, right where they had landed when Whitman assaulted her. They noticed that wires leading to the phone mounted on the east wall had been ripped, and knew there would be no communications from the reception area. Martinez and Crum then moved to the west window in an attempt to attack Whitman from a covered position. They could not see him, but they could see his footlocker and the vast array of supplies Whitman had carried to the deck. It was an awesome sight.[10]

After leaving Mr. Gabour on the ground floor, Jerry Day returned to the twenty-seventh floor to join the other officers, who had decided to remove the wounded before storming the deck. As McCoy entered the stairway he, too, came across the Gabours and Marguerite Lamport. Mike, now energized by the help around him, asked McCoy for his shotgun, "Let me shoot the son-of-a-bitch!" The officer replied that he'd shoot the bastard for him. Mary did not appreciate that kind of language at all. McCoy assured her that they would get her to the hospital as soon as possible. Officers Moe, Shepard, Conner and Shoquist moved Mike and Mary to the twenty-seventh floor as Houston and Jerry Day provided cover. The men, nearly all of them prior service veterans, were horrified at the gruesome scene. George Shepard estimated that the Gabours lay in about two inches of coagulated blood. Phillip Conner, a former medic in the military, was charged with administering first aid. He later said the blood on the floor was so deep it oozed over the top of his penny loafers.

As Houston McCoy gazed at the door of the reception area, Day mentioned, almost in passing, that a civilian with a rifle was with Martinez. It probably saved Allen Crum's life. Had McCoy entered the reception area earlier, or if Crum had returned to the landing, he likely would have been shot on the spot. McCoy was looking for a civilian, in plain clothes, with a rifle. If the first person he saw had been Allen Crum, he would have "blown him away." McCoy's first thought was that they needed to get Crum out of there. Houston was now even more convinced that he had better get up there as soon as possible.[11]

Houston still hoped for a plan. He thought it was a good idea to go to the very top and storm the sniper, or snipers, from above. But things were moving too fast and everyone had to improvise. Only minutes earlier, when entering the receptionist area, Martinez and Crum had discovered the body of Edna Townsley. She was still alive, but barely. She moaned and groaned during her struggle against death. Martinez and Crum heard shots from the northwest corner. They looked through windows on the southwest and south sides and could see "a lot of stuff" out there. As Crum stood against the interior south wall he covered the west window. Martinez went for the glass-paneled door on the south side but Whitman had wedged the Austin Rental Service dolly against it. As Martinez struggled to open the door, McCoy and Jerry Day entered the room. Day covered the window on the west side; Crum moved towards the south door to join Martinez. Phillip Conner would join them shortly. Martinez began kicking the door, making enough noise to concern the other officers in the room. Finally, the dolly fell, making even more noise. McCoy, Crum, and Day gazed at the windows, waiting for the sniper to appear. Martinez gazed at the glass-paneled door.[12]

IV

In defense of his department, Police Chief Bob Miles said, "In a situation like this, it all depended on independent action by officers." Other than some coordination at 21st Street and Speedway there was no plan. No documentation exists of Chief Miles's actions during the crisis. Neither are there any accounts of his going to the campus. That is not to say that he should have been there. The fact is that the Austin Police Department was not prepared for the incident. Whether they should have been could be forever debated. No other city had ever been faced with a crime such as the one Charles Whitman inflicted on Austin from his perch at the University of Texas Tower.

The bulk of APD officers responded first by clearing the area. Traffic was cut off at various intersections, forming a large circle around the campus. Other officers on the campus ran through the grounds getting people into buildings and behind barricades and out of the line of fire. More than one hour after the firing had begun, APD had to dispatch an officer to a restaurant several blocks from the Tower to restrain a civilian from returning fire with a high powered rifle.

The record does show that some Austin policemen actively took part in getting people out of harm's way. Officers Still and Baylor, for example, risked gunfire to help the wounded. Other witnesses told of people being led to safety by policemen. Jerry Day, Bob Day, Ramiro Martinez, Houston McCoy and others ran through open areas to do their jobs. Billy Speed died in the line of duty. Of all of the policemen on the campus, most were off-duty and not in direct communications with headquarters. Walkie-talkies used by a few of them were of poor quality anyway. Communications had to be conducted by telephone at a time when Austin's phone lines were jammed with a record number of incoming phone calls. Without the luxury of being able to prepare, an effective coordination of the police response would have been a virtual impossibility. Chief Miles was right. Progress did depend on the individual actions of each policeman.

One of the more famous and daring but completely unsuccessful attempts to get at Charles Whitman came about from the air. The use of helicopters was considered by the APD but rejected as too dangerous, as choppers were thought to be too vulnerable to gunfire. After receiving a call from Tim's Airpark, however, APD did decide to try to assault Whitman from a small plane. APD sent sharpshooter Lieutenant Marion Lee to the small air strip north of Austin near a little town called Pflugerville. There, Lee and a flight instructor and a part-time Williamson County Deputy Sheriff named Jim Boutwell boarded a very small Champion Citabria airplane and took off for the Tower. The Champion Citabria was a cloth-covered aircraft and, like the rejected helicopters, wholly unsuited for an assault involving gunfire. As Boutwell put it, his only protection was "the fabric side of the airplane and a blue shirt." Before takeoff Boutwell turned to Lee and asked, "In case I got hit could you land this airplane?"

"Sure I could. Let's go," replied Lee, who had never landed a plane in his life.[13]

Circling 1,200 feet above the ground, Lee and Boutwell were able to confirm that there was only one sniper. Unfortunately, the lack of communications throughout the campus meant that this timely information never made it to the men on the twenty-eighth floor. As Boutwell approached the concrete jungle, the light airplane began to bounce, making it nearly impossible for Lee to aim. The turbulence was caused by "thermal lift," or a convectional system of hot air rising from the pavement. Lee had to be concerned about the consequences of missing Whitman, and possibly the entire Tower. His rounds could have eventually hit the ground near the Tower, possibly injuring or killing an innocent bystander. Boutwell watched for other aircraft and other snipers. He would later remember: "We kept his [Whitman's] attention but then he kept ours too. The plane was bouncing too much for Marion to get him in the scope. But we had the best seat in the house." The little plane did catch the attention of Charles Whitman. Looking up, he fired at least two rounds that went completely through the fabric-covered plane. Whitman came dangerously close to shooting an aircraft out of the sky. Surely, had he been successful, at least two more people would have been killed and possibly many more on the ground. Whitman would have liked that. Wisely, Boutwell backed off and awaited instructions. And then they saw men walking onto the deck through the glass paneled door.

---

[1] Files: *SOR*s by G. Shepard, Phillip Conner, H. Moe, M. Shoquist, M. Ferrell, and Houston McCoy, 1 August 1966, *McCoy Statement*, n.d.

[2] Ramiro Martinez; APD Files: *SOR*s by J. Day, R. Martinez and B. Day, 1 August 1966, *Allen Crum*, 2 August 1966.

[3] APD Files: *SOR*s by J. Pope, 4 August 1966 and H. F. Moore, 5 August 1966.

[4] APD Files: *SOR* by L. Janetzke, 3 August 1966; *Newsweek*, 15 August 1966; *Daily Texan*, 1 August 1991; *Texas Monthly*, August 1986; *Austin American-Statesman*, 3 and 4 August 1966, 1 August 1976.

[5] Chief Miles quoted in *Austin American-Statesman*, 7 August 1966.

[6] Houston McCoy; *Austin American-Statesman*, 1 August 1986.

[7] Houston McCoy; APD Files: *McCoy Statement*, n.d.

[8] Ramiro Martinez; APD Files: *SOR*s by R. Martinez, H. Moe, J. Day, 1 August 1966; *Newsweek*, 15 August 1966; *Austin American-Statesman*, Allen Crum quoted on 7 August 1966, Houston McCoy quoted on 1 August 1986.

[9] Ramiro Martinez; APD Files: *Allen Crum*, 2 August 1966, *SOR* by R. Martinez, 1 August 1966; Lamport Interview; *Austin Citizen*, 1 August 1977; Spelce Tapes.

[10] Ramiro Martinez; APD Files; *Allen Crum*, 1 August 1966, *SOR* by R. Martinez, 1 August 1966; Allen Crum.

[11] Houston McCoy; Phillip Conner; APD Files: *SOR*s by H. McCoy, P. Conner, H. Moe, M. Shoquist, and G. Shepard, 1 August 1966.

[12] Houston McCoy; Ramiro Martinez; APD Files: *McCoy Statement*, n.d., *SOR*s by H. McCoy, R. Martinez, J. Day, 1 August 1966, *Allen Crum*, 2 August 1966.

[13] APD Files: *SOR* by Marion Lee, 1 August 1966; Time-Life, p. 38; *Austin American-Statesman*, 1 August 1986.

[14] Jim Boutwell quoted in *Dallas Morning News*, 1 August 1986; *Austin American-Statesman*, 7 August 1966, 1 August 1986; *Daily Texan*, 1 August 1991; *Texas Monthly*, August, 1986.

14

The White Headband

Telling the story takes longer than it took to do it. I'm not talking about minutes; I'm talking about seconds.
—Houston McCoy

I

After Ramiro Martinez knocked down the dolly Whitman had wedged outside the door, the men on the twenty-eighth floor stared at the windows and listened carefully. They could hear shots coming from the northwest corner, but each of them knew that at any moment someone could appear at the window. Each of Martinez's raps on the door produced noises that the others

209

thought would surely get the attention of the sniper. Every "bang" caused McCoy, Crum and Day to grasp their rifles a little tighter and to look a little closer. "God damn! He's making a lot of noise," McCoy thought.[1] Each of them had seen what the sniper was capable of doing. Outside the Tower they had seen bodies shot from incredibly long distances; inside they had seen what Whitman had done at close range: Edna, Mark, Marguerite, Mary, and Mike.

Ramiro Martinez never hesitated. Armed only with a 38 revolver, he walked through the glass-paneled door and out onto the deck. For the first time in over ninety minutes Charles Whitman had company—company he must have known would arrive eventually. Although Martinez made a considerable amount of noise getting the glass-paneled door to open, Whitman may have heard nothing. The return fire on the west side was fierce and Whitman had tuned his radio, with the volume as high as it could go, to Neal Spelce's broadcast on KTBC. It is even possible that Whitman had lingered on the west side in order to hear some part of the radio broadcast, unknowingly allowing Martinez, Crum, and McCoy time to enter the deck undetected. The news reports Whitman would have heard by that time probably pleased him.

On his hands and knees, and with his pistol in his right hand, Officer Martinez crawled around the southeast corner and headed north. Crum, clutching the rifle that had been handed to him by W. A. Cowan, stood at the door. At different moments both Martinez and McCoy had told Crum to watch the southwest corner and to shoot anything that came that way. Almost immediately after Martinez turned the first corner, Crum told McCoy, "Your fellow officer . . . might need your help." For the second time in a matter of seconds McCoy thought he had better hurry. Things were happening faster than he wanted. But it was too late; Martinez was already headed for the northeast corner towards the sniper. And indeed, McCoy did want to help his fellow officer.[2]

After rounding the first corner, the two officers were on the east side. Phillip Conner then entered the reception area and covered the west window. Jerry Day stepped outside and joined Allen Crum. While Day watched the southwest corner, intending to shoot anyone who should show up there, Crum noticed a pump rifle on the floor of the deck. He retrieved the weapon and immediately noticed that the gun itself had been shot and made inoperable; Lt. Bert Gerding had shot Whitman's gun off the ledge.

Whitman, near the northwest corner, decided to change his position, as he had done almost continuously since walking through the glass-paneled door. He ran from the northwest corner along the west towards the southwest corner. If his plan had been carried out, Whitman would have exposed himself to Phillip Conner, still inside the reception area guarding the west window and waiting to shoot anyone who came into view. There must have been a lull in both the ground fire and the radio broadcast because, miraculously, Crum heard the crunching of bits of limestone beneath Whitman's sneakers as he ran in a southerly direction. Crum also heard yelling, which he thought must have been the sniper. Much like Conner, Day and Crum waited, determined to shoot anyone who came around that corner. Before Whitman reached Conner's window, Crum, unfamiliar with the rifle he had been handed, fired a round into the interior southwestern corner of the parapet. Conner later remembered that Crum's shot "scared the shit out of Jerry Day." He also remembered Crum clumsily trying to ready his rifle for another shot. Luckily, Whitman immediately turned and headed back towards the northwest corner.[3]

Years later, when describing Houston McCoy, Ramiro Martinez would say, "He's a tall boy." McCoy stood erect as he rounded the corner onto the east side of the deck. As Martinez crawled to the right and saw McCoy coming up from behind, he waved his hand as if to plead with McCoy to stay low. It was good advice. As McCoy would later remember, "Three million splats reminded me that we still had ground fire." He got down, but barely. He bent his knees slightly but otherwise stayed erect. Still not certain that there was only one sniper, McCoy kept his eye on the columns above—just in case. He also wanted to be in a position to fire over Martinez if that became necessary.

In spite of his low position, Martinez was still vulnerable. The most accurate return fire came from the east side of the Tower where officers like Nolan Meinardus had nearly shot Whitman through a porthole. Also, return fire from that area came from higher vantage points than from the south and west sides. As Martinez reached the rain spouts, he scooted to avoid incoming fire. McCoy, not wanting to get shot in the foot, did the same. He saw at least one round from the ground funnel through a spout and hit the wall between Martinez and himself.[4]

Other dangers surrounded the officers. The clocks on each of the inside walls of the deck jutted out and created blind spots. In fact, Martinez and McCoy could not see large portions of the east side of the deck. A sniper could have been on the other side of the clock. More than once it entered McCoy's mind that maybe Mike Gabour was wrong. Maybe he had seen only one of many snipers.

No safe way existed to end the madness. Martinez wanted McCoy to get down; McCoy wanted Martinez to get into a better firing position. Neither had time to realize that they actually complemented each other quite well, although not as the result of any plan or considered thought. As Chief Miles later described, their operation resulted from individual actions. After Crum fired into the parapet, Whitman retreated to the northwest corner, knowing he was no longer alone on the deck. Assuming a defensive position, he sat with his back against the north wall of that corner. He bent his legs enough to rest his carbine on one of his knees, aiming for the southwest corner. Since Crum had fired from that area, Whitman apparently believed that an attack from that direction was imminent. He waited.

McCoy continually checked a red button near the trigger of his shotgun to see if it was off safety. He experienced odd flashing thoughts of Ruth and his boys. As Martinez continued to crawl, McCoy aimed over his head toward the northeast corner. The bullets of well-meaning police and civilians "zinged" by. Martinez had reached the northeast corner, but because of the clock portion of the north wall that jutted out, he needed to move away from the corner, well out into the view of the sniper. Whitman, still seated in the northwest corner, with his back against the north wall, fixed his sights towards the south. Martinez thought immediately of Crum. Had he left his position? Was the sniper ready to shoot Crum? Without looking at McCoy, Martinez leveled his revolver and began to shoot towards Whitman as fast as he could. He later remembered being on his knees, but McCoy called the shooting position a "cheerleaders's split."[5]

McCoy and Martinez agree though, that the shots were "Pow, pow, pow, pow, pow, pow"— as fast as you can say it. Reports conflict as to whether Martinez fired all six rounds in his revolver before McCoy turned the corner, but given the obvious rapidity of the firing, it is likely. From the corner Whitman turned his head to the left, clearly seeing Martinez firing at him. He tried desperately to wheel the carbine in that direction to return the fire, but for some reason he could not bring the rifle down. Instead, he uncharacteristically shot wildly into the air. Martinez saw fiery flashes spurting from the gun. Then Whitman saw McCoy turn the corner. After watching Martinez fire, McCoy had some idea where the sniper was and in what general direction to aim. From a better firing position and with a more appropriate weapon, McCoy leveled and aimed for the first and most obvious target he could see on the sniper—the white headband.

For a split second Whitman and McCoy eye-balled each other. McCoy fired the 12-gauge loaded with 00 buckshot and sent nine pellets toward the sniper.[6] They hit Whitman on a flat plane across both eyes and through the top of the nose, only an inch or so below the white headband. Whitman's blue eyes were gone. Then like an inverted pendulum, Whitman's head sprung back and to the right. McCoy instantly chambered another shell and fired again, this time hitting the left side of Whitman's head. The force of the second shot caused the sniper to slump even more. In an instant the white headband turned red.

Still holding the carbine, Whitman's large body twitched in a *danse macabre*. McCoy jacked in another shell and again looked above for more snipers. Martinez, still in a low firing position, threw his empty pistol to the floor, reached up with his left hand, and grabbed the shotgun out of McCoy's grasp. Stunned, McCoy let go and grabbed his revolver as Martinez ran towards Whitman. Controlled by adrenalin, he screamed as he ran towards the flopping body. McCoy later called it a "war cry." Martinez fired nearly point blank into Whitman's upper left arm, nearly blowing it off. Pellets destroyed the humerus before entering Whitman's chest. This third shotgun blast lifted Whitman's body several inches off the floor and away from the wall. He lay flat on his back with both arms above his head. At 1:24 P.M., the Eagle-Scout-turned-mass murderer lay dead on the red tiled floor of the observation deck.[7]

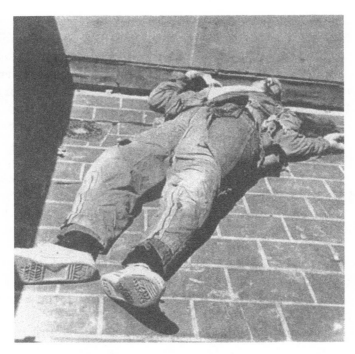

At 1:24 P.M. the terror came to an end when Austin policemen Houston McCoy and Ramiro Martinez turned the northeast corner of the observation deck and killed Whitman, who wore coveralls over his clothes to look like a janitor. More ammunition and another gun would be found hidden in Whitman's clothing after his body had been taken to Cook's Funeral Home. *Austin Police Department Files.*

II

Charles Whitman was dead; no more shooting would come from the Tower. But the ground fire continued, and the deck was still exceedingly dangerous. Police and civilians below continued to shoot at anything that moved, namely Martinez and McCoy. For a second Martinez stood over Whitman, now completely sprawled out on the deck. Emotion overwhelmed him, and he threw Houston's shotgun onto the floor. As Chief Miles would say later, "He got the shakes." He began to scream, "I got him! I got him!" as he stood up straight. He may not have been as tall as McCoy, but Martinez was still nearly six feet tall. Ground fire began hitting the walls all around him. This time, it was McCoy's turn to get his fellow officer to duck for cover.[8]

After administering first aid to the wounded inside the Tower, DPS Officer Cowan and APD Officers Shoquist, Moe, and Shepard had begun to climb the stairs. The gunfire from above was so loud that they took cover and prepared for a gunfight in the stairways and halls. On the south side of the deck Jerry Day and Allen Crum could hear the shooting. They braced themselves and prepared to shoot anything that rounded the southwest corner as both Martinez and McCoy had instructed. Inside the reception area, Phillip Conner pointed his rifle at a window near the same southwest corner; he, too, was prepared to shoot anyone he saw. After all of that shooting it was a safe bet that someone else was dead or severely wounded, but they had no way of knowing whether it was the sniper or Martinez and McCoy. Their muscles tensed as they clutched their rifles and continued to focus on the southwest corner. The hope, of course, was that Martinez and McCoy would come back around the southeast corner, from where they left the glass-paneled door, to let everyone know that the sniper was dead and everything was over.[9]

Martinez still had the shakes. "I got him! I got him!" he continued to scream in a vain attempt to halt ground fire. It did not take him long to realize that no one could hear him. McCoy told him to tell Jerry Day to call the radio stations to halt ground fire. Running in a southerly direction towards the heavily guarded southwest corner, Martinez came into Conner's view through the window. A fraction of a second later, Martinez rounded the corner itself, coming face to face with Day and Crum. Finally Martinez reached Harold Moe and reported an end to the sniping; Moe called it in on his walkie-talkie. In his report Officer Shepard wrote that Martinez had nearly been shot by his fellow officers.[10]

Meanwhile, McCoy picked up Martinez's pistol and discarded the empty shells onto the deck floor, placed the pistol in his belt, and walked towards Whitman. McCoy picked up his shotgun and leaned it against the corner of the north and west walls. He knelt over the sniper's bullet-ridden body and checked the pockets for identification. He noticed the blood from Whitman's body flowing over the white grout between the floor's red tiles. It got closer and closer to McCoy's new Wellington boots. He talked to the dead sniper as he went through the pockets, "If you get blood on my boots, I'll throw you over." Phillip Conner, who came upon McCoy talking to Whitman's dead body wondered whether McCoy would actually do it. After retrieving the billfold and the contents of Whitman's pockets, McCoy was able to make a tentative ID from the documents and the stenciling on the footlocker. Then it dawned on him: "He planned everything that day, even how we would get him. He could have killed Martinez and me pretty easy. It was almost as if he was waiting for us."[11] Officer McCoy sat on the floor and leaned against the west wall as he continued to look through the contents of the wallet. He discovered the sniper's name—Charles Joseph Whitman.

Crum grabbed a green towel from the footlocker and waved it in an attempt to signal an end to the siege. At other moments, Day and Martinez waved handkerchiefs as well. But so many people were firing towards the Tower that an end to the shooting did not occur until some time later. While waiting for the firing to stop, Day joined McCoy near Whitman, whose blood continued to flow over the grout and into a drain on the floor. McCoy did not notice it, but one of the items in the wallet was an index card on which was scrawled, in a handwriting that was not Whitman's, the name and address of a business Officer McCoy had visited twice that morning:

Everett's Hardware Store
2820 Guadalupe
GR8-5365[12]

Slowly, more officers arrived: Conner, Shoquist, Cowan, Moe, and Shepard. Day and McCoy continued to wait for the firing to stop. "Should we throw the son-of-a-bitch over?" McCoy asked facetiously. Day said they had better not. Conner had a similar conversation with McCoy and still wondered whether he was serious. Day asked Officer McCoy who "got" Whitman; McCoy's answer, "Martinez," modestly excluded his own role in bringing down the sniper. As the two officers listened to Neal Spelce's broadcast over Whitman's radio, Day asked if any officers were killed. McCoy told Day that he had seen Billy Speed get shot, but that it was a shoulder wound, and he looked like he would be okay. At almost that exact moment, Joe Roddy, reporting live, announced that Officer Billy Speed was dead on arrival at Brackenridge Hospital. After a moment of stunned silence, McCoy asked again, "Are you sure you don't want to throw the son-of-a-bitch over?"[13]

III

It was over, but word was slow to get out. Those who had radios heard Neal Spelce announce "the sniper is dead." The number of people Charles Whitman had pinned down with his fire soon became evident as hundreds of people emerged from dozens of buildings, from behind hundreds of trees, bushes, and parked cars. Dozens still carried their pistols and rifles. The South Mall was teeming with humanity. In the midst of the crowd it occurred to Spelce that if he were wrong and there *was* another sniper up there, a lot more people could easily be killed. The sniper could hit anywhere and not miss a shot.

In the midst of the crowd, Larry Fuess was thinking about his friend Charlie. He wanted to talk to him about the shooting and ironically, he thought "Charlie would have done it that way." Then, Larry heard the unthinkable. Spelce announced the identity of the sniper—Charles Joseph Whitman. Larry stood silently, in utter shock.

From the second floor of Calhoun Hall, the second building from 21st Street on the west side of the South Mall, Officer Bobby Simpson had been returning fire with a scoped rifle when he found out that the sniper was dead. He located two doctors, Robert C. Stokes of the Student Health Center, who had already faced considerable danger helping other victims, and Richard Alexander, a local psychiatrist. Officer Simpson escorted them to the Tower, along with a Catholic priest, Father David O'Brien, the Director of the Catholic Student Center. An *Austin American-Statesman* reporter named Al Williams accompanied the group on the elevator ride to the twenty-seventh floor. After boarding the elevator, a policeman told the doctors to "look for those who are still alive." The doctors, Williams, and Father O'Brien were not prepared for what they saw when the elevator doors opened. Dr. Stokes later wrote, "The entire floor was so blood-soaked that one had to step with caution to avoid slipping." Likewise, Williams wrote of having to step over and around bodies to avoid the blood. Phillip Conner remembered that Mark Gabour's body had "dammed up" so much blood on the stairway that when he was removed the blood flowed down the stairs. Father O'Brien immediately began to administer Extreme Unction, the last rites of the Catholic Church. On the floor near the elevator Dr. Stokes began to treat Edna Townsley. He observed "ecchymotic" eyelids (bluish due to hemorrhaging) and shallow respiration. The "scrapper" was still alive, but she had been viciously attacked and the doctors and policemen instinctively knew she had no chance of surviving. She would be taken to Seton Hospital for emergency surgery, where she would die at 3:18 P.M. Dr. Alexander was taken to Mary Gabour. Although her condition was not much better than Edna's, Mary would survive. She would be permanently crippled and legally blind.[14]

Al Williams moved past the bloody stairway towards the reception area. He saw the trail of blood that Cheryl Botts and Don Walden had stepped over. Someone had moved Edna's desk completely away from the door and placed her glasses and nameplate on the top. Williams stepped out onto the deck followed shortly by Dr. Stokes, who had been warned to walk in a stooped position, just in case some vigilante had not yet heard the news that the sniper had been killed. Williams noticed six bullet holes in the face of the Tower clock and saw Whitman lying on his back with the binoculars draped around his neck. Stokes was able to confirm the obvious; Charles Whitman was dead. Later that same week, in a statement to the Food and Drug Administration, Stokes wrote: "In my thirty-four years of practice I have never before seen such violence manifested by a human being."[15]

Indeed, Dr. Stokes had seen much that day. But in a couple of hours he would make one more shocking discovery.

IV

Merle Wells, APD's head of homicide, supervised the Tower crime scene and the removal of evidence and bodies. He asked Jerry Day to get a camera to take photos. McCoy stayed with Whitman until Wells instructed policemen and ambulance attendants to wrap up the body and remove it to Cook's Funeral Home. Officer Martinez, still suffering from the shakes, nearly collapsed. Wells instructed Lieutenant Lowell Morgan to assist Martinez downstairs. Morgan reported that Martinez appeared exhausted. He had been running and for the first time in quite a while he realized that it was damn hot. Morgan brought him to the west entrance of the Main Building. There, John Pope, a somewhat large man, placed his arm around Martinez and assisted him to a squad car. Many onlookers assumed that he had been wounded; he had blood on his shirt from moving the Gabours and he needed Pope's assistance. Neal Spelce remembered that Martinez's eyes were glazed and his legs were like jelly. Once back at the police station, he suffered from "dry heaves" for about thirty minutes. His stomach was empty. Back home the "piece of meat" he had started to cook for lunch was still in the oven.[16]

Finally, the ground fire ended and officials on the deck could walk erect. Nearly everyone looked at the contents of Whitman's pockets, including a small container of pills which police immediately assumed were illicit drugs of some sort. Whitman's pockets also contained a poll tax receipt dated 19 October 1965 which listed his address as 1001 Shelley Avenue. Soon, police, reporters and curious spectators converged on the address.

As time passed, the crowd on the South Mall grew. Throngs of Austinites, many of whom were relatives of someone in the university family, joined employees, students, and faculty. Cries of "kill" and "lynch" could be heard, but for the most part and despite their huge numbers, the emotional crowd stayed under control. When the time came to bring ambulances to the Main Building, officers had to move—sometimes shove—people away. Removing bodies from the building proved to be even more difficult than expected. The narrow halls and stairways and the small elevators prohibited the normal use of stretchers and gurneys; turning corners was nearly impossible. Some of the victims had to be carried on blankets until they reached the first floor. The sheet-covered body of Mark Gabour was carried out to the South Mall to an ambulance on Inner Campus Drive. As the crew walked down the steps where Dr. Robert Boyer had been shot and near the spot where Billy Speed had been mortally wounded, Mark's foot fell over the edge of the stretcher and jiggled with the bounce of each step. The shoe that was once on his foot had been placed on the stretcher. M. J. Gabour, laboring to make his way through the crowd cried, "That's my boy."[17]

The crowd fell silent as Marguerite Lamport's body, covered except for her blood-streaked legs, was taken to a vehicle. And then the horror of Mary and Mike Gabour's bullet-ridden bodies and Edna Townsley's twisted, beaten face paraded past the crowds. Shortly afterwards, at Brackenridge Hospital, Harold Moe would see a dazed William Lamport still clutching Marguerite's purse. Clearly in a state of shock, Lamport explained that he was looking for Marguerite but he could not find her. According to Moe, Lamport had "believed her to be dead." Officials on the deck, where Whitman's body still lay on the floor, wisely decided to call for an ambulance to park on the north side of the building. Much of the crowd wanted a glimpse of the body of the sniper. Concerns about the reaction of the crowd were valid. Many civilians with guns were part of the crowd.

Larry Fuess went to the north side of the Tower and saw two ambulance attendants and three policemen carry Whitman's blanket-covered body out of the building. Earlier, while in the elevator, Cook Funeral Home attendants had had to stand the stretcher with Whitman's body upright. Additional wrapping covered his head, but the blood still soaked through.[18]

At the Austin Police Department, Ramiro Martinez recovered. After assuring Vernell by phone that he was all right, he wrote his report. He then retreated to his brother's home in Austin, away from the rush of news reporters demanding to speak to him. There he drank an entire bottle of gin. It did not faze him.

Houston McCoy was one of the last officers to leave the Tower. He walked back to his squad car and drove himself to the station. While checking in his vehicle, he noticed the clothes and shoes he had collected near Lake Austin when he had first received the call to report to the University of Texas. In his pocket he still had the Social Security card of an Hispanic male. "Oh, hell," he thought, and threw the clothes in the trash. (The body of an Hispanic male, about six feet tall and weighing about 175 pounds, was discovered in the river on Wednesday, 3 August 1966.)

After writing his reports, McCoy accompanied a few police friends, including Jerry Day and Phillip Conner, to a vacant lot near Interstate 35. Still dressed in blues, they were off duty and had a couple of beers—even the usually abstemious Phillip Conner. It was finally time to go home. On the way, the tough West Texan broke down and allowed himself to cry for a second or two. He was all right by the time he got home, and like Martinez, he drank more and even got a little drunk. Only then would Ruth McCoy learn of Houston's heroics. On the next day, he reported for work as usual.[19] It would be anything but a usual day.

[1] Houston McCoy; Ramiro Martinez; APD Files: *SOR*s by J. Day, R. Martinez, Houston McCoy, 1 August 1966, *Allen Crum*, 2 August 1966, *McCoy Statement*, n.d.

[2] Houston McCoy; Ramiro Martinez.

[3] Allen Crum; APD Files: *SOR*s by J. Day, P. Conner, R. Martinez, and H. McCoy, 1 August 1966; Phillip Conner.

[4] Ramiro Martinez; Houston McCoy; APD Files: *SOR* by Nolan Meinardus, 2 August 1966.

[5] Ramiro Martinez; Houston McCoy.

[6] Ibid.; The shotgun Houston McCoy carried onto the deck is on display in a showcase in the Austin Police Department Headquarters.

[7] Houston McCoy; Ramiro Martinez; APD Files: *SOR*s by H. McCoy and R. Martinez, 1 August 1966 and *McCoy Statement*, n.d.; *Autopsy Protocol*, Charles Joseph Whitman, Case #MLS-62-1966, 2 August 1966, in Austin History Center files (hereafter cited as *Autopsy Protocol*); The APD Files also have pictures of Charles Whitman at Cook's Funeral Home with his clothes removed. The wound on his left arm inflicted by Martinez's shotgun blast is only slightly larger than a silver dollar. Thus, Martinez had to have fired from near point-blank range.

[8] Houston McCoy; Ramiro Martinez.

[9] Ibid.; APD Files: *SOR*s by J. Day, P. Conner, G. Shepard, H. Moe, M. Shoquist, 1 August 1966; Texas DPS Files: *Interoffice Memorandum* by W. A. Cowan, 2 August 1966.

[10] APD Files: *SOR*s by J. Day, P. Conner, G. Shepard, H. Moe, M. Shoquist, 1 August 1966.

[11] APD Files: *SOR* by H. McCoy, 1 August 1966 and *McCoy Statement*, n.d.; Houston McCoy; Phillip Conner; Houston McCoy quoted in *Dallas Morning News*, 1 August 1986.

[12] Houston McCoy; APD Files: *McCoy Statement*, n.d. A copy of the contents of Charles Whitman's billfold are part of the Austin Police Department Files.

[13] Houston McCoy; APD Files: *McCoy Statement*, n.d.

[14] APD Files: *SOR* by B. Simpson, 3 August 1966, *CAPOR* by B. Landis, 1 August 1966 and *Food and Drug Administration Statement*, Robert C. Stokes, MD, 5 August 1966; Phillip Conner; *Daily Texan*, 1 August 1991; *Summer Texan*, 2 August 1966; *Austin American-Statesman*, 2 August 1966.

[15] APD Files: *Food and Drug Administration Statement*, Robert C. Stokes, MD, 5 August 1966; *Austin American-Statesman*, 2 and 3 August 1966.

[16] Ramiro Martinez; Houston McCoy; APD Files: *SOR*s by L. Morgan, R. Martinez, 1 August 1966 and John Pope, 3 August 1966; *Palm Beach Post*, 3 August 1966.

[17] *Daily Texan*, 1 August 1991; *Austin American-Statesman*, 2 and 7 August 1966, 1 August 1976.

[18] Lawrence A. Fuess; APD Files: *SOR* by Harold Moe, 2 August 1966; KLBJ Radio, *The Paul Pryor Show*, 1 August 1995; Time-Life, pp. 40 and 54; *Newsweek*, 15 August 1966.

[19] Ramiro Martinez; Houston McCoy; Phillip Conner; APD Files: *McCoy Statement*, n.d.; *Texas Monthly*, August 1986; *Austin American-Statesman*, 3 August 1966; Ruth McCoy, in a conversation with the author on 31 August 1996.

15

To Whom
It May
Concern

I

Charles Whitman began shooting from the deck at 11:48 A.M. Ninety-six minutes transpired before his shooting spree ended, enough time for major news organizations to cover some of the tragedy live. Bulletins interrupted regular programming all over the world. In Lake Worth, Florida, Charles's grandmother Whitman heard a bulletin and summoned Charles's brother Patrick to the television. Twenty years later, Patrick remembered it this way:

> I went in to listen to
> the TV, but the news

bulletin didn't come right back, so I called the station, and I asked them to repeat the news bulletin. At first they wouldn't repeat it, so I said, "My name is Patrick Whitman. Would you please repeat it." Then I broke up and went and got my father. From then on it was turmoil. They had to sedate me.[1]

It probably went exactly as Charles would have hoped. Much of the world's media began to ask questions, many of them directed at C. A. Whitman of Lake Worth, Florida. The glare of publicity for the Whitman family was only beginning. Still to be discovered were the notes Charles had left at 906 Jewell Street and Penthouse Apartment #505.

"Johnnie Mike" Whitman was still on a cross-country trip with his friend Jim Poland when his brother Charles began his killing spree. After the news of the sniping broke, the Whitman family began a search for the youngest Whitman boy, eventually locating him in Asbury Park, New Jersey, a small town along the Atlantic Coast. Immediately, "Johnnie Mike" and Jim Poland began the long drive to Lake Worth to attend funerals.[2]

As Whitman had anticipated, media attention immediately turned to his father, C. A. Whitman, in Lake Worth, Florida. *UPI/Corbis-Bettmann.*

Oddly enough, obtaining a positive identification of the world's most famous corpse took nearly an hour and a half, much of which was spent locating someone at the university who knew Charles. Professor Leonardt Kreisle, Whitman's former academic advisor, along with UT Security Chief Allen R. Hamilton and APD Sergeant T. J. Allen, eventually drove to Cook's Funeral Home to make the positive identification.[3] By then the name Charles Whitman already headlined the news.

Back in Needville, Raymond W. Leissner heard his son-in-law's name on the radio at about 2:00 P.M. He immediately called 906 Jewell Street in a desperate, yet futile, attempt to reach his daughter Kathy. When he was unsuccessful, he thought of Kathy's summer job at Southwestern Bell Telephone Company. The supervisor on duty told him that Whitman had called earlier in the day to report that Kathy was ill and would not be at work. Mr. Leissner then called the Austin Police Department; his call was forwarded to Detective Donald Kidd. Leissner identified himself and expressed a concern for Kathy's safety. In the course of their conversation Leissner revealed that Whitman's current residence was 906 Jewell Street and not the Shelley Avenue apartment. Leissner asked that someone go there to check on Kathy. Kidd realized he had no transportation and asked his fellow officer Bolton Gregory to drive him to the south Austin address.[4]

Kathy's friends were concerned for her as well. One of her colleagues at Lanier High School, a speech and drama teacher named Mayda Nell Tupper, called the Police Department and asked Officer Betty Hamm if Kathy was at headquarters. She identified herself as a close friend and offered to sit with Kathy through the ordeal. Officer Hamm told Tupper that an attempt would be made to locate Kathy, and that APD would likely call on her. In the Jewell Street neighborhood, Mrs. D. W. Nowotny, a resident of 910 Jewell Street, walked over to the Whitman residence.

> I thought so much of Mrs. Whitman that I went to her house so she wouldn't be by herself. But there was no answer at the door. I looked through the little glass in the door and everything was as neat as a pin like it always was.

Mrs. Nowotny turned, walked off the little porch and headed back home.[5]

In a short time, two *Austin American-Statesmen* reporters, Don Vandiver and Mike Cox, arrived to find another reporter from the *Houston Chronicle* already there. They, too, tried the door and found it to be locked. Only minutes later Officers Kidd and Gregory arrived. They knocked several times, walked around the house, and peered through the windows. Kidd was struck by how neat and orderly everything was. Looking through a window near the southwest corner of the house into the front bedroom, Kidd saw Kathy lying in the bed. He cut the screen and climbed into the room where Kathy lay, covered to the neck with a sheet and bedspread. She had obviously been dead for some time; rigor mortis had set in and her body was cold to the touch. A brief investigation established the identity of Kathy's murderer. On Kathy's death bed, Gregory found an envelope with a partially typed, partially handwritten note entitled "To whom it may concern" signed by Charles J. Whitman, the person they knew to be the sniper on the UT Tower deck. The most shocking part of the note, the first sentence of the third paragraph, read, "Similar reasons provoked me to take my mother's life also."[6]

When Donald Kidd and Bolton Gregory called APD to report what they had found, they discovered another unfolding drama, an investigation into the whereabouts of Margaret Hodges Whitman. Upon hearing the news of the shooting and the identity of the sniper, Wyatt's Cafeteria manager had immediately called APD to report that Charles had called earlier to say that his mother was ill. Margaret's friends at Wyatt's began to fear for her safety. Meanwhile the manager of the Penthouse Apartments, Margaret Eilers, called APD after she recognized the name Whitman. Looking into Margaret's file, she noticed C. J. Whitman listed as her son and next of kin. When Eilers went to Apartment 505, she found the note to "Roy" posted on the door. Lieutenant Bill Sterzing assigned Sergeant Frank Monk to proceed to the Penthouse. At Cook's Funeral Home near the corpse of Charles Whitman, Chief Miles asked an employee if he could use the phone. He dialed a few numbers and waited as a phone in Penthouse apartment 505 rang. There was, of course, no answer. Miles then hung up the phone, looked at the employee and said, "He killed her, too."[7]

When Frank Monk arrived at 2:55 P.M., Eilers, Penthouse owner Reuben H. Johnson, and Reverend B. Molloy, a resident of apartment 808, handed him the note that had been posted on the door of Apartment 505. Johnson, Molloy and Monk knocked and called out to Margaret. When no one answered, Monk instructed Johnson to unlock the door. Once inside the apartment, Monk located Margaret's body in the south bedroom. She, much like her daughter-in-law, was covered to the neck and appeared to be asleep. When Monk felt her cold face, he knew that she had been dead for some time. Before long Sergeant Dwight L. Moody arrived to conduct the investigation. He slowly removed the floral bedding that covered Margaret's lifeless body, exposing the extent and brutality of the assault from her eldest son. Moody also uncovered a note written on a yellow legal pad. Like the one found with her daughter-in-law, Margaret's note was also entitled "To whom it may concern." Reuben Johnson immediately identified the murdered woman as Margaret Whitman.[8]

Meanwhile, Lieutenant Merle Wells, the head of APD's homicide squad, and Frank W. McBee, the Justice of the Peace of Precinct 5, arrived separately at 906 Jewell Street. Donald Kidd and Bolton Gregory briefed them both. McBee's inquest determined the obvious—Kathy had been killed by "multiple stab wounds in the chest." An autopsy to determine the cause of death was clearly unnecessary and none was ever performed. A close friend of the Whitmans, Ronald Macon, arrived on the scene and positively identified Kathy. Larry and Elaine Fuess arrived to see if they could be of assistance to Kathy. Instead they discovered that she was dead. Larry then told Kidd of their visit to Whitman the night before. Officer Kidd placed a call to Raymond Leissner and informed him of Kathy's death. He asked that his daughter's body be sent to a local funeral home for transfer to another in Rosenberg, Texas. At headquarters Chief Miles instructed Officer Hamm to tell Mayda Nell Tupper of her friend's death.[9]

On Jewell Street, Mrs. Johnny Whitaker informed Kidd and Gregory that she had seen Whitman take two guns into the west side of the garage in the back yard. Gregory attempted to enter the garage, but Whitman had locked it earlier that morning, so he used Mr. Whitaker's hammer to break off the lock. Inside the garage, the investigator found the butt of a Sears 12-gauge shotgun and metal shavings from the cut-off barrel lying on the floor. Later, one of the neighborhood children would be discovered playing with the piece of barrel Whitman had cut from his shotgun. Gregory knew exactly where he had earlier seen the rest of the altered gun—on the deck near the body of its owner. He also saw what young Mark Nowotny had called "a whole bunch of army stuff." Lieutenant Wells instructed Gregory to nail the door shut. Johnny Whitaker supplied the three nails Gregory used to secure the garage.[10]

Late in the afternoon the investigation at the Jewell Street house came to a close, at least for the day. After the officers and ambulance attendants lifted Kathy onto a stretcher, they took her out of the neat little house and wheeled her over the sidewalk through the front yard. Neighbors, including the children she had loved and who had loved her, and the little boys Charles had taught to climb a rope "marine style," stood silently as Kathy began the journey that would take her back home to Needville.

II

As afternoon became early evening at the University of Texas, the sunshine diminished and the temperature "cooled" to the low nineties. From all over the world, parents of UT students called for their children. Most of the students, now perfectly safe, had joined the throngs of people assembled on the South Mall. Dorm workers spent the rest of the day talking to desperate parents, many in tears, trying to locate their children. Ironically, some of the residual burden from the crime committed by Charles Whitman fell on Kathy's colleagues at Southwestern Bell Telephone. August 1, 1966, set a record for the largest number of long distance calls placed in a single day in Austin. Of 34,228 calls, the company completed approximately 20,500, or about sixty percent.[11]

In Lake Worth, Florida, C. A. Whitman learned that his eldest son Charles was dead, as did most of the world. At 3:30 P.M., in a telephone conversation with APD Captain J. C. Fann, he learned that Margaret and Kathy were also "tentatively identified as dead." C. A. asked that the Jewell Street home and the Penthouse apartment be secured. About a half hour later, the elder Whitman called again. He indicated that he would fly from Lake Worth to Austin in order to claim the bodies of Charles and Margaret. For a second time, he requested that the residences be locked. Two hours later, at 6:37 P.M., C. A. called again to inform APD of the funeral arrangements he had made in Lake Worth and West Palm Beach. He asked Captain Fann for a third time to be sure to lock the residences. He explained that Margaret had valuable property in her apartment and an automobile parked nearby. During that phone call, C. A. stated that he could think of no reason why his son did what he had done. He explained that Charles was an Eagle Scout, an honorably discharged ex-marine, and an honor student at the university.[12]

III

After pronouncing Whitman dead, Dr. Robert Stokes had joined some of the other police officers on the deck in looking through Whitman's wallet. In a statement to the Food and Drug Administration, Stokes would later write:

> I found the name to be Charles Joseph Whitman and then I left to return to the first floor where I learned in the auditor's office that he was a student registered in the university for the summer session.
>
> I returned to the Health Center where I immediately looked up Whitman's medical records, found that he had been seen by a psychiatrist on March 29th and went to the psychiatry office where I read the report to the psychiatrist.[13]

So began a hellish period in the life of Dr. Maurice Dean Heatly.

Early the following day, on 2 August 1966, the University of Texas summoned reporters to what many assumed would be a routine press conference. None of the reporters were prepared for the drama about to unfold. Before introducing Dr. Heatly, Dr. Charles LeMaistre, Vice Chancellor for Health Affairs for the University of Texas System distributed the following statement:

Editors, Correspondents & Newscasters:

Having learned late yesterday that Mr. Charles Whitman had visited the University Health Center on March 29, 1966, and at that time had been referred to Dr. M. D. Heatly, staff psychiatrist, for private consultation, the University administration has directed the Health Center to make available to law enforcement agencies and the public the complete confidential records of this visit with Dr. Heatly, his only psychiatric appointment at the University.

Mr. Whitman was told to make an appointment for the same day next week, and was informed that if he needed to talk to the therapist, he could call on him at any time during the interval. However, he never returned and was not seen by this therapist or by any other University physician after March 29, 1966.

The University Health Center is a voluntary operation provided by the University for the benefit of students. Psychiatric, as well as medical care is available; but no student is required to take advantage of it. Each student has the right and privilege to select a physician and hospital of his own choice.

Unless a student demonstrates a behavior pattern which would legally justify involuntary commitment, the University has no alternative except to suggest that the student take advantage of its services, and it is up to the student to decide whether he wishes to do so. In this case, the attending physician saw no indication of any legal grounds for commitment, and although he suggested further consultations, the student did not take advantage of them.

Dr. Heatly's conclusion on March 29, 1966, that there was no indication at that time that Whitman was a danger to either himself or the community was consistent with the impressions of his teachers, his employer, and his associates, none of whom observed anything during the intervening 4 months which reflected unusual behavior.

Whitman completed 19 hours of engineering work in May 1966 with a B average, which indicates he was a better than average student. Since that time, he has been carrying a normal work load in the College of Engineering this summer with satisfactory results. At the same time he performed his duties as Laboratory Assistant in a way that was entirely satisfactory to his supervisors. This normal situation prevailed at least through Friday, July 29, which was the last day he attended classes and performed his regular work assignments.

In reporting to the University, Dr. Heatly explained that if a student chooses to visit the Health Center for psychiatric consultation, the alternatives following such consultation are: first, to determine that he is not a psychiatric case; second, to schedule serial visits for further observation but the visits must be voluntary on the part of the student; and third, to determine that the patient is psychotic and/or dangerous to himself or others, in which case it is necessary to separate him involuntarily from society. Where this latter situation has been indicated, that procedure has been followed. In this case, there was no psychiatric basis at the time of the interview on March 29 for pursuing this last alternative.

During the four months which have elapsed since Whitman was last seen by Dr. Heatly, no University physician has had any opportunity to observe or evaluate his condition.[14]

The statement was clearly designed to prepare the correspondents for the statement of Dr. Heatly.

Under the glare of lights, before nine microphones and six television cameras, the round-faced, bespectacled psychiatrist read the report he had written after his now infamous session with Charles Whitman.

> This is a new student referred by one of the general practitioners downstairs. This massive, muscular youth seemed to be oozing with hostility as he initiated the hour with the statement that something was happening to him and he didn't seem to be himself.

> Past history revealed a youth who was one of two [sic] brothers that grew up in Florida where the father was a very successful plumbing contractor without an education, but who had achieved considerable wealth. He identified his father as being brutal, domineering and extremely demanding of the other three members of the family. The youth married four or five years ago, and served a hitch in the Marines during his married life. He expressed himself as being very fond of his wife, but admitted that his tactics were similar to his father's and that he had on two occasions assaulted his wife physically.

Heatly then left the text to explain that the preceding sentence really meant that Whitman admitted to beating Kathy on two occasions. He looked back at his written statement and continued:

> He referred to several commendable achievements during his Marine service, but also made reference to a court martial for fighting which resulted only to [sic] his being reduced several grades to a private. In spite of this he received a scholarship to attend the University for two years, and remain a Marine at the same time. He said that his wife had become more comfortable with him and he says that she really has less fear of him now than in the past because he had made a more intense effort to avoid losing his temper with her.

> The real precipitating factor for this initial visit after being on the campus for several years seemed to stem from

the separation of his parents some thirty days ago. Although there has been gross disharmony through the years, his mother summoned him to Florida to bring her to Texas, and she is now living in Austin, but not with her son and daughter-in-law. The youth says that his father has averaged calling every forty-eight hours for several weeks petitioning him to persuade his mother to return to him. He alleges to have no intentions of trying to do that and retains his hostility towards his father. Although he identifies with his mother in the matter above, his real concern is with himself at the present time. He readily admits having overwhelming periods of hostility with a very minimum of provocation. Repeated inquiries attempting to analyze his exact experiences were not too successful with the exception of his vivid reference to "thinking about going up on the tower with a deer rifle and start shooting people."

At that moment the heads of many reporters lifted. Their mouths opened. "Could you please repeat that entire sentence?" Heatly repeated the only direct quote from Whitman in the report. In their follow-up questions the reporters emphasized the word "shooting."

"Whitman was describing his temper tantrums," Heatly stated. "My interpretation of the remark was that it was quite transient. It meant that he was hostile enough to knock down anything in his way." Heatly continued:

He recognizes, or rather feels that he is not achieving in his work at the level of which he is capable and this is very disconcerting to him. The youth could talk for long periods of time and develop overt hostility while talking, and then during the same narration may show signs of weeping.

OBSERVATIONS: This youth told numerous stories of his childhood and of involvement with his father that were not repeated, and it was felt that this relationship together with the genetic feature is largely responsible for this present predicament. Although his father is semi-literate, he is a perfectionist in other respects and extremely expansive. The youth has lived for the day when he could consider himself as a person capable of excelling [sic] his father in high society in general. He long ago acknowledged that he had surpassed him in educational fields, but he is seeking that status in versely [sic] all fields of human endeavor. He has self-centered in egocentric [sic], and at the same time he wants to improve himself. The degenerated state of affairs with his parents plus his repeated recent failures to achieve have become extremely frustrating to him which he (and his father) would express his hostility; thus some of the experiences noted above.

No medication was given to this youth at this time and he was told to make an appointment for the same day next week, and should he feel that he needs to talk to this therapist he could call me at anytime during the interval.

M.D. Heatly, M.D./dms[15]

During the question-and-answer portion, Heatly described Whitman as someone who looked like he could have been a professional football player. Then he made a remark that would dominate nearly all future descriptions of Charles Whitman. "His features and the flat top or burr haircut suggested the all-American boy." Combined with the earlier statement containing descriptions of Whitman as an honor student and a dependable young man, and subsequent stories of how he was an Eagle Scout, a model marine, a hard-working newspaper boy, a talented musician, and an all-around nice guy, a myth emerged. The unsavory side of Charles Whitman's life took a back seat to the image of an "all-American boy."

When asked if, in retrospect, he saw any psychosis, Heatly replied, "I found no psychosis symptoms at all." Instead, he suspected an "organic" or physical malady which could have led to a sudden episode of violence. After a number of questions Heatly summed up his impressions back in March of 1966, the same impressions he had the day after Charles Whitman committed the largest simultaneous mass murder in American history. "I am unable to account for the chain of events on a pure and uncomplicated psychiatric basis."[16]

The Heatly press conference lasted about forty-five minutes. Disturbing questions followed: Should Maurice Heatly have known that Charles Whitman was a dangerous individual? Should Dr. Heatly have had Whitman committed? Was Whitman crying for help? Were those cries ignored? Those questions haunt the University of Texas to this day. Since the incident, only a few fellow UT staff and faculty members, in hushed tones, have engaged in criticism of Dr. Heatly, and much of that criticism could conceivably be attributed to wrenching emotion. Robert Ressler, an author and criminologist, has suggested that Heatly should have "soft committed" Whitman. But the relevant literature of the event nearly unanimously absolves Dr. Heatly's actions.

Charles Whitman was a psychiatrist's worse nightmare. A University of Chicago psychiatrist, Dr. Robert Daniels, summed up the feelings of the medical family. "Thousands of people—and I mean literally thousands talk to doctors about having such feelings." Most do not go through with their inclinations, and when they do their medical records are seldom, if ever, the subject of public scrutiny. In 1965, according to *Time* magazine, of the nearly 2,500,000 Americans treated for mental illnesses, nearly one-third were classified as psychotic. Psychosis exists in varying degrees. Minimally, psychotics lose touch with reality.[17]

When Charles Whitman visited Dr. Heatly in March, he had not lost touch with reality. It appears that he continued to be in touch with reality through his conscious decisions to protect himself and to cover his crimes. Had anyone suspected he was mentally ill, yet another quandary would have emerged. As criminologist James Alan Fox has pointed out, mental illness is not a crime; neither is having a violent fantasy.[18] Successful treatment of mental illness, even when obvious, most often involves confidentiality in order to gain the trust of the patient, who in turn, like Charles Whitman, determines the extent of treatment. Even when mental illness is suspected, how mentally ill should a person be to justify involuntary commitment? And who should authorize commitment?

Answers to those questions in reference to Charles Whitman are easy. Committing himself would have been most uncharacteristic, and, if an attempt had been made to commit him involuntarily, who would have done so? Neither Kathy nor Margaret would have done it; both women trusted and felt safe in Whitman's company to the very moment he killed them. None of his friends or teachers considered committing him. Some people thought he was intense, but most thought he was a nice guy. Those close to him would have given testimony to his sanity, not insanity.

Second guessing Dr. Heatly would have been extraordinarily easy on 2 August 1966 and it may still be tempting. But on 29 March 1966, any commitment of Charles Whitman would have been the result of a "hunch" that most doctors would have found unscientific and most Americans would have found inconsistent with the principles of a free society. Ironically, with the tragic exception of what Dr. Heatly considered a "transient feeling," his report and observations of Charles Whitman were quite insightful and accurate. Arguably, even the "transient feeling" notation was accurate. The sniping did not take place until four months later, and during that time, no one, not Kathy, not Margaret, not his closest friends, imagined that this all-American boy could be capable of such violence.

---

[1] Patrick Whitman quoted in *Austin American-Statesman*, 1 August 1986.

[2] APD Files: *SOR* by G. Phifer, 3 August 1966; *Austin American-Statesman*, 4 August 1966.

[3] APD Files: *SOR* by T. J. Allen, 8 August 1966; Connally Report, p. 4; *Daily Texan*, 1 August 1986.

[4] McBee Inquest, 1 August 1966; APD Files: *CAPOR* by D. Kidd and B. Gregory, 1 August 1966, *SOR* by B. Gregory, 1 August 1966.

[5] APD Files: *SOR* by B. Hamm, 3 August 1966; Mrs. D. W. Nowotny quoted in *Austin American-Statesman*, 2 August 1966.

[6] Mike Cox is now the Public Information Officer of the Texas Department of Public Safety. In 1966 as a cub reporter he wrote of his experiences on 1 August. He graciously made available his writings on the incident. Hereafter cited as Cox Papers; APD Files: *SOR* by B. Gregory, 2 August 1966; *Austin American-Statesman*, 4 August 1966.

[7] APD Files: "The Tower Incident" is an unidentified and undated document that appears to be the script of a television broadcast. It is not clear as to why the document is in the file. *SOR* by F. Monk, 1 August 1966; *Austin American-Statesman*, 2 and 7 August 1966. The unidentified Cook Funeral Home employee called in to KLBJ Radio: *The Paul Pryor Show*, 1 August 1995.

[8] APD Files: *SOR* by F. Monk, 1 August 1966; APD Files: *HOR* by D. L. Moody, 1 August 1966.

[9] APD Files: *SOR*s by B. Gregory and D. Kidd, 1 August 1966, B. Gregory, 2 August 1966, and by B. Hamm, 3 August 1966; Lawrence A. Fuess.

[10] APD Files: *SOR*s by B. Gregory and D. Kidd, 1 August 1966, B. Gregory, 2 August 1966, and by B. Hamm, 3 August 1966; Phillip Conner.

[11] *Austin American-Statesman*, 7 August 1966.

[12] APD Files: *SOR* by J. C. Fann, 1 August 1966.

[13] APD Files: *Food and Drug Administration Statement*, Robert C. Stokes, MD, 5 August 1966.

[14] Copies of the University's statement and Dr. Heatly's report can be found in AHC, BHC and APD files.

[15] UT Health Center.

[16] Dr. Maurice D. Heatly quoted in *Austin American-Statesman*, 3 August 1966.

[17] Dr. Robert Daniels quoted in *Time*, 12 August 1966.

[18] *Time*, 12 August 1966; Connally Report, p. 16; Robert Ressler's and James Alan Fox's observations are from AJS.

16

APD

I

Somehow, it seemed pathetically appropriate. Flags on the University of Texas campus had already been lowered in tribute to fifty-six-year-old retired Army Reserve Lieutenant Colonel Richard Bryant Pelton, who had died of a heart attack on the previous Friday. If Don Walden and Cheryl Botts still wondered why the flags were lowered, they could have read about Pelton in the *Austin American-Statesman* in a small article, hidden in the midst of an entire issue on the Tower sniping.[1]

The city of Austin and the University of Texas became the

focus of world news. TASS, the official Communist Party news organ of the Soviet Union, used the occasion to highlight the problem of crime in the United States: "Murders, armed attacks, robbery, and rapes have become common in present-day America." Richard Speck and Charles Whitman dwarfed coverage of the White House wedding of Luci Baines Johnson and Patrick Nugent. When reminded that the Speck murders in Chicago had been called the "Crime of the Century," APD Chief Bob Miles replied, "It isn't anymore." Reporters from all over the world interviewed witnesses, victims, and victims' families.[2] Charlotte Darenshori, the secretary pinned down behind the base of a flagpole on the South Mall, remembered: "I had a call from Dan Rather wanting me to be on the afternoon news, from the networks and from newspapers everywhere. I just didn't understand the interest."[3]

Reporters converged on Needville as well. Undoubtedly, many had to locate the hamlet on a map first. Kathy's mother stayed secluded. Mr. Leissner, struggling to hold back tears, candidly admitted his inability to explain what happened: "He [Whitman] was just as normal as anybody I ever knew, and he worked awfully hard at his grades. There was nothing wrong with him that I knew of. It's just a sad tragedy that happened to a very nice family."[4] Later in the week Kathy's body returned to Needville for services at the white, wooden Methodist church she had attended as a little girl. A large crowd attended her burial at Greenlawn Memorial Park in Rosenberg during a driving rain storm. Several classmates from her graduating class carried her body to its final resting place near a small oak tree.

Charles Whitman's body had been taken to Cook's Funeral Home for an autopsy. As layers of clothing were removed, APD Sergeant Bill Landis found several 30-caliber M-1 Carbine clips and a 25-caliber automatic pistol. The autopsy did not take place until 8:55 A.M. the next day, *after* Whitman had been embalmed.[5]

II

The University of Texas fully disclosed everything—Whitman's transcripts, medical records, and employment applications. Chancellor Harry Ransom ordered an inquiry of the events leading to the incident, down to the "minute detail." But Texas Governor John

Connally had an even larger investigation in mind and pre-empted the study.

Considered by many to be the greatest governor Texas ever had, John Connally was remembered by most Americans as the man who sat on a jump seat in a limousine in front of John F. Kennedy on 22 November 1963 in Dallas. By 1966, he had tired of talking about the Kennedy assassination. Upon hearing the news about the Tower sniper on 1 August 1966, Connally, in Brazil as part of a trip to several South American countries, immediately cut short his excursion and returned to Austin. He formed a commission of some of the nation's leading medical and psychological experts and charged them with investigating the medical aspects of the Charles Whitman murders.

In Washington, D.C., President Lyndon B. Johnson, a son of the Texas Hill Country, sent personal notes to the families of the victims. He called J. Edgar Hoover, the Director of the FBI, and personally ordered an investigation into the Whitman tragedy.[6]

III

By Thursday, 4 August 1966, John Michael Whitman had returned home to Lake Worth, Florida, to attend the double funeral of his mother and oldest brother. In Catholic tradition, a rosary was recited at the funeral home the night before the funeral, which took place on Friday, 5 August 1966. Approximately 300 people filled Lake Worth's Sacred Heart Catholic Church. Father Eugene Quintan served as the celebrant of the Mass and double funeral. He reminded friends and family, and informed the world, that both Margaret and Charles were once people of deep religious devotion. After the High Mass, Father Quintan led a procession to the waiting hearses and thirty-three other cars on a trip to Hillcrest Memorial Cemetery in West Palm Beach. Because church officials presumed that Charles Whitman was deranged at the time of his death, his coffin was draped by the flag of the United States. The funeral was an occasion for prayer and song. The only show of emotion, other than weeping, came from Johnnie Mike when he shook his fists at cameramen. The caravan motored a few miles to Hillcrest Memorial

L–R, Patrick, John, and Charles A. Whitman, brothers and father of mass killer Charles J. Whitman, at the funeral of Whitman and his mother on 5 August 1966. The priest who celebrated the funeral mass stated that the Roman Catholic Church gave Whitman a Christian burial because "God in His mercy does not hold him responsible" for his final actions. *UPI/Corbis-Bettmann.*

Park in West Palm Beach without incident. There, Charles and his mother were laid side by side.[7]

At 12:43 A.M. on the day after the funeral, C. A. Whitman called the Austin Police Department and left a message for Major Herbert to call collect at 11:00 A.M. that same morning. When the call was returned C. A. asked for a Monday morning (8 August 1966) meeting. Again, he requested that the Jewell Street home and the Penthouse apartment be locked. At 7:50 A.M. he called again to inform APD that he and his father-in-law would arrive in Austin at 8:50 P.M. under the names "R. Smith and A. Smith." He asked that the Penthouse be made available at that time, but APD could not guarantee its availability.[8]

On the following Monday morning, 8 August 1966, while shaving for work, Ramiro Martinez began to shake. For a moment he did not know why. Then he realized it had been a week since his trip to the Tower. It was not a big deal; he got over it. What he did not yet know was that C. A. Whitman was now in Austin. Later that day at APD headquarters, C. A. would ask to meet the policeman who had killed his son, saying it was one of his reasons for coming to Austin:

> I came to Texas to express my sympathies and regrets to all concerned and to cooperate to the fullest with all law enforcement officers and I have met personally and embraced the man that killed my son and I have no animosity, in fact, I have respect for him for doing his job. . . . I think this will help this boy [Martinez] in years to come.[9]

It was a kind gesture, and Ramiro Martinez was very gracious to the man from Lake Worth who sobbed and said that he just did not know what happened, that his son was just not like that. Martinez had always known that police work might involve killing someone. "It is why they give you a gun; it is part of the job. No one likes killing, if they do they're sick. It's just part of the job. I had a job to do and I did it." He would never question the need to bring Charles Whitman down, and once he got over a temporary spell of the "shakes," his recovery was complete and permanent.[10]

While in Austin, C. A. Whitman cooperated completely. He consented to every request made of him by the Austin Police Department and other law enforcement agencies. On 9 August 1966 Chief Miles gave C. A. the following letter:

> To whom it may concern:
> Mr. C. A. Whitman of Lake Worth, Florida, the father of Charles J. Whitman, has cooperated fully and graciously with the Police Department in their efforts to complete their investigation of the tragedy which occurred on the Campus of the University of Texas on August 1, 1966. His attitude and assistance is appreciated and gratefully acknowledged.
> Sincerely,
> R. A. Miles
> Chief of Police

On the same day, C. A. was taken to 906 Jewell Street where he met the Leissner family. As Mr. Leissner remembered: "We more or less took some personal things that we wanted, and he [C. A. Whitman] took what he wanted. There wasn't much. They were just kids." Nowhere to be found was Kathy's little dog Schocie. A neighbor called APD early on the morning after the murders to report that Schocie had mysteriously disappeared on 1 August 1966 after Kathy's body had been removed from her home.

C. A. Whitman would neither see nor hear from the Leissners again. By the end of the day he had located Margaret's new Mercury Park Lane automobile, which had been taken to the Austin Police Department's impounding yard for safekeeping. It was released to him at 6:05 p.m.[11]

On the next day, 10 August 1966, C. A. penned a short note to most of the victims and their families. The note he sent to Robert Heard, the Associated Press reporter who had been gunned down in an open area north of the Tower read, "Dear Mr. Heard, May we express our most sincere regrets. C. A. Whitman, Jr. and family."[12]

IV

Events like the Charles Whitman murders bring out the best in people. The reaction of the people of Austin revealed the town's character. Immediately after the shooting stopped someone picked up Alex Hernandez's newspapers and sold them at double the list price. The money was later delivered to him at Brackenridge Hospital, where fifty stitches had been required to repair a huge gash from his hip to his knee. Less than five minutes after Joe Roddy announced a need for blood, a traffic jam formed around the Travis County Medical Society. Some motorists passing through Austin went out of their way to give blood. APD had to be called to the downtown area to handle the congestion. Two hours later an estimated 1,000 donors, including mothers holding babies, students, businessmen in suits, and soldiers in uniform from Bergstrom Air Force Base, lined the streets.[13]

Police Chief Bob Miles asked the world to believe that "this could have happened in any city in the United States, or any city in the world for that matter." It was a period of kindness. The police and even the Travis County Grand Jury sought to protect C. A. Whitman from his son's vitriolic notes:

> We have instructed the police to release the notes left by Charles Whitman only to authorized investigating agencies, since they contain unverified statements of an insane killer which could be misunderstood if publicly released.[14]

But C. A.'s own statements to the press contained numerous incredibly candid and injudicious declarations. Reporters found him quotable; he admitted to beating his wife, spanking his children, being a "fanatic" about guns, and personally training his boys in marksmanship. His speech had strength and assertion but no emotion, even though he had just been told that his son had killed his wife, daughter-in-law, and scores of others before being gunned down by policemen. It all seemed rather odd. Had Charles's notes been released in their entirety on 1 August of 1966, C. A. Whitman's life would have been intolerably more complicated.

The most remarkable group of people to emerge from the tragedy were the survivors of Whitman's gunshots. In an article for the *Texas Observer* written less than three weeks after the incident, Bill Helmer wrote that he knew no one who had any hatred towards Whitman—only pity and dismay: "It is hard to hate a pain-tormented animal that strikes out indiscriminately as it dies."[15] Mary Gabour had the greatest right to descend into anger and bitterness. For months she languished in hospitals and recovery centers enduring painful rehabilitation procedures. She emerged permanently crippled and legally blind. Her physical recovery was complicated by the end of her marriage to M. J. Gabour. And, of course, she had lost her youngest child, Mark, whose funeral she was unable to attend. But she forgave the sniper. Ten years after the incident, she told a reporter: "I don't feel any bitterness towards Charles Whitman. I can only feel a sort of pity for him—to have had to face his judgment with the blood of so many on his hands." Once Mike Gabour was able to talk to reporters he was asked if he had any resentment towards the man who shot him. Mike only replied, "He's dead."[16] The Gabours were remarkable people.

However, an attempt by the community and its commentators to explain what happened and, to a lesser extent, to find someone or something to blame, did follow. Janet Paulos, whose wedding to Abdul Khashab had to be postponed, became dismayed at American culture. "There must be something wrong somewhere when in a civilized country like this a guy can get guns like he did and do what he did."[17] Some time later the young couple moved to Khashab's native country, Iraq.

The Whitman murders coincided with the beginning of a period in U. S. history when Americans began to lose their "school boy's" view of their country. Revisionist interpretations of American history began to replace traditional and "patriotic" histories. JFK assassination theories began to replace hard facts found in the Warren Commission Report, and as a new conspiracy industry began to flourish, Chief Justice Earl Warren was slowly transmuted from a hero of the Civil Rights Movement to a major player in a sinister cover-up. American institutions—the FBI, the CIA, the military, corporations, and the Presidency itself—were portrayed by some as murderous institutions. As John Connally observed, conspiracy advocates saw "evil." America entered a period of doubt and self-flagellation. And so, in an atmosphere of suspicion and cynicism, during a time of war against individual guilt, some embraced and others were conditioned to accept the notion that Charles Whitman was, indeed, an all-American boy.

Most attempts to apply blame focused on the Austin Police Department. Phone calls and telegrams for "heads to roll" flooded APD and the offices of the *Austin American-Statesman*. Specifically, there were calls for the resignation of Chief Bob Miles. The bulk of local criticism, some of it fueled by rumor and misinformation, came from University faculty members. Dr. Irvin Spear, an assistant professor of botany, enumerated one of the longer lists of concerns in a letter to the *Austin American-Statesman*. He claimed that very little was done by APD to keep people from walking into the area, that no one was ever rescued by police but by civilians instead, and that police in the Biology Building (apparently where Professor Spear was located) were armed with only shotguns rather than rifles. He also complained that police had no organized communication with one another and had no plan for ending the siege other than firing back, that scores of civilians with high-powered rifles were immediately allowed to wander the campus after the incident, and that Charles Whitman was finally stopped by an off-duty officer and a civilian.

Other students and faculty asked whether ninety-six minutes was a much longer than necessary time period for police to take to get to the top of the Tower. There were many questions as to why Allen Crum, a civilian, was up there at all. A UT student named Richard Solem asked, "Is Austin so short of responsible policemen that it must deputize a middle-aged businessman to do the work policemen are trained for?" Still other questions involved the use of the University's tunnels; shouldn't they have been used much sooner to get into the Tower? Stanley Werbow, a Law Professor, called on Governor Connally to appoint a commission to study the reaction of the Austin Police Department. His concerns were essentially the same as those enumerated by Spears.[18] All of the questions were fair and the Austin Police Department was held accountable for answers to them. The pressure to explain fell on Chief Bob Miles. For the most part, he rose to the occasion.

The easiest and most obvious question was whether the Austin Police Department was prepared for the magnitude of the crime. Clearly, they were not. A more relevant question was whether they *should* have been prepared. More specifically, should APD have had plans for handling a sniping or any crime of that magnitude?

A fair assessment of APD's performance requires an appreciation for the enormous area over which the crime took place and the number of people involved. Whitman hit people in an area covering five city blocks, or the area of a circle around the Tower with a diameter of at least 1,200 yards. It was an enormous crime scene; likely the largest in American history for a crime perpetrated by a single individual. The area included virtually all of the University and a substantial portion of some of the most congested sections of Austin. It involved every kind of landscape including trees, alleys, tall and short buildings, streets, construction sites, stairways, hills, statues, roofs, automobiles, windows and tunnels. The danger zone, or the total area over which Whitman could have inflicted injury, can only be estimated, but has to be considerably larger than the actual crime scene, possibly a half-mile squared, or about 300 acres. The crowds covering the South Mall after Whitman had been killed represented only a small portion of the number of people who were pinned down. The perception that APD did little or nothing to get people out of harm's way is likely the result of the large area involved. Numerous reports by officers detailed efforts to get people into buildings and keep others off the campus.

The size of the crime scene also contributed to the impression that very few officers ran into the open to rescue the wounded. Certainly, any given individual was more likely to have been wounded or killed near a civilian than a policeman. Logically, at least according to some critics, if an officer did his job, he had people around him take cover, making a rescue less likely, which is what many officers indicated that they had done. Numerous accounts of officers rescuing individuals who were trapped, but not wounded, did exist. The *Daily Texan* later related a story of an unidentified coed huddled under shrubs and crying in terror as she held her bruised and bleeding knee. An unidentified policeman led her to safety.[19]

The assertion that APD's weapons were inadequate for the crime does have merit. The entire department had fifteen rifles, but they were 35-caliber Remingtons that had not been used for law enforcement for twenty years. In his review of Whitman's arsenal, noted writer Russell Tinsley pointed out that Whitman's own 35 Remington was hardly better than a pistol from the top of the Tower.[20] Had APD's Remingtons been used from the ground they would have been even less accurate. In any case, premium deer rifles, accurate over long distances, were fired by seasoned hunters at Whitman to no avail. No more appropriate type of weapon could have been used from the ground. The inability to get Whitman by shooting from the ground was less related to the quality of the weapons used than the quality of the fortress he had chosen. No one so much as wounded Charles Whitman from the ground; he was killed by APD officers in the only way he could be reached—from a distance of about fifty feet—by shotgun blasts from an APD-issued weapon. What does seem reasonable to assume, however, is that a police department should have weapons of better, or at least equal, quality than those available to the general public, even if they are not likely to be used.

The siege lasted ninety-six minutes, but for those who were there, it seemed to last all afternoon. Critics wondered what took so long.

APD's complete display of Whitman's materials. *Austin Police Department Files.*

The questions were reasonable. Ninety-six minutes might have been too long to get to Whitman, if that were all APD had to do. Some attributed the length of time to inadequate communications and a lack of planning. Unfortunately, trying to establish communications between APD and UT Security took time and kept officers anchored to positions. W. A. Cowan kept security on the phone while Harold Moe had a walkie-talkie. The phone effectively immobilized Cowan and the noise made by the walkie-talkie would have made bringing it to the deck dangerous.

The need to evacuate the Gabours and Lamports and university employees further complicated the whole operation. Assuming an inevitable gunfight, APD could not have allowed anyone to stay on the twenty-seventh floor. Moreover, it would have been heartless to walk past Mike and Mary Gabour and not remove them to an area where they could receive aid. Once those tasks had been accomplished, the officers faced other uncertainties: how many snipers were on the deck and what were their positions?

Could the officers have gotten to the Tower faster by using the tunnels? Probably not. The first three officers in the Tower, Bob Day, Jerry Day, and Ramiro Martinez, dashed over open ground to reach the Main Building. The tunnels were safer, but not faster. Houston McCoy and his team had to be led through the maze of tunnels to the Tower by a university employee. Without the guide they could have gotten lost.

Why was it that the team that finally stormed the deck and killed the sniper consisted mainly of off-duty policemen and a civilian? Technically, all of the policemen were on duty. Shepard, Shoquist, Moe, and Conner reported to APD first and were assigned to report to UT Security to form a team to storm the deck. Martinez called APD and was told to report to the campus to handle traffic control. A review of the reports shows that the officers already on duty when the firing began were likely to be assigned to traffic and crowd control. The idea was to remove Whitman's targets by getting people out of the way, something officers with communications capabilities, i.e., a motorcycle or squad car radio, were likely to be asked to do, and something some critics maintained APD should have done more of. Off-duty officers, like some who brought their own weapons to return fire, or like Ramiro Martinez, often engaged in direct, independent actions.

Finally, why was Allen Crum, a civilian, on the deck when Whitman was killed? He was there because he insisted on going. Allen Crum guided the lawmen through hallways and passageways leading to the deck. None of the policemen knew the layout of the twenty-seventh and twenty-eighth floors. Only Jerry Day and W. A. Cowan knew Crum to be a civilian from the time they met him. Shortly after reaching the twenty-seventh floor, Jerry Day was forced to escort a very distraught M. J. Gabour downstairs and then had trouble keeping him there. As Cowan struggled to establish communications with UT Security, Martinez saw that the rifle-wielding Crum ascended the stairs with him "military style," reinforcing Martinez's assumption that Crum was with UT Security. It was not until a moment before they entered the reception area that Martinez discovered who Crum was and deputized him.

Allen Crum had demonstrated extraordinary courage. He placed himself in danger from Charles Whitman and inadvertently from all of the officers accompanying Houston McCoy who agreed that the sniper needed to be killed. McCoy, by his own account, came dangerously close to killing him. Once Crum had stepped onto the deck, Charles Whitman actually charged in Crum's direction when Crum fired a round from a gun he had been handed and with which he was unfamiliar. Luckily, Whitman reacted by turning around and running in the opposite direction. Had he turned the southwest corner, Crum or Day would have killed Whitman, or Whitman would have killed Crum or Day or both. In either case, a tremendous public outcry would have taken place. Arguments as to whether Allen Crum should have been on the deck should not supplant the crucial role he played as the navigator of the team that ended the tragedy. Without Allen Crum the siege would likely have lasted even longer.

Time and norm referencing should also be applied to a fair analysis of APD's performance. In 1966, could any other police department of comparable size have reacted any better? Probably not. Was there any information routinely collected by other comparable police departments that APD should have had that they did not? Not really. Chief Miles did react to the sniper incident by saying that the department would secure blueprints of the top floors of all of Austin's tall buildings, but before 1 August 1966 they would never have been used, and in the thirty years that followed the Tower incident they have not been needed for any other serious crime.

Moreover, as Jack Levin and James Alan Fox have pointed out in their book *Mass Murder*, sniping is a very infrequent crime in America. Single-victim homicides, robbery and property crimes encumber far more police resources and time. To plan for Whitman-like crimes would certainly siphon resources from more immediate problems.

V

Not surprisingly, rumors began to circulate. The most shocking was that three to four years prior to the Tower incident Whitman had approached a businessman on the Drag for the purpose of selling pornography. The *Texas Observer* was the first to print the off-the-record story of the unnamed businessman who claimed to have thrown Whitman out of his establishment. The account would later be expanded in Time-Life's series of books on True Crime:

"He said he had a nice supply of pornography," the merchant recalled. Whitman then took some pictures out of his pocket and showed them to the man. He told me there was tremendous profit in them. I said, "I don't think I am interested." He treated the whole darn subject as though it were imported sugar cane from South America. He was very technical about it. No sentiment whatever. I asked him what market he had in mind, college kids? "No," he said. "High school and grade school children." He was like some guy trying to sell an ad in the Yellow Pages.[21]

The story cannot be disproved, but it is suspect. At the time of the alleged incident Whitman was a NESEP scholar enjoying a relatively generous income from the marines and an allowance from his father. Additionally, his job as a counselor in Goodall-Wooten Dorm allowed him to lodge rent-free. Other than his tour of duty in Cuba, when there were no other job opportunities, it is the only period of his adult life where he sought no employment. He did not need the money. It was also during that period that he began to date Kathy. Shortly afterwards, he moved to Fort Lejeune, North Carolina, for the remainder of his hitch in the marines. More significantly, however, after an exhaustive investigation into his past, including very candid statements by his closest friends, the APD, Texas DPS, and FBI files on Whitman contain no reference to pornography. No pornographic materials of any type were found in his home or garage.

Further, there is more evidence that Whitman could be prudish. In his notes, diaries and numerous lists, he often chastised himself for cursing. On 31 January 1964 he wrote in his notebook, a precursor to his *Daily Record*, that he left the showing of a movie because "the animals [some other marines] make so much noise and comments that you can't enjoy anything."[22] Undoubtedly, the comments included vintage marine obscenities. Finally, the businessman was apparently never asked, nor was it ever explained why he failed to report an attempt to sell child pornography at the time the event took place.

A connection to child pornography would satisfy an urge to bring congruency to understanding Charles Whitman, since the evil of it would fit the enormity of his crime. But there is no hard evidence to support his involvement.

Another persistent rumor involving Charles Whitman was that on Thursday, 28 July 1966, Whitman entered the First National Bank Building in Dallas and signed the register on the forty-ninth floor. The implication was that he "scouted" the high rise. The rumor was patently false. On the day in question Whitman reported for work in the Experimental Science Building as usual. On that day a classmate, Tom Brightman, asked to see Whitman's notes from a class they were taking together. Additionally, Whitman attended classes and reported for work on the next day. Without question, Charles Whitman was in Austin on 28 July 1966. Moreover, the name on the bank register was "Chas. Whitman, University of Texas Campus, Austin." Whitman never signed his name in that manner. The incident was clearly a prank.[23]

One of the more ludicrous rumors involved a Volkswagen dealer from Memphis, Tennessee, named William C. Dewey. The 16 September 1966 issue of the *Memphis Press-Scimitar* prominently pictured a smiling Dewey holding a five dollar bill. Allegedly, before going out for coffee, he checked his wallet and found the bill with writing in blue ink that stated "I Charles Whitman have killed my wife and mother." In another place was written "Charles Whitman, Aug. 1, 1966." Also included on the bill was an official-looking stamp in black ink which read "August 1, 1966." But the real tip-off that the bill was a hoax was on the backside; the Lincoln Memorial had been labeled "U. of Texas" and a tiny arrow pointed to the top of the monument next to the word "me."[24]

---

[1] *Austin American-Statesman*, 2 August 1966.

[2] *Dallas Morning News*, 2 August 1966.

[3] *Austin American-Statesman*, 2 August 1966.

[4] Ibid.

[5] APD Files: *SOR* by B. Landis, 1 August 1966; *Autopsy Protocol*.

[6] *Austin American-Statesman*, 6 July 1986.

[7] FBI Files: *Cole Report*, 17 August 1966, p. 6; *Palm Beach Post*, 3 and 6 August 1966.

[8] APD Files: *SOR* by R. C. Wilkes, 6 August and amended 7 August 1966.

[9] Ramiro Martinez; C. A. Whitman quoted in *Austin American-Statesman*, 9 August 1966; C. A. Whitman.

[10] Ramiro Martinez.

[11] APD Files: Letter of R. A. Miles dated 9 August 1966, *VIR*, 9 August 1966 and *SOR* by L. Morgan, 3 August 1966; Raymond W. Leissner quoted in *Austin American-Statesman*, 1 August 1986; *Dallas Morning News*, 1 August 1986; C. A. Whitman.

[12] *Dallas Morning News*, 4 September 1966.

[13] Fahrenthold and Rider, *Admissions*, p. 90; *Summer Texan*, 2 August 1966; *Austin American-Statesman*, 2 and 6 August 1966.

[14] APD Files: *Travis County Grand Jury Special Report*, n.d.; Chief Bob Miles quoted in AJS.

[15] *Texas Observer*, 19 August 1966.

[16] Mary Gabour quoted in the *Austin Citizen*, 1 August 1977; Lamport Interview; Mike Gabour quoted in *Austin American-Statesman*, 4 August 1966.

[17] Janet Paulos quoted in *Austin American-Statesman*, 4 August 1966.

[18] *Austin American-Statesman*, 7 August 1966.

[19] *Daily Texan*, 1 August 1991.

[20] See Russell Tinsley in *Austin American-Statesman*, 4 August 1966.

[21] *Texas Observer*, 19 August 1966; Time-Life, p. 42.

[22] APD Files: Whitman's Notebooks, entry of 31 January 1964, and separate notes in Whitman's personal papers; Lawrence A. Fuess.

[23] *Austin American-Statesman*, 4 and 7 August 1966.

[24] A copy of the *Memphis Press-Scimitar* article is in APD Files along with a letter dated 21 September 1966 from Chief Miles to James C. MacDonald, the Chief of Police of the Memphis Police Department. The file also included an enlarged photocopy of the bill. It is clearly not Charles Whitman's handwriting.

17

Why Did He Do It?

Often the test of courage is not to die but to live.—Conte Vittorio Alfieri (1794–1803), Italian playwright and poet

I

Once he returned to Austin, Governor John Connally assembled a blue-ribbon commission to look into every medical aspect of the Tower incident. The commission members were giants in their respective fields. Fact-finders consisted mostly of medical school professors. Dr. R. Lee Clark, Surgeon-in-Chief of the University's M. D. Anderson Hospital in Houston, served as the chairman. The work of the eleven fact-finding members was reviewed by twenty-one other blue-ribbon physicians from throughout the United States.[1] The Connally Commission (for want of a better name) established four investigative objectives:

1   To determine the events and circumstances which surrounded the actions of Charles J. Whitman on August 1, 1966.
2. To explore the findings and to make such additional examinations as might be indicated by the factual information which is available.
3. To prepare the material for its maximal utilization in evaluating the problem for our society.
4. To make recommendations aimed at the detection and prevention of circumstances which might lead to similar incidents.[2]

The commission looked carefully at Whitman's background, health, and overall behavior throughout his life. His elementary, high-school and university transcripts were analyzed. Teachers, classmates, family, and old and recent friends were interviewed.

The conclusions reached by the commission reinforced what many of Whitman's associates already knew about him and also exposed the nice facade he had developed around himself. Its portrait of Charles Whitman was that of an "intelligent, intense and driven" young man, but someone who had been encased in internal and external predicaments causing personal turmoil.[3] The internal goal of outdoing his father in all areas, not just education, had become an unhealthy obsession, a source of anxiety he inflicted upon himself. The separation of his parents, which had been out of his control, only exacerbated his internal struggles. Margaret's move to Austin exposed Whitman to her misery on a daily basis, and his father's constant phone calls only made things worse. Cumulative frustrations made him more dangerous, but his "nice" facade had effectively concealed that explosive state from his family and closest friends. Whitman realized that many of his cohorts in their mid-twenties were already college-educated, on their own, and supporting a wife and family. Aside from his own low-paying jobs, his family was being supported by the two jobs his wife held and the regular allowance sent by his father. For someone who had tried desperately not to bite his fingernails because it was not manly, who had a disdain for government workers because they had no ambition, and who had a general disrespect for anyone who did not accomplish, Whitman must have hated facing that reality.

As an adolescent he had often resorted to taking dares to draw attention to himself. Knowing that in an adult those behaviors would be seen as silly and childish, he had displayed a facade of seriousness and maturity to his teachers, probably because he saw them as authority figures and wanted to please them. Charles Whitman was always who he was expected to be. He could act extraordinarily immature and indulge in juvenile behavior in front of friends who were equally juvenile. His immaturity should not be underestimated. In many ways his physical development was what had made him face the cold world of adulthood, which he had entered without goal-setting and decision-making skills. Even the frustration of controlling his own weight had once become an occasion for lashing out at Kathy. Some of his pictures included one in which he was shown walking with a little boy (probably Kathy's baby brother), along the sidewalk adjacent to Austin's famous Barton Springs. Another had him seated along the walkway with his feet dangling in the Springs' famous sixty-eight-degree water. Both depicted a pronounced "gut" pouring over Whitman's belt line and "saddlebags" above both hips; he must have hated that.[4]

Whitman's frustrations, according to the commission, had led to "profound personal dissatisfaction" and a poor self-concept.[5] Numerous notes he wrote display his need to berate himself in regard to his shortcomings. His childhood in Lake Worth, Florida, and his service in the marines as a young adult had been filled with taking orders from domineering authority figures. His notes to himself, consisting of lists of ways to improve, had become pathetic replacements for those authority figures. Consequently, freedom, self-reliance, intrinsic motivation, and persistence—without the goading of an authority—had become occasions for failure.

Another result of his inability to focus on goals was that he could not decide what he wanted to do with his life. He went through career aspirations like many children go through favorite toys. Within a period of less than five years, his plans shifted from mechanical engineer, to career marine officer, to architectural engineer, to real estate agent, and finally to lawyer (with an engineering degree). In an eighteen-month period from 1964–65 he held six different jobs— all menial and inconsequential. His best friend believed he wanted to be a lawyer with an engineering degree—not for any love of the law or engineering, but for money. Additionally, he had once confided to a friend that he would return to Lake Worth to work for his father. As an avocation, music seemed to give him respite, but he mostly repressed urges to play and often refused the requests of his closest friends to do so. On yet another occasion of extreme despair, he had decided to become a bum. Charles Whitman had what career counselors call a "flat" interest profile: he could do many different things, but *loved* nothing. As a result, from a career standpoint, he knew a little about and was fairly good at many things, but he excelled at nothing. (Except, of course, guns.)

Whitman's indecision had not been limited to career options. The frequency with which he wrote the word "definitely" in his diary is striking. For instance, he had once written, "I am definitely going to learn more about electronics," but of course, he never did. There had been nothing definite in Charles Whitman's life. Consequently, there had been few accomplishments.[6]

The only person that Charles Whitman ever truly loved was Kathy and, without question, she loved him. Her attempts to get him to help himself had been limited to her gentle pleas to see a psychiatrist. Other than a single reference in his diary to her having been angry at him for gambling, getting himself court-martialed, and locked up in the brig at Camp Lejeune, there are no references or other documented occasions of her having been assertive with him. On the contrary, he wrote pages of gushing prose about how perfect she was in every respect. In neat penmanship he groped for superlatives to detail her physique and how she had satisfied him.[7] He clearly worshiped her, but his love for her had been immature as well. He sought to dominate her and in many ways he had succeeded, even recording in his notebook how he had "taught" her to satisfy him.

Kathy Whitman, as Charles wrote on the note he left on her dead body, had been as good a wife as any man could hope for, though it is obvious that she feared his temper and was disturbed at the extent and frequency of his bouts of deep depression. But Kathy had also engaged in what we now call "enabling" behaviors. Her laudable attempts to support her troubled husband had supported his frustrations, depression, and immaturity instead. He had hit her, probably on the two occasions he related to Dr. Heatly, and their arguments often reached a volume that could be heard beyond the walls of their home, but there is no testimony by neighbors, family or friends that his physical abuse of her had been constant. Most likely he had exerted control over her through mind games and taking advantage of her seemingly endless supply of patience and support. Moreover, she had certainly known of his sleep deprivation and had probably known that he took Dexedrine or some other substance to stay awake. Most likely, like her husband, she made herself believe he could handle it. Like many spouses in a troubled relationship, she probably also believed that she could eventually change him, and she may even have been heartened by how he was able to control himself during the last few months of their lives together. In reality, his laudable self-control had been dangerous repression.

The Connally Commission's final report contained the collective expertise of some of America's premier physicians and behavioral scientists. It included accurate observations and detailed data on the life and death of Charles Whitman. But in the end the commission could not explain why he had comitted what was at the time America's largest mass murder: "Without a recent psychiatric evaluation of Charles J. Whitman, the task force finds it impossible to make a formal psychiatric diagnosis."[8]

II

So why did he do it?

The explanations that have emerged tend to reveal the agendas of their advocates. The anti-military crowd, at the time growing as the Vietnam War escalated, offered Whitman's marine training as the culprit. Even the Connally Commission issued a recommendation that combat-trained personnel, in effect, be deprogrammed in order to "re-learn in such a way as to de-emphasize in their minds those hostile acts taught as laudatory in time of war."[9] Consisting largely of academics and university administrators, the commission may have betrayed an anti-military slant just beginning to flourish on campuses throughout the United States. Other faculty, like Dr. Alfred Schild, noting that Lee Harvey Oswald had also been a marine, called for the abolition of the Marine Corps.[10] The question remained. Had Whitman's military training contributed to his crimes?

Several elected officials saw the Tower sniping as an occasion to lament the prevalence of violence in the media, especially television. United States Senator Ralph Yarborough of Texas mourned:

> The sharp increase in crimes of violence against the person and in murder in recent years are likely to continue unless America stops teaching violence to her people. Every night T.V. programs stress homicide. Murder, sudden and quick, is piped into every home as "entertainment."

Yarborough elaborated by saying that television was building a "Frankenstein" which, left unchecked, would destroy America. He also pointed out that newspapers were hardly better and that even the United Nations and countries at war, like the United States, reported "kill ratios" as routinely as traffic accidents.[11]

The Connally Commission, clearly not wanting to advocate censorship, called upon the media to conduct a self-study on how news of violent acts is disseminated. The impetus to review the effect of violence depicted on television was given a jolt when on 5 August 1966 a fifteen-year-old boy was arrested for shooting a night watchman in the West Texas town of Roscoe. "I've been thinking about why I did it. I wanted to have fun like the guys in Chicago [Richard Speck] and Austin who had fun killing people," said the pathetic youngster.[12] The question is as old as the mass media itself: Does violence depicted in the media breed real-life violence?

Public officials and some members of the medical community, alarmed by the drastic rise of the "drug culture," quickly and strongly argued that Whitman's use of illicit drugs, namely Dexedrine [dextroamphetamine], contributed to his violent explosion. The Connally Commission concluded that there was no evidence of acute drug toxicity on 1 August 1966, but Whitman did have six Dexedrine tablets in a metal container on his person while on the deck. Further, after a review of the autopsy data, the Federal Bureau of Drug Abuse Control concluded that "failure to recover the urine, etc., made analytical proof of amphetamines impossible." The report indicated that while Whitman's blood analysis had not suggested drug toxicity, other fluids like urine and the contents of his stomach would have been better indicators of the presence of drugs. Because Whitman had already been embalmed at Cook's Funeral Home at the time of the autopsy on the morning after the snipings, the contents of his stomach and his urine had already been discarded.[13] Had they been analyzed they would almost certainly have contained traces of Dexedrine. But would that have explained what he did?

Gun control advocates pointed to Whitman's weapons as the real culprit. News reports with a bevy of statistics followed the incident. Americans learned that from January through July of 1966, 175,768 pistols had been sold in the state of Texas alone. In 1965, an incredible 571,058 hunting licenses had been issued; another 160,000 exemptions from licenses were issued to children under the age of seventeen and the elderly over age sixty-five. In 1965, the only requirements for the purchase of a gun were a name, address, and the age of the buyer. In America, approximately 100 million handguns and other firearms were already in the hands of private individuals in 1966, and about one million additional "dangerous weapons" were being sold every year. Mail order purchases of dangerous weapons were commonplace, the most infamous purchase being the rifle used to kill President Kennedy. Lee Harvey Oswald had bought his rifle without incident using the alias "A. Hidell." Charles Whitman had purchased all of his guns through transactions which were perfectly legal, using his own name. Gun control, normally associated with liberal causes, picked up a strange bedfellow in FBI Director J. Edgar Hoover, who stated shortly after the Tower incident, "Those who claim that the availability of firearms is not a factor in murders in this country are not facing reality."[14]

Other gun control advocates saw the 750,000-member National Rifle Association (NRA), of which Whitman was ironically not a member, as the chief obstacle to a safer American society. NRA backers envisioned an assault on a constitutional right by Communists and other radicals. Individuals reacted in different ways. Claire Wilson's father reportedly sold all of his guns, but most Americans, as is common after high profile murders and crime waves, purchased more guns in order to protect themselves.[15] The question remained: Had the availability of weapons and the ease with which Charles Whitman purchased his arsenal caused or at least contributed to the Tower incident?

Those concerned with child welfare and with the victims of domestic abuse quickly used Charles Whitman's upbringing as an example of the dehumanizing effect of spanking and other corporal punishment. Children's rights advocates saw the Tower incident as a forum to demonstrate what childhood abuse and domestic violence could do to an adult. The incident helped to give rise to the "abuse excuse." Many opponents of corporal punishment consider spanking, as such, abusive. Others, many of them successful parents of well-adjusted children who grow to become responsible adults, see spanking as immediate negative reinforcement for unacceptable behavior. The larger question remained: Had Charles Whitman's upbringing helped to condition him to become a mass murderer?

The most startling discovery, however, occurred during the autopsy of Whitman's body, when Dr. Coleman de Chenar noted that Whitman's skull was unusually thin (2 to 4mm) and found a tumor "in the middle part of the brain, above the red nucleus, in the white matter below the gray center thalamus," which was "a fairly well-outlined tumor about 2 x 1.5 x 1 cm in dimensions, grayish-yellow, with peripheral areas of red as blood." In his report Dr. de Chenar described the tumor:

> The tumor of the brain is composed of elements of the connective tissue of the brain (glea) and of blood vessels of enlarged calibers. Some of these blood vessels have thick walls, others thin ones, with defective construction of the layers and microscopically small bleedings into the surrounding intercellular spaces, however, only a dozen or less red blood cells enter those spaces around. The cells are rather small, round or elongated, with a small amount of cytoplasm and mostly well staining nucleus. The chromatin substance of the nucleus is well organized, round or

somewhat elongated or, in some places, vesicular. Cell divisions occur only very exceptionally, indicating a minimal level of activity, just on the borderline to malignant formations. There are areas of cell death (necrosis), surrounded by a fence-like arrangement (palisade formation) of elongated cells.[16]

Dr. de Chenar did not think that the tumor had any correlation to psychosis or persistent pains, like headaches.[17] For many of Whitman's friends and family, the tumor has become the culprit—something in his brain had made him somebody else. Many have been comforted by the fact that in his notes he asked for an autopsy to explain what he did. The suggestion was that he knew, as one of his teachers stated, that "something was wrong with his head." This case became part of a much larger ongoing debate over whether brain disease can cause violent behavior. In this case, could the tumor, or his intuition that something was physically wrong with him, have caused him to go berserk?

Victims' advocates and law enforcement officials, hardened by the evil they see on the streets and in some homes, have simpler explanations. Maybe Charles Whitman made a deliberate decision to kill people; maybe he knew exactly what he was doing and that it was wrong. Maybe he was just mean as hell.

III

Or was he crazy?

Mrs. L. J. Hollorn, a neighbor of the Whitman family in Lake Worth, Florida, thought, "He must have just lost his mind." C. A. Whitman asked reporters and the world to realize that his son was clearly a sick man: "I am at a loss for what reason he had. I feel he was definitely sick. I can say nothing but that he was a wonderful lad in the past. I am proud that I had a son like him up to this point."[18]

Robert Kennedy, a former U. S. Attorney General and Senator from New York, candidly asserted that had Whitman lived he would have undoubtedly been acquitted because "he was so clearly insane."[19] Dr. Robert Stokes, an eyewitness to the carnage, and the doctor who officially pronounced Whitman dead, believed he suffered from an acute schizophrenic break.[20]

Less than three weeks after the incident, Bill Helmer wrote in the *Texas Observer* of his experiences during the shootings. In his article he offered his own theory:

> A crackpot, a nut, a maniac almost never possesses the skill of a Whitman, or the manner. He was cool, efficient, and totally rational in every way except his impulse to kill, and in that he was determined, unflinching, and extraordinarily competent. He planned his deed with more good sense than most people can bring to bear on the job of packing a suitcase for a trip. He executed his plan with no sign of indecision or compromise. Another sniper might have indulged himself in shooting into the bodies on the mall, or knocking out a tempting plate glass window, or lobbying a few bullets into the Capitol or downtown Austin. Whitman did absolutely nothing for dramatic effect; he labored only to kill, in the "one shot, one man" military tradition.[21]

Helmer's observations voiced a sentiment common among eyewitnesses; Whitman made them angry. Another of Helmer's observations was that if Whitman had only done something trivial, like shooting a car or breaking a number of windows; if he had only shot the statue of Jefferson Davis or tried to shatter the "bubble gum" lights atop police cars, just for the hell of it, it would have been easier to think of him as crazy. But because Charles Whitman had done none of those things, he made people extraordinarily uncomfortable. The *Texas Observer* wrote, "If Charlie was a monster then so are we all."[22]

Barton Riley, the faculty member who likely had spent the most time with Whitman and who had gone to extraordinary lengths to help his troubled student, believed in a much simpler explanation:

> I don't think he was insane. He was fed up with everything. He hated his father, his mother was miserable. Something was wrong with his family. . . . [H]e decided to

quit it all. I feel like the only thing he wanted was to bring shame down on his father.[23]

But Gary Boyd, a classmate, candidly admitted, "That's not the Charlie Whitman I knew. When he got up there he was somebody else."[24] The opinions of those who knew Charles Whitman ran the full spectrum, from belief that he had suffered a complete mental breakdown and total insanity to belief that he was a cold-blooded mass murderer.

The verdict on Charles Whitman's insanity lies in the definition of insanity itself, for which there is no common standard. If defined by the act itself, Charles Whitman was clearly insane, as Senator Robert Kennedy had suggested. He could not have known the particulars of the Whitman case at the time of his comments. Using the act as the standard, the argument would have been that no sane person would amass an arsenal, go to the Tower and kill people. That was simply a crazy thing to do. The application of such logic, however, could be extended to an absurd degree. If no one in his right mind could kill anyone, maybe murder, as such, is not a crime but a manifestation of mental illness. Charles Whitman's actions on 1 August 1966 obviously had grossly deviated from the norm. Some acts were insane, but was Charles Whitman insane?

In his book *In Cold Blood*, Truman Capote wrote about the rule many states apply to determine insanity in criminal cases, called the McNaughtan Rule, an "ancient British importation." In *Mass Murder: America's Growing Menace,* Levin and Fox quote the postulate:

> A defendant must be shown to be labouring under such a defect of reason, from disease of the mind, as to not know the nature and quality of the act he was doing, or if he did know it, that he did not know he was doing what was wrong.[25]

As Capote pointed out, the rule is that if a defendant understands the nature of the act, and more importantly, knows that it is wrong, then he is competent to stand trial and should be held accountable for his crime. It would have been extraordinarily difficult for Charles Whitman to effectively argue insanity via the McNaughtan Rule.

The evidence and his behavior suggest that Whitman had made a decision to become a mass murderer no later than the early afternoon of 31 July 1966 when he purchased a Bowie knife and binoculars at Academy Surplus. From that moment on he made hundreds of deliberate and conscious decisions. He successfully covered up the murder of his mother by leaving a note on her door and calling Wyatt's Cafeteria to report her illness. He did likewise in Kathy's case. He clearly knew that he should hide what he was doing because it was wrong.

As Capote had illustrated in the question of insanity for Smith and Hickock in *In Cold Blood*, if the insanity plea were applied as a result of the much more lenient Durham Rule, which states that a defendant is not responsible for his crimes if he suffers from mental disease or defect, Charles Whitman would have had a much greater chance of successfully pleading not guilty by reason of insanity.[26] Unquestionably, he suffered from severe bouts of depression. Many of his friends, family, teachers, and a university psychiatrist could have provided testimony and documentation to that effect.

The harder question is whether he could have prevented himself from killing. The process of getting to the deck and controlling it required planning, patience and discipline, hardly the attributes of someone incapable of preventing himself from killing. Whitman's behavior towards Cheryl Botts and Donald Walden removes any doubt about his control. He could have killed them in an instant. Instead, he let them walk over Edna Townsley's blood and out of the reception area. Minutes later, he gunned down the Gabours and Marguerite Lamport. Such behavior was not random, but instead quite the opposite. Walden and Botts were leaving—getting out of his way; the Gabours and Lamports were arriving—getting in his way. Charles Whitman did what he had to do to secure the twenty-eighth floor.

The insanity plea, as Fox and Levin have pointed out, "assumes an absolute: you are either insane or not."[27] Charles Whitman's behavior does not suggest insanity. He did too many things requiring clear thinking, a sense of right and wrong, and judgment. Even "temporary insanity" is without foundation because his crimes were spread over a period from 12:15 A.M. to 1:24 P.M.—over thirteen hours. His actions would have required him to turn his temporary insanity on and off several times during the day to accomplish what he did.

Whitman fits the definition of a sociopath, someone who is not just mentally ill or, as Levin and Fox explain, "grossly out of touch with reality." Sociopaths are "bad, not mad." They care only for themselves. They can make themselves nice, but they cannot feel passion or empathy. Sociopaths are typically held accountable for their actions.[28]

IV

Charles Whitman disturbed Americans, who had previously thought of a mass murderer as a "glassy-eyed lunatic who kills innocent and helpless people in order to satisfy sadistic and lustful impulses." Whitman taught Americans that murder was seldom a crime of hardened criminals, but of usually law-abiding citizens. In 1965, the American public learned, a total of 9,850 murders had been committed in the United States, a large majority of which were instances of domestic violence by "normal" people with little or no criminal record.[29] In many ways Whitman forced America to face the truth about murder and how vulnerable the public could be in a free and open society. He caused everyday Americans, most of whom were never affected by the horror of mass murder, to question their assumptions of safety, especially in public places. Now America could see the "face" of mass murder, and it was the handsome face of a nice, all-American boy with no serious criminal record. "From that point on the concept of mass murder was real. . . . It really changed Americans' feelings of safety," stated James Alan Fox.[30] The criminal justice system responded as well. Before 1966, mass murder was so rare that the system had no special category or documentation for it. Statistics and procedures had treated such criminals and their crimes in the same manner as a single murder. Whitman also forced law enforcement agencies to acknowledge realistically the firepower that existed in the hands of ordinary citizens. It could not be denied that Charles Whitman had held off an army. Throughout the United States, especially in urban jungles where structures could be turned into fortresses, police departments began to take inventories of their weapons, training and personnel and to attempt to match the expertise and weaponry of the citizenry. For most of the larger police departments those efforts took the form of special weapons and tactics teams called SWAT.[31] Unfortunately, since 1966 SWAT teams have become extraordinarily useful.

V

In the search for a reason for Charles Whitman's actions of 1 August 1966, it has seldom been postulated that he just decided to do it. The historical record has been complicated by emotional acquaintances and writers seeking to "discover" a "cause" for the Tower incident. The influences most often cited as contributing factors—his military training, the depiction of violence by the media, his drug abuse, his fondness for guns, spankings by his father (and probably his mother as well), and the tumor on his brain—cannot, at least by themselves, explain what he did.

Millions of young men experience the regimen of the United States Marines and other branches of the armed forces. Virtually all Americans Whitman's age watched television as a child, read the newspapers and listened to the radio. Hundreds of thousands of young people took "goofballs" to stay awake for exams or just to get giddy. Hunting and collecting guns, indeed "loving" guns is common, more common than many Americans would like. But there was only one Charles Whitman.

The effect of Whitman's brain tumor will probably be debated forever. The type, and very existence, of a tumor had been questioned. Violence caused by brain disorders, although rare, is usually sudden or episodic; but Whitman's crime, as James Alan Fox has pointed out, was neither sudden nor episodic.[32] He did not "suddenly" pack a footlocker. His physical health during the months before the snipings and his actions on the deck effectively eliminate any notion that the tumor had a physical effect on him. The coordination required to aim and shoot as well as he did was astounding. The tumor could possibly have given him headaches, but most people deal with severe headaches by going to a doctor, not by shooting nearly fifty people. For nearly thirty years after the discovery of the tumor, most of those who knew Whitman and who thought he was not capable of such a slaughter have cited the growth as the cause: a pecan-sized demon that took possession of him. But in the past thirty years nearly all of the physicians and criminologists who have made themselves familiar with the case have pronounced the tumor "innocent."

Whitman's excellent hand-eye coordination on the deck also effectively eliminates drug intoxication. According to numerous classmates, when under the influence of drugs, Whitman's motor and cognitive skills had been sharply reduced. Given his known activities the night before, it is safe to assume that he had not slept. Since Dexedrine was found on his body, there is a good chance that he had taken something during the morning to combat fatigue. But if he had taken any drugs, he could not have taken enough to have a significant effect on his movement, cognition, or judgment. Like insanity, a drug-induced psychosis would most likely have resulted in a loss of touch with reality. Given his actions during his murderous spree, he would have had to control his psychosis, which is oxymoronic.

Calls for gun control following the Whitman murders implied that if firearms had been regulated the crime could have been prevented. Sadly, the regulation of firearms would not have prevented Charles Whitman from getting guns because no conceivable set of regulations would have disqualified him from his purchases. Any background check would have described a young, literate man with an honorable discharge from the marines, who had no history of violent crime, who could produce a history of hunting licenses, and who could assemble an army of character witnesses. To think that he needed classes in firearm safety (which has often been attached to gun control legislation) would be ludicrous; he could easily have qualified to teach the classes (which he had done as a Boy Scout leader). Only the confiscation of over 100,000,000 privately-owned handguns, rifles, and shotguns nationwide might have prevented the University of Texas tragedy; it is a degree of gun control that, even if possible, would never find political acceptance in the United States. One week after the murders President Lyndon Johnson called for the speedy passage of gun control legislation "to help prevent the wrong persons from obtaining firearms." But before 1 August 1966, Charles Whitman would not have been considered one of those "wrong" persons.[33]

VI

Charles Whitman knew that what he was doing was evil. Explanations for his crime describe the source of his frustrations, but they do not excuse his killing. Almost every premeditated murder results from a frustration of some sort, and Whitman's troubles were not particularly remarkable. College campuses are filled with students who work at odd jobs to get through college, take schedules that are too heavy, and who work extraordinarily hard maintaining or improving their grades. Many young people, even in 1966, faced the hurt of watching their parents go through separation and divorce. None became mass murderers.

Charles Whitman became a killer because he did not respect or admire himself. He knew that in many ways he was nearly everything he despised in others, and he decided that he could not persevere. He climbed the Tower because he wanted to die in a big way; not by suicide, but by taking others with him and making the headlines. He died while engaging in the only activity in which he truly excelled—shooting. His murders of Kathy and Margaret represented "suicide by proxy." He wanted to spare them the embarrassment of what he would do, just as he had written, probably because he loved them.[34] Margaret and Kathy's murders have been advanced by some as an indication of Whitman's insanity; why would he kill those he loved? This argument ignores America's experience with mass murderers, who often kill loved members of their own family. Given the folklore of his own personal religious beliefs, which trivialized the value of life, he likely thought that he and Kathy would be reunited in a less frustrating hereafter. Fully conscious of his mother's deep religious devotion, he may have created a notion in his mind that he was hastening her trip to heaven. After the breakup of his parents' marriage he had no such benevolence towards his father, whom he had never developed the courage or the maturity to deal with. In his mind it was just as well that the elder Whitman, alone, would be left to answer the questions. In other words, Charles Whitman was an extraordinary coward.

Charles J. Whitman ushered in a new era in which what Bill Kurtis called a "rare and frightening crime" became more common.[35] He also intensified a debate over an issue America never really addressed: What are we willing to accept as an excuse for murder? Whitman and some other high-profile killers, like Ted Bundy, gave mass murder a normal, even handsome look. Richard Speck motivated many thousands of Americans to question notions of safety in our homes; Charles Whitman stole from us the comfort of believing in the safety of public places. Together they robbed us of the luxury of initiating a pleasant conversation with a stranger, and the consolation that no member of the human family can be completely void of virtue and conscience. Through our fear they made us pay a high price for living in a free society.

[1] Connally Report, pp. 21–23.

[2] Ibid., p. 1.

[3] Ibid., pp. 9–10.

[4] The pictures are part of the Austin Police Department files.

[5] Connally Report, pp. 9–10.

[6] Lawrence A. Fuess; FBI Files: *Cole Report*, 4 August 1966; APD Files: *The Daily Record of C. J. Whitman*, passim.

[7] See APD Files: Charles Whitman's Notebooks, passim, and *The Daily Record of C. J. Whitman*, entry of 23 February 1964.

[8] Connally Report, p. 11; Cox Papers.

[9] Connally Report, p. 15.

[10] *Texas Observer*, 19 August 1966.

[11] Ibid.

[12] Connally Report, p. 15; *Austin American-Statesman*, 6 August 1966.

[13] Connally Report, passim; APD Files: Lab Request by Bill Landis and letter of K. R. Herbert to D. Tisdale, 10 August 1966.

[14] *Palm Beach Post*, 5 August 1966; J. Edgar Hoover quoted in *Time*, 12 August 1966.

[15] *Time*, 12 August 1966; *Austin American-Statesman*, 1 August 1976; FBI Files: *Cole Report*, 5 August 1966.

[16] *Autopsy Protocol*, p. 3.

[17] Ibid.; *Austin American-Statesman*, 5 August 1966.

[18] Mrs. L. J. Hollorn quoted in *Austin American-Statesman*, 2 August 1966, C. A. Whitman quoted in 9 August 1966.

[19] *Time*, 12 August 1966.

[20] APD Files: *Food and Drug Administration Statement*, Robert Stokes, MD, 5 August 1966.

[21] *Texas Observer*, 19 August 1966.

[22] Ibid.

[23] Ibid.

[24] *Life*, 12 August 1966.

[25] Truman Capote, *In Cold Blood*, p. 318; Jack Levin and James Alan Fox, *Mass Murder: America's Growing Menace* (New York: Plenum Publishing, 1985), pp. 200–201.

[26] For a discussion of Durham's Rule see Capote, *In Cold Blood*, pp. 377–78.

[27] Levin and Fox, *Mass Murder: America's Growing Menace*, pp. 198 and 207.

[28] Ibid., p. 71; James Alan Fox and Jack Levin, *Overkill: Mass Murder and Serial Killing Exposed* (New York: Plenum Press, 1994) p. 42.

[29] Ibid., p. 3; *Time*, 12 August 1966.

[30] James Alan Fox quoted in AJS.

[31] Levin and Fox, *Mass Murder: America's Growing Menace*, p. 219.

[32] Ibid.; Dr. Albert Lalonde; Fox and Levin, *Overkill*, p. 139.

[33] *Newsweek*, 15 August 1966; *Texas Observer*, 19 August 1966.

[34] For a discussion of "suicide by proxy" see Levin and Fox, *Mass Murder: America's Growing Menace*, p. 100.

[35] Bill Kurtis quoted in AJS.

18

Who Killed Charles Whitman?

I

In 1985 two sociologists from Northeastern University, Jack Levin and James Alan Fox, completed a "comprehensive exploration of the characteristics of and the circumstances which precipitate mass murder," producing a work entitled *Mass Murder: America's Growing Menace*. In 1994 they followed up with *Overkill: Mass Murder and Serial Killing Exposed*. In the foreword of *Mass Murder* noted defense attorney F. Lee Bailey wrote that Americans know little about mass murder and that much needs to be done to understand and prevent it.[1] In their work Levin and Fox present a composite profile of a mass murderer: a white male, in his late twenties or thirties, whose motives to kill include money, expediency, jealousy, or lust. American mass murderers, hardly ever career criminals but sometimes with a history of property crimes, often commit their murders following lengthy periods of frustration. For some, like Charles Whitman, guns become a solution to this frustration and are seen as the "great equalizer."[2]

Of course, people are classified as mass murderers only *after* they have committed the murders. Hence, the prevention of mass murders could only be accomplished through predicting who will become one and intervening before the crime. That requires the identification of variables found to have a cause-effect relationship with mass murder. Levin and Fox candidly admit that their profile of a mass murderer fits hundreds of thousands of individuals and that attempts to make the profile more detailed subtract from its accuracy. Moreover, the more prevalent character traits of mass murderers tend to be hidden. Like other mass murderers, Charles Whitman battled feelings of powerlessness and a lack of accomplishment, a brand of impotence Whitman thought made his life not worth living.[3] Accepting any of the sources of frustration as an excuse for his actions is to suggest a cause-effect relationship which should manifest itself in many hundreds of other individuals.

Trying to identify potential mass murderers through observable physical features and societal status continues to be folly because they run the spectrum of looks and conditions, from the charming and the attractive, like Whitman and Ted Bundy, to the ugly, like Richard Speck. Some mass murderers have homes and some are drifters. Some are married and some are single. They include tall and short, rich and poor, urbanites and country boys, literate and illiterate. They love and hate kids, dogs, their parents, their neighbors, and their country. Trying to identify childhood characteristics associated with individuals who grow to be violent is also fraught with danger. For example, the MacDonald Triad—which includes bedwetting, firesetting, and torturing small animals—denotes a group of common characteristics in children who grow to become violent adults. The triad has often been attributed to poor parenting. But many well-adjusted, nonviolent adults were children who wet their bed and liked to play with fire; some might even have been cruel to animals. Yet few become mass murderers.[4]

In general, predicting the behavior of individuals is extraordinarily difficult and inexact. (Predicting the behavior of groups of people is much easier. For example, insurance companies can predict the losses of particular groups very accurately.) Usually, predictions for individuals are accurate only when they are based on measurements under standardized conditions and when the measurements are similar to those of the predicted behavior. Exams, like college admissions tests, pose questions that duplicate the thought processes and the problems examinees will later face in college. A test's design and content result from a great deal of science and data. It can be altered and field tested; its effectiveness can be measured and demonstrated. On the other hand, there is no "test" for mass murderers (or for most other anti-social behavior). While teams like the FBI's Behavioral Science Unit have amassed information on known mass murderers, the relative infrequency of the crime and the lack of direct measurements makes prediction problematic.

In predicting mass murderers, there would be four possible outcomes: 1. False-Positive: Someone who is predicted to become a mass murderer but does not become one. 2. True-Positive: Someone who is predicted to become a mass murderer and does become one. 3. True-Negative: Someone who is predicted not to become a mass murderer and does not become one. 4. False-Negative: Someone who is predicted not to become a mass murderer and does become one.

The accurate prediction of a mass murder, or early identification of a potential mass murderer, is nearly impossible because of the large number of false-positives (an inaccurate prediction) and the small number of true-positives (an accurate prediction). Simply put, the more prevalent characteristics of mass murderers, variables like the MacDonald Triad and those "causes" of the Whitman murders, are also common in the general population. Statistically, the accurate prediction of any condition as infrequent as mass murder from a large general population is extraordinarily difficult, if not impossible. Societally, the consequence of error in predicting such a horrendous behavior is intolerable. It would lead to labeling, baseless discrimination, and unwarranted suspicions among friends, neighbors, and family.[5]

Charles Whitman provides a good example of the severe limitations of prediction. All of the variables associated with the cause of his murders are common in the general population. There are too many others who engage in those activities or suffer from those conditions who proceed to develop into normal, productive adults. Charles Whitman *decided* to become a mass murderer.

II

During the week of 1 August 1966, attention fell on the unlikely person of Ford Clark of Ottumwa, Iowa, little-known author of a book entitled *Open Square*. The paperback, published in the early 1960s at about the time Charles Whitman first moved to Austin as a NESEP scholar, was a fictional account of Ted Weeks, a psychotic student who happened to hate his parents. In a haunting coincidence, the Weeks of *Open Square* climbed a tower on a university campus somewhere in the Midwest and began firing a high-powered rifle at students and faculty below. As the real-life drama unfolded in Austin, Clark was working on a new publication:

> I was writing when my fiancée called me and told me they were acting out my novel on the University of Texas campus. This must have been about noon. I completely misunderstood her. I thought they were making a play of the book.

Shortly afterwards Clark received an anonymous phone call from someone with a Southern accent: "If you ever come down to our country we're going to put a bullet in your head. I know he read your book. He was a good boy. You're to blame for all of this."[6]

On 5 August 1966, the *Austin American-Statesman* listed an astounding list of similarities between Charles Whitman and the fictitious Ted Weeks: the sniper's nest had food; Weeks had an overly loving mother and a perfectionist for a father; he could not live up to the expectations of his father; he was trained to shoot in the military (ROTC); he hauled his supplies in a suitcase, the contents of which included water, gasoline, and five hundred rounds of ammunition; and he used ventilation slits as portholes to fire through.

Astoundingly, the fictitious sniper Ted Weeks was killed by a police force headed by a "Chief Miles."[7]

Dr. Coleman de Chenar, the physician who performed the autopsy on Charles Whitman, was reported to have postulated that the book had given Whitman the idea. Ford Clark replied that de Chenar's statement was irresponsible. Each finally apologized to the other after the physician claimed to have been misquoted. After the eerie similarities became common knowledge, the Austin Police Department obtained a warrant to search 906 Jewell Street for a copy of *Open Square*. The search was conducted on 3 August 1966 and no copy was found.[8] No evidence was ever uncovered that Charles Whitman might have read the book, by checking it out from a library for instance, or even that he might have known such a book existed. In any case, clear evidence does exist that Whitman had immediately recognized the value of the Tower as a fortress the first time he saw it in 1961, almost certainly before *Open Square* was published.

The first attempt to dramatize the Tower incident occurred nine years later. Antonio Calderon produced a made-for-television movie entitled *Deadly Tower*. The film focused on Ramiro Martinez, played by an actor named Richard Yniguez, as the central figure and hero. Kurt Russell played a dazed, almost robotic, Charles Whitman, who had few lines in the entire feature. Ned Beatty played Allen Crum. No other real names were used in the production. In August of 1974 Houston McCoy was approached by the studio, but he refused to sign a release for his name to be used. McCoy proposed more factual script changes. In a letter to Antonio Calderon dated 18 September 1974, Ben Neel, representing McCoy, summarized McCoy's objections and proposals:

> Houston's entire objection to your movie, Mr. Calderon, revolves around the actual shooting of Whitman by Martinez in your film. If you will study our position, I will be glad to discuss it with you again. This proposed change in your tower scene would in no way discredit Martinez or your movie, but it would disclose the truth at long last.

This is our position, Mr. Calderon. If you go ahead and film the movie and have Martinez's one shot with Houston's shotgun killing Whitman, either pay Houston the royalties or entirely delete Houston from the film and do not substitute any other character by a different name that even remotely resembles Houston McCoy in any manner or action. If you wish your movie to be a documentary that tells the truth about the sniper in the tower, Houston will be glad to remain in the movie and help you as a technical advisor. If you make the proposed script change, Houston will be glad to assist you. If you don't make the movie at all, that will be fine with Houston, too.[9]

Antonio Calderon did not accept the changes. The University of Texas also refused to cooperate by disallowing filming on the campus. As a result, UT was not mentioned in the movie. Interim President Lorene Rogers issued this statement:

I did not want to bring back bad memories that are still vivid in the minds of many of our students, their families and the people of Austin. It would just be opening up old wounds, and I did not want the university to be a part of it.[10]

Antonio Calderon, however, saw the *Deadly Tower* as more than just a movie. "The most positive aspect of this picture is that for the first time in the history of television, the subject and hero will be a Chicano."[11]

The production cost about $1 million and was filmed in Baton Rouge, Louisiana, on the grounds of the state capitol, which served as the Tower. Although the Louisiana State Capitol is considerably larger, the building and the surrounding sunken gardens bore some resemblance to the Tower and the South Mall. The production schedule ran from 16 June through 4 July 1975, a time of year in Baton Rouge that was hot. *Deadly Tower* very accurately portrayed the heat battled by the police and civilians, but that was about as far as accuracy went. The made-for-TV movie was first broadcast on Saturday, 18 October 1975 on NBC.

Calderon never intended to make a documentary. But immediately, major players in the real crime universally decried the movie as uninformed and inaccurate. The real-life hero of the film, Ramiro Martinez, became incensed at the portrayal of the Austin Police Department as racist and at his depiction as a victim of discrimination in the awarding of promotions. "This business about being passed over for a promotion is just a lot of malarky," he said. Ramiro was especially sensitive to that issue because he had fond memories of good friends he had made while an Austin policeman and good times his family had shared with the families of other policemen. Years later he would remember, "Oh, I'm sure some people may not have liked me because I was Hispanic, but some people don't like anybody."[12]

Equally infuriating to Ramiro, and his wife Vernell, was how she was depicted. The movie portrayed her character as a nervous, pregnant, Hispanic housewife who immediately pleaded with her husband not to go to the campus, an action resulting in an argument. "Mrs. Martinez" is later overcome by an overwhelming need to go to the Tower just as Ramiro is being led out. In fact, Vernell is of proud German heritage and was a working professional at the time of the Tower shootings. Ramiro was at home alone when he heard Joe Roddy reporting the incident on television. Ramiro and Vernell Martinez sued MGM Studios, the NBC Television Network, and Antonio Calderon. Their original complaint detailed the major points of the suit: 1. The movie showed Ramiro having made the highest score on a competitive exam for a promotion and not having been promoted. It also depicted a vigorous objection by Ramiro and an argument over the issue with a superior (played by Pernell Roberts). In general, *Deadly Tower* depicted Ramiro Martinez as having a troubled relationship with the Austin Police Department and his fellow officers and that the cause was racial discrimination. 2. Ramiro repeatedly discussed inaccuracies with Antonio Calderon and other agents of MGM. 3. MGM and NBC advertised a film as historic fact but presented a film with substantial portions of fiction and, in the process, adversely affected the reputations of Ramiro and Vernell Martinez. 4. Ramiro and Vernell asked for an injunction on further broadcasts of the *Deadly Tower*. The couple later settled out of court, the terms of which have never been made public, but the film, which still airs occasionally on the TNT network, differs slightly from the original. One of the opening scenes informs viewers that "both the character and personality of Ramiro Martinez's wife and certain scenes about the Martinez family have been fictionalized for dramatic effect."

Years later, Houston McCoy sued Turner Broadcasting for airing *Deadly Tower*. He claimed that even though he was never mentioned by name, the character "C. T." could only have been him. The character, Houston alleged, was portrayed as a coward. "They made me look like Gomer Pyle." Houston maintained that he was unable to see the movie without "slipping into deep depression." He also admitted to having become an alcoholic. For Houston, however, the case was not settled but thrown out of court. His troubles were compounded when the judge ordered him to pay attorney's fees for Turner Broadcasting. "Can you believe it? I owe Ted Turner and Jane Fonda money," he later lamented.[13]

III

Since 1 August 1966, the most enduring, and at times tragic, controversy involving the Tower incident involves Ramiro Martinez and Houston McCoy, and which of the men actually fired the fatal projectiles that killed Charles Whitman. For ten years after the tragedy, resentments would ferment. Some felt that Ramiro Martinez, who had received the bulk of the recognition for ending the siege, had not killed Whitman. There was a sense that, somehow, Houston McCoy had been overlooked and his role in bringing down Whitman had been unappreciated. The controversy hit the news on the 10th anniversary of the incident when Bob Miles, then the former Police Chief, was quoted in the *Daily Texan*. "The newspapers sort of took over, they didn't ask anybody. They gave all the credit to Ramiro Martinez."[14]

On the 10th anniversary of the shootings, Houston McCoy was in a hospital bed in West Texas, where a Dallas reporter found him and interviewed him while—Houston claims—he was under the influence of medication and not fully aware of what he was saying. A few days later in the *Daily Texan* article with the Miles statement, Houston was quoted. "All I can say is if he [Martinez] had been up there by himself, he'd be dead right now."[15]

Since 1976 nearly every anniversary and feature article involving the Whitman murders has included a section on "Who Killed
Charles Whitman?" Some of the articles appear to be flagrant
attempts by reporters to create and report controversy. The 29 July
1994 issue of the *Los Angeles Times* headlined a story entitled "In
Texas—Massacre and Myth—Who Killed Charles Whitman?" The
subtitle reads: "One man ended Charles Whitman's coldblooded
Austin slaughter. Was it the hero of legend, or a second officer in the
tower who says he fired the crucial shots?" The article compares the
saga of Martinez and McCoy with John Ford's classic western movie
The Man Who Shot Liberty Valance. In that movie Lee Marvin played
Liberty Valance, a feared and despised thug; James Stewart played a
mild-mannered lawyer who openly detested the violence of the West;
John Wayne played a strong, moral pillar of manhood, the only decent person able to stand up to Liberty. The climax of the movie is
an unavoidable gunfight between the characters played by Marvin
and Stewart, in which, miraculously, Stewart guns down Marvin.
Stewart is subsequently honored as "the man who shot Liberty Valance." The Stewart character moved on to enjoy a successful
political career. Later, in a flashback, the truth emerges: Liberty Valance had really been shot by John Wayne from a position no one
could see. The wrong man had been honored.[16]

The comparison of the Tower incident and *The Man Who Shot
Liberty Valance* is absurd. Even more absurd are connections made
between fatal projectiles and bravery. "Whomever it is, the man who
shot Charles Whitman was the bravest of them all." Such a statement assumes that Charles Whitman could only have been shot by
one man, either Martinez or McCoy, and that only the fatal bullet
defines the extent of bravery.

The controversy took a sad turn when Martinez became a Texas
Ranger and it was later suggested by others that his induction into
the elite group resulted from his role in bringing down Charles
Whitman, a role which had been exaggerated because he was Hispanic. Bob Miles fanned the flames of controversy when he was
quoted as saying:

> I think Ramiro quit [the Austin Police Department] and
> went to work as manager of a cafe. He failed at that and

went around to several different jobs. Finally, they had an opportunity to appoint him as a Texas Ranger so they could have a Mexican American in the job.[17]

It was during the same interview that former Chief Miles strongly and disingenuously asserted that "the newspapers sort of took over" and "gave all the credit to Ramiro Martinez."[18] Miles must not have given a great deal of prior thought to what he said. On the next day he angrily refused follow-up questions by saying that he did not "have a damn thing to say about the Whitman Case, who shot the sniper, or why he felt the news media had wrongly given Martinez credit for ending the tragedy."[19]

Other APD officers have candidly shared their feelings about the issue. Jerry Day asserted, "Houston was definitely the one who killed Whitman."[20] In October of 1975, Lieutenant Bolton Gregory, one of two officers who discovered Kathy Whitman's body, maintained that the autopsy showed that a shotgun blast killed Whitman. He went on to explain that Martinez fired six times but hit the sniper only once in the arm.[21] (Dr. Coleman de Chenar, the pathologist who performed the autopsy, did note that "pellets" were found in the brain; there is no notation, however, concerning a 38-caliber round in Whitman's arm.) Houston's advocates in this controversy are sincere in their beliefs but none of them has ever questioned Martinez's bravery.

There are many facts about the shooting of Charles Whitman that Ramiro and Houston agree on: Ramiro led the way, turned the corner first, and from a very low position fired all six rounds in his revolver as quickly as he could pull the trigger; Houston fired two blasts from a 12-gauge shotgun loaded with 00 buckshot; Ramiro subsequently grabbed the shotgun from Houston's grasp and ran towards Whitman and fired into Whitman's upper body. The area of disagreement concerns Whitman's reaction once Ramiro started firing. Ramiro recalls that Whitman "sprung like a cat" and from a standing position tried to level his carbine to fire back, while Houston recalls that Whitman stayed in a seated position as he tried to level the carbine.[22] The disagreement is believed to be significant because if Whitman were standing it is more likely that Ramiro wounded him. If he were seated the large deck lamps would have obstructed his line of fire, and furthermore, only Houston would have had a clear view of the sniper's head to fire the fatal blasts.

There are other facts that are not in dispute. A total of thirty-three missiles were fired at Whitman by Ramiro and Houston. Ramiro fired six rounds from his revolver; Houston fired eighteen pellets in two shots. Ramiro fired another nine pellets at very short range from one shotgun blast. To seek to determine which of the two men killed Charles Whitman is to search for the pellet or bullet that inflicted not only a fatal injury, but the first injury that might have been fatal. Even if possible, such a search would be extraordinarily unproductive, serving only to legitimize the notion that such a discovery is a prize to be won. Chief Miles initially stated that no one should seek or take "credit" for killing another human being, a wise statement he should have stuck to. Regardless of how justified or necessary, the killing of a person, even someone as evil as Charles Whitman, should not be an occasion for celebration. Selflessness, courage, and the rescue of an entire university from the clutches of a killer deserve recognition. In that respect, two Austin policemen, Ramiro Martinez and Houston McCoy, side by side, faced identical dangers to bring the madness to an end. Killing and death are not measures of courage; if so, Whitman would have been the bravest—an absurd notion. Would Martinez and McCoy have demonstrated less courage had they taken Whitman alive?

It can hardly be denied, however, that Ramiro Martinez has received the bulk of the recognition for killing Charles Whitman. The *Deadly Tower* movie ended the politeness of the debate. The controversy has focused some attention on the role Houston McCoy played in ending the incident, but unfortunately, more space and time have been focused on the argument than the deed. Some who resent how Houston has been overlooked have postulated a number of different reasons for the historical oversight. Houston has suggested that, in part, he is to blame; West Texans grow up in a culture "where you just don't talk a lot about yourself."[23] Others claim that the Hispanic community adopted Ramiro Martinez as a hero, and that fact somehow exaggerated the recognition he received. Unlike many controversies associated with the Whitman case, the evidence is clear: the reason Ramiro Martinez was identified as the slayer of Charles Whitman cannot be traced to the actions of newspaper reporters or Hispanic groups, but a single, most unlikely, individual—Police Chief Bob Miles.

In the Austin Police files on the Whitman case there is only one reference to the whereabouts of Chief Miles during the shootout. Apparently he and a "Major Biggerstaff" proceeded to Brackenridge Hospital, most probably as a result of the shooting of fellow officer, Billy Paul Speed.[24] Not surprisingly, requests for statements were directed at Chief Miles even before the incident came to an end, and his first statements contained a number of inaccuracies. For example, on the next day, citing a statement by Miles as their source, the *Austin American-Statesman* incorrectly reported that Martinez and Jerry Day, with Houston McCoy, were led through tunnels beneath the UT campus.[25]

At 3:00 P.M. on 1 August 1966, only about one and a half hours after Miles could have found out that Whitman was dead, he issued the following statement via teletype:

ALL PUBLIC NEWS MEDIA

SNIPER ON TOP OF UNIV OF TEX AS [sic] TOWER
WAS DOA 1 22 PM THIS DATE
ATTEMPTED APPREHENSION MADE BY OFFICER
RAMIRO MARTINEZ PATROLMAN AUSTIN POLICE
DEPT & OTHERS
SUBJECT TENTATIVELY IDENTIFIED AS CHARLES
J WHITMAN CAU-MALE DOB 6-24-41 RESIDENT OF
AUSTIN SEVEN KNOWN DEAD
ESTIMATED 27 INJURED

CHIEF R A MILES
PD AUSTIN TEXAS   OPR CUNNINGHAM   8 1 66
3 PM[26]

At that time Ramiro Martinez could hardly have been seeking sole credit for killing Whitman—he had been taken to APD headquarters where he was suffering from dry heaves. From that moment, however, being the only officer named in Miles's release, Martinez became the focus of attention. Reporters from all over the world wanted to know more about him and what he had done. They also wanted to talk to him. Chief Miles replied: "He's too shook up. I wonder how you'd feel if you had just crawled past four bodies on the stairs, one a child with his tongue protruding, en route to the parapet." Either Miles could have pointed out that Houston McCoy had a great deal to do with killing Charles Whitman and did not, or he was not in command of the facts when he issued his statement.

The next day's edition of the *Austin American-Statesman* had the caption "Shoots Slayer" below a picture of Ramiro Martinez that was even larger than the picture of Charles Whitman. Martinez had neither issued any statement nor spoken to any reporter. On the contrary, he chose to stay at his brother's home in order to avoid reporters. Reports about what Houston McCoy had done were limited to textual references. His picture did not appear in the newspaper until the following Friday, when he arrived to testify before the grand jury. If, indeed, there is injustice in the recognition of Ramiro Martinez as the lone slayer of the sniper and in the lack of recognition given to Houston McCoy, it is due to the first statements issued to the mass media from the Austin Police Department—statements issued by Chief Miles.

The words of both men should be remembered by those who would continue this silly and senseless debate, which distracts from the incredible acts of courage and heroism displayed by both Martinez and McCoy.

> Ramiro Martinez in 1975: "We were both shooting and we were both scared. I don't know who actually killed him. Only God knows that."

> Houston McCoy in 1986: "I want to be remembered as someone who did his job to the best of his ability, that's all."

> Ramiro Martinez in 1986: "Who fired the fatal projectile? I could care less. I don't get into that type of argument."

Houston McCoy in 1986: "Ramiro was a brave man and I take nothing away from him. As for me, you can't make too many mistakes with a shotgun."

Ramiro Martinez in 1991: "I think we were equally important out there together. I have nothing but admiration for Houston McCoy."[27]

Both men deserve the peace of knowing that each did his job heroically. The recognition that Ramiro Martinez received for his part in ending the Tower incident was richly deserved. It is unfortunate that Houston McCoy did not receive similar recognition, which he also deserved. The bitterness of the debate overshadowed the obvious: they made a great team. Ramiro served as a catalyst for Houston's firepower, and both were necessary to kill Charles Whitman.

------

[1] Levin and Fox, *Mass Murder: America's Growing Menace*, pp. ix and 7.

[2] Ibid., p. 55.

[3] Ibid., pp. 47–48, 53–68, 118.

[4] Ibid., p. 60. For an excellent discussion of the MacDonald Triad see pp. 27–29, 36–37.

[5] I am indebted to Dr. Richard Sawyer of Iowa City, Iowa, for his valuable assistance in the construction of the prediction model. See also Ibid., pp. 35–36; Fox and Levin, *Overkill*, p. 89.

[6] *Austin American-Statesman*, 4 August 1966; Ford Clark and anonymous caller quoted on 5 August 1966.

[7] Ibid.

[8] Ibid.

[9] Ben Neel to Antonio Calderon, letter dated 18 September 1974 in APD Files. Apparently McCoy sent a copy of his personal papers to the Austin Police Department for inclusion in the Whitman File.

[10] Dr. Lorene Rogers quoted in *Daily Texan*, 10 June 1975.

[11] Antonio Calderon quoted in Ibid.

[12] Ramiro Martinez quoted in the *San Antonio Standard*, 22 October 1975; Ramiro Martinez.

[13] Houston McCoy; *Austin American-Statesman*, 29 November 1990.

[14] Bob Miles quoted in *Daily Texan*, 3 August 1976.

[15] Houston McCoy; Houston McCoy quoted in Ibid.

[16] *Los Angeles Times*, 29 July 1994. A copy of this article was given to the author by Houston McCoy.

[17] Bob Miles quoted in *Daily Texan*, 3 August 1976.

[18] Ibid.

[19] Bob Miles quoted in an unidentified clipping in APD Files.

[20] Jerry Day quoted in Ibid.

[21] *San Angelo Standard*, 22 October 1975.

[22] Ramiro Martinez; Houston McCoy; Spelce Tapes.

[23] Houston McCoy.

[24] APD Files: *SOR* by F. Monk, 4 August 1966.

[25] *Austin American-Statesman*, 2 August 1966.

[26] The teletype is in the APD Files.

[27] *San Angelo Standard*, 22 October 1975; *Austin American-Statesman*, 1 August 1986.

EPILOGUE

The Writer From Austin

The evil that men do lives after them; the good is oft interred with their bones.—Marc Antony in William Shakespeare's *Julius Caesar*, Act III, Scene II.

Austin, Texas

Thirty years after the Tower incident, people on the Austin Police Force still think of Charles Whitman, and they still get angry. At APD headquarters, a typical government building, visitors walk into the lobby through front doors facing the access road of Interstate Highway 35, where Houston McCoy sped toward the Tower from

Holly Street. A sign tells visitors to walk around to the back of a large circular desk for assistance. A trophy case on the left commemorates victories by Austin Police teams at shooting contests. Some of the trophies are old and tarnished, as are some of the frames which hold pictures of APD officers killed in the line of duty. Uniformed officers work the reception area near the elevators, which visitors cannot board without a numbered sticker identifying the floor to which the visitor has been given access. A large matted frame near the elevator holds a black and white picture of Billy Paul Speed. He looks his age—twenty-three. Few know that at the time of his death he was ready to quit police work and go back to school.

Austin and the University of Texas have more than doubled in size since Charles Whitman was a resident. Both have prospered and grown even more diverse. Nineteenth Street is now Martin Luther King Boulevard; First Street is now Cesar Chavez Street. Residents celebrate June 19th as a significant holiday called "Juneteenth" to commemorate the date in 1865 when Texas slaves learned they were free. Comparing Austin to the rest of Texas uncovers about as many similarities as comparing the equally Greek cities of Athens and Sparta. Austin is still different.

Charles Whitman assaulted not only individuals, he also assaulted Austin. And in many ways he continues to fire from the deck. Virtually all who were on the campus on that damn hot day in August still look at the Tower and see the face of Charles Whitman. Many still hear the shots and feel the terror. Whatever good Whitman may have done in his life is buried with him in West Palm Beach, Florida; his evil continues to live in Austin, Texas. He attacked youth and promise when he gunned down Mark Gabour, Alex Hernandez, Karen Griffith and the others who had not yet celebrated their eighteenth birthdays. He attacked love itself when he put bullets into lovers holding hands: Adrian and Brenda Littlefield, Paul Sonntag and Claudia Rutt, and Claire Wilson and Thomas Eckman.

In some ways Charles Whitman inhabits the Tower. It has a "bad karma." That curse reaches all those Whitman hurt, even those he did not shoot. In the early 1980s, Patrick Whitman, while on a trip through Texas, found himself attracted to the University of Texas. He told the *Austin American-Statesman*, "For some unknown reason, if I had gone to Austin and if the Tower was reopened, I would have gone. I don't know why. It's just like a driving force." Patrick's daughter talked him out of making the trip.[1]

Tragically, that driving force has attracted others. During the first thirty years of its history, a total of three people committed suicide from the Tower; in a six-year period from 1968 to its reclosing in 1974, four more people chose to end their troubled lives there.[2] In 1967, the University of Texas spent $5,000 repairing the bullet holes on the exterior walls of the building,[3] and in February of 1976, the University of Texas Regents permanently closed the observation deck,[4] but repairing the image and easing the pain will require much more than official closings and money.

The University of Texas demonstrated, immediately following the Whitman tragedy, the value of revealing controversial facts rather than hiding them. It must have been tempting to hide the fact of Whitman's visit to Dr. Heatly and to shred the report about Whitman's urge to "go to the Tower and shoot people," but UT did not. Public institutions faced with similar situations today should take note.

The university also wisely avoided making Charles Whitman an obsession. As soon as possible, teachers returned to teaching and students returned to class. The South Mall holds no memorial to the many who died, and perhaps that is best.

C. A. Whitman

In Lantana, Florida, in an area where wooded tracts were being thinned out to provide for a new neighborhood, the traffic slowed where the road had been torn up. Near the center of activity an old man sat on a green golf cart. I recognized him right away, even though all of the pictures I had seen of him were from 1966. He did not have the look of someone who might be the only person Charles Whitman hated, or of someone a police department and a grand jury would seal documents in order to protect. He looked like what he was, a plumbing contractor, and one in the process of building. Where the road's shoulder had been dug out it looked like a large dry moat that could swallow my small rental car. C. A. Whitman motioned for a small bulldozer to move gravel and crushed stone along the edge of the road so that I could drive through. The men moved quickly; C. A. Whitman is still tough.

Now approaching his late seventies, he wears glasses and his hair is gray and longer than it had been when he came to Austin in 1966. "I am the writer from Austin who spoke to you earlier this week, Mr. Whitman. It is a pleasure to meet you," I said. The old man smiled and extended his left hand. He asked that I park up the driveway a bit and wait just a few minutes to allow him to conduct a little business. From a distance I positioned the car in order to watch the old plumber from my rear view mirror. Mr. Whitman did all the talking. The large, burly construction workers stood silently and nodded their heads. They listened intently, in spite of the sounds of hammers and heavy equipment. The air smelled of fresh dirt. Soon the green golf cart pulled up beside the car. "Follow me."

The long white driveway led to a modest home nearly surrounded by a large nursery. The hissing of sprinklers replaced the sounds of construction, and the scent of wet plants and cool, oxygen-rich air overpowered the smell of dirt. C. A. Whitman escorted me to his home. Near the living room door an antique milk jug held a number of walking canes. Sofa pillows depicted horses, and equestrian pho-tographs were everywhere. A horseshoe was nailed to the kitchen door frame and to the left hung a large circular thermometer deco-rated with paintings of ducks. In the center of the room an old coffee table covered with magazines was topped with a license plate that read, "Love Thy Neighbor, But Don't Get Caught."

The elder Whitman sat and talked graciously. His belt, a wide leather strap with a large buckle in the shape of a German Luger pistol, distracted me. After all that has happened to this man, why on earth would he wear a buckle in the shape of a gun? But then I have to remember, I am here to talk to him about things that hap-pened nearly thirty years ago.

C. A. Whitman began the questioning. "So what do you pro-pose to do?" He gradually began to repeat the same story he has told a million times. No wonder it sounded so matter-of-fact, so cold. "I had three sons and they are all dead," he said to me. Patrick, he revealed, had died of AIDS several years earlier. Of the three surviving Whitmans, Patrick was most affected by the Tower trag-edy, which Mr. Whitman called "the accident."[5] I recall reading that

Patrick used to go to Mass each August 1st, but later he despaired, saying "I don't think I know what happiness is."[6]

Oddly, C. A. Whitman spoke more about Johnnie Mike than about his more infamous eldest son. But I already knew that by 1971 John Michael Whitman had straightened himself out and returned to work with his father. Before then, however, he had led a troubled life which included several arrests for offenses ranging from speeding to breaking and entering. He once told West Palm Beach deputies, "You've heard of my brother, well, you haven't seen any reputation yet."[7] On 4 July 1973, Johnnie Mike, by then a husband and father, decided to take a break from his studies by taking his wife out for a drink. Inside "Big Daddy's Lounge" an argument broke out that moved outside to the parking lot, where someone shot John in the stomach. He died in an ambulance en route to the hospital. Later that night C. A. Whitman identified the body of his youngest son. Lake Worth Police Sergeant Bill Openshaw later shared with reporters that the elder Whitman was grief-stricken.[8] In 1995, C. A. Whitman recalled, "He was killed on a Friday outside of Big Daddy's. He was gonna take his plumber's exam on Saturday."[9]

In a telephone conversation only a few days before my trip to Florida, I had awkwardly introduced myself as a writer from Austin. C. A. agreed to sit and talk with me. But during my visit the old plumber did not say much, merely repeating the same facts that a high school student could easily find out doing research for a term paper. Suddenly I found out the reason for his reticence; he told me he wanted to make "financial arrangements." It would not have been inconsistent with my temperament to get a little angry at that point, but I did not do so and I do not know why. As politely as I could I said, "Mr. Whitman, I need to make clear to you that I do not intend to pay you anything for this interview." He looked surprised. He told me of others who had paid him for his time and pictures. Shortly, I began to pack my case. It was enough, I decided, just to meet this most remarkable man and say, "Hello."

Just before I left we shook hands and exchanged business cards. The old plumbing contractor walked away and went back to work. He has been in business since 1940 and has earned the right to rest, but he is still driven; he is still tough.

Larry Fuess

Like Austin, the town of Dallas has grown dramatically since 1966. It is still the hometown of Lawrence A. Fuess, who is now the President of L. A. Fuess Partners Engineers, a business housed in the Oak Lawn section. He was once described as one of the brightest engineering students at the University of Texas, a superlative that was easy to believe after entering his suite of offices. The jewel tones of the carpet and furniture were fashionable, consistent with the style, dress and dignity of the man who emerged from the back offices into the anteroom saying: "Gary, I'm Larry Fuess."

As we came to the front desk, Mr. Fuess stopped and asked about the lunch he had requested for us. Because of a mixup it had not been ordered. He sent someone out to get it, and it arrived in minutes. We talked and ate. Larry Fuess was an extraordinarily personable man. "I cannot imagine or conjure up a reason *that would satisfy me*," was his reply to an invitation to muse about why, in 1966, his best friend became America's deadliest mass murderer. The mystery, however, has not changed his feelings. "Charlie" was his friend.

This was the first interview Larry Fuess has granted on the Whitman saga in nearly thirty years, but he says he still remembers everything. When asked about his visit to Jewell Street on 31 July 1966, Fuess recalled it as:

> one of the more pleasant times we had with him in the preceding couple of months. We were with him, he had the whole plan in mind. He was writing the letter as calm as could be; he was funny; he was engaging. He was calmer than he had been in weeks, maybe even months before that. . . . He seemed so together and calm that night.

Every now and then, Fuess says, something happens to make him think of Charlie. He does not feel betrayed. Larry said the sign on the wall of Charlie's study summed up his friend's problem: "Strength has no quarter." Charlie wouldn't ask for help.[10]

Ramiro Martinez

People still recognize him as the slayer of Charles Whitman. He has slowly become resigned to the notion that "you just can't escape it," deciding that one of the most effective ways to deal with what has happened to him is simply to get it over with, answer the questions and talk openly about it.

As one of his first official duties after the Tower incident, Ramiro Martinez was assigned to be among the APD officers attending the burial of Billy Paul Speed. Shortly after returning to his duties as an Austin police officer, Ramiro Martinez received a frantic radio dispatch calling for him to respond as quickly as possible to an area of Austin where "shots were being fired." As he had done a few days earlier, Martinez took a deep breath and headed to the area as fast as he could. Was history going to repeat itself? Was it going to happen again? Was there a nut out there who wanted to outdo Charles Whitman? The answer to each of these turned out to be "no." Martinez had been dispatched to a place where a number of little boys were "popping firecrackers in the back of a red wagon."[11]

Ramiro Martinez as he looks today. *Gary Lavergne.*

Less than two years after his heroics on the Tower's deck, on 5 July 1968, Ramiro Martinez, then a Sergeant Investigator, announced his intention to resign from the Austin Police Department. His last day on duty was 26 July 1968. He had become disgruntled with the Austin City Council's new policy that called for the automatic suspension of any officer who discharged his weapon. Reports were that he was also dissatisfied with the pay and retirement offered by APD. He quickly denied that his resignation had anything to do with his relations with other officers. "I enjoyed the work and we officers always got along well."[12] When he left police work, he first went into the restaurant business. Later he joined the Texas Department of Public Safety. On 5 September 1973, at 9:00 A.M., he was sworn in as a Texas Ranger. At the time Texas had only eighty-eight Rangers. Contrary to popular myth, he was the third, not the first, Hispanic Ranger in Texas history. His colleagues and others called him "Ranger Ray."[13]

By August of 1991, Ramiro Martinez was described by the *Austin American-Statesman* as "burned-out." Shortly afterwards he retired from the Texas Rangers. Today, he is the Justice of the Peace of Precinct #2 in Comal County, Texas. Occasionally people write to him and ask for his autograph; he signs the little cards and sends them back. "You just accept it. You can't escape it."[14]

As recently as 8 May 1994, *Parade* magazine published a question from a reader: "Whatever became of Ramiro Martinez, the Texas policeman who shot the berserk sniper Charles Whitman at the University of Texas in 1966?" In February 1994, Robert Draper published an article in *Texas Monthly* about the Texas Rangers; page eighty-one was a magnificent picture of "Ranger Ray."

Ramiro Martinez has never second-guessed what had to be done nor has he ever lost a night's sleep or dreamed of Charles Whitman. He often sees the Tower when he visits his brother in Austin, and it does not affect him.[15]

Outside a Luby's Cafeteria in New Braunfels, Texas, I awaited his arrival. At exactly the appointed hour, he drove up and we met. He was dressed for work in a sports coat, white shirt and tie. He now wears glasses and has lost much of his hair, but he is still a handsome man. And again, he answered the questions in a methodically calm and patient style. He still had no doubts. But he was clearly saddened by how often reporters and others pit him against Houston McCoy. When I asked the predictable question about who shot Charles Whitman, he blurted out a sincere, but nonetheless frustrated answer: "Who cares, as long as he's dead!"[16]

Therein lies the secret to how Martinez has adjusted. He killed Charles Whitman only once.

Houston McCoy

Houston McCoy as he looks today. *Gary Lavergne.*

One hundred and fifty miles west of Austin, drivers heading north from the little town of Junction, towards Eden on Highway 83, cannot help but be impressed by the vast expanse of Texas and the hardiness and gut determination it must have taken for pioneers to settle the area. Seeing this region makes it easier to understand Houston McCoy. The only thing between Eden and Junction is the even smaller town of Menard, which takes drivers by surprise as they motor over a hill and see it all at once. Menard looks much like it did when Houston McCoy grew up there five decades ago. The antiquated water tower looks rusty, but it is painted yellow to honor the Menard High School Yellow Jackets. The homes have been placed in no particular pattern; many look crooked. The businesses are old, except for a few major oil company "mini marts" that look out of place.

I parked my truck at what must be a Menard landmark, the Navaho Inn, near the center of town. It looked like a good place for breakfast so I went inside. There, seated by the window facing the street, I waited for Houston McCoy. A few minutes later, I saw a "long drink of water" strutting toward the Inn from a few blocks away. He must have seen the strange truck and known it did not belong to anyone who lived in Menard. He figured it had to be the writer from Austin he had spoken to earlier in the week.

"Go ahead and finish your breakfast. We've got time," McCoy said as he watched me devour my favorite meal, a real West Texas breakfast: eggs (the kind that looked like they came out of a real chicken), ham, and grits with real butter. He never let me call him "Mr. McCoy," insisting on just "Houston" instead. He wore a blue western shirt and brown polyester pants. I do not know why, but I knew they were his best clothes. Immediately, he began to talk.

"I don't want any money. I just want my grandchildren to know the truth," McCoy said as he was explaining that we needed to go to the home of his friends, Hugh Bob and Mary Lee, to continue the interview. We arrived at the lovely home at 9:00 A.M. and got comfortable at the dining room table. While I hooked up the tape recorder McCoy excused himself and went to the kitchen. I could see him moving things in a cabinet. McCoy was clearly at ease at Hugh Bob's house. He returned with a nearly-full liter of whiskey and an empty eight-ounce glass. Pouring a considerable amount of warm brew into the glass, he closed his eyes, took a sip, and said, "Okay, what do you want to know?"

He sipped straight whiskey for the rest of the morning. I studied him carefully for nearly four hours and I never saw even the beginnings of intoxication. Some of my sources documented McCoy's problems over the years. He had admitted in 1991 that he was an alcoholic; he admitted it again in 1995. But on this day McCoy was ready and able to talk. Because of his tragic past, and the bottle before me, I baited him with questions I already knew the answers to. His responses were flawless. Hell, he even corrected me on some elements of the story. Mary Lee beams, "You sound so good today."

"I'm a pilot and I got to talk in directions," McCoy said as he explained the events of 1 August 1966 by pointing to a map of the University of Texas campus. Once he located north he began. Again, he was flawless. When he got to the part where he and Martinez shot Charles Whitman, he left the dining room chair, sat on the floor with his back against the fireplace, and re-enacted the position Whitman took on the northwest corner of the deck. He turned his head to the left and eyeballed me, just as Whitman had done to him twenty-eight years earlier, and McCoy's head snapped back as he told the story, only to return and snap back again. I did not know what the hell to do.

A chill filled the silent room. McCoy was no longer in Hugh Bob's house. He was on that deck, killing Charles Whitman again. I felt the unsettling realization that Houston McCoy kills Charles Whitman every day. It saddened me because an authentic hero like Houston McCoy does not deserve that much pain, and Whitman does not deserve that much attention.

It was time for a break. Mary Lee and I talked about Cajun food. Hugh Bob invited everyone to lunch at the Navaho Inn.

"Just send this back when you're finished with it," McCoy told me, handing me an envelope filled with personal mementos. Outside of the Navaho Inn I bade farewell to Houston McCoy, but before leaving I pretended to pack things in a tool box bolted to the bed of my truck. I wanted to watch the hero of the Tower cross the streets from whence he came.

His friends hope to see justice; they hope that his heroics will one day be appreciated, and they have a point. It is a point, however, that does not have to come at Ramiro Martinez's expense.

The truth is that on 1 August 1966, Houston McCoy and Ramiro Martinez together participated in one of the most courageous acts in American law enforcement history. They, and the world, should remember that one fact and forget about whose bullet actually killed Charles Whitman.

Maybe the day will come when Houston McCoy will find peace, but for now the killing repeatedly and unceasingly haunts him. During the early part of our interview, he had gazed at me, his piercing frontier eyes looking into my soul, becoming watery and red. His large, wrinkled hands shook slightly as he took a deep breath and yet another sip from that eight-ounce glass filled with straight, hot whiskey. Then Houston McCoy said something I will never forget: "If I meet Charles Whitman in heaven, I'm gonna have to kill him again."[17]

---

[1] Patrick Whitman quoted in *Austin American-Statesman*, 1 August 1986.
[2] *UTmost*, September, 1991.
[3] *Austin American-Statesman*, 30 July 1967.
[4] Ibid., 1 August 1976.
[5] C. A. Whitman.
[6] Patrick Whitman quoted in *Austin American-Statesman*, 1 August 1986.
[7] John Michael Whitman quoted in an unidentified clipping in AHC.
[8] Unidentified clipping in AHC.

[9] C. A. Whitman.
[10] Lawrence A. Fuess.
[11] Ramiro Martinez.
[12] *Austin American-Statesman*, 7 July 1968; Sherman *Democrat*, 2 July 1973; Unidentified clipping in AHC.
[13] Ibid.; Ramiro Martinez.
[14] Ramiro Martinez.
[15] *Texas Monthly*, February, 1994; Ibid.
[16] Ramiro Martinez.
[17] Houston McCoy.

Notes on Sources

In his landmark work on the Kennedy Assassination entitled *Case Closed*, Gerald Posner effectively demonstrated how the passage of time and repeated exposure to large amounts of coverage of an infamous incident tend to blur the recollections of eyewitnesses. Oral history is necessary, but as an historian I am often suspicious of memories that are thirty years old. A great deal of folklore has surrounded the Charles Whitman case, so wherever possible, I have given preference to primary documents from 1966 rather than relying on the 1995–96 recollections.

Interviews

I conducted three formal interviews: one with Houston McCoy on 10 March 1995, in Menard, Texas; one with Ramiro Martinez on 3 April 1995, in New Braunfels, Texas; and one with Lawrence A. Fuess in Dallas on 6 June 1996. All three gentlemen were interviewed as much for an update on their lives since 1966 as for their recollections of the Tower incident. I also had brief meetings with Phillip Conner, one of the members of the McCoy Team, on 18 August 1995, at my office in Austin; Dr. Albert Lalonde on 30 June 1995, at his home in Austin; and Robert Heard and Jack Keever, former Associated Press reporters, on 16 March 1996, at the 1996 South by Southwest Media Conference in Austin. Other, very brief, conversations are endnoted through the book. None of the interviews produced dramatic new information relative to the Whitman murders.

On 26 January 1995, I met Mr. C. A. Whitman at his home in Lantana, Florida. It is my personal belief that news and history should not be purchased, so when he indicated that in the past he has received payments for interviews and pictures, I explained that I could not pay him for any information. We then had a pleasant conversation which yielded no information that had not already been published or was otherwise well-documented.

Primary documents

The bulk of the information of this work is taken from the Whitman Case File, offense number M968150, of the Austin Police Department. The original documents are still locked in an evidence room vault on the second floor of the Austin Police Department headquarters. Wisely, APD asked for evidence of my qualifications to review the material. I presented a resumé and volunteered other personal information to gain access to the original documents.

The APD file on the Whitman Case consists mostly of reports completed by virtually all of the officers involved in any way with the incident and related investigations. The Whitman Case is more completely documented than most crimes, not only because of its notorious nature, but because Police Chief Robert Miles sought to answer criticisms of his department's performance by requiring detailed reports from all officers involved as to their movements and actions. They completed hundreds of pages of forms including *Supplementary Offense Reports, Crimes Against Persons Reports, Hospitalization Offense Reports, Details of Investigations*, and *Vehicle Impounding Reports*, in addition to various statements and affidavits to other government agencies, including the FBI, Food and Drug Administration, Texas Department of Public Safety and others. The record is extraordinarily complete.

The Texas Department of Public Safety file on the Charles Whitman Case, file number 4-38, is larger than the APD file in that it includes its own reports as well as the FBI files and the APD files. My access to FBI reports was through this body of material.

The APD and Texas DPS files also contain a wealth of copies and original primary documents related to Charles Whitman's childhood and adolescence, as well as his life as a marine and as a University of Texas student. They include health and education records from Sacred Heart Elementary School, Lake Worth, Florida; Saint Ann's High School, West Palm Beach, Florida; and the University of Texas at Austin. There are also documents pertaining to his hitch as a marine, including tablets he used as notebooks for his marine classes and the scorebook he used that certified him as a marine sharpshooter.

Whitman's own writings provide an astonishing look into his mind and character. The earliest example of his writing is his *Autobiography of Charles Joseph Whitman*, dated 1 March 1956, followed chronologically by numerous calendars, notebooks, and diaries, the richest of which is *The Daily Record of C. J. Whitman*. Charles Whitman was an obsessive listmaker and notemaker; dozens of examples are in both the Austin Police Department and Texas Department of Safety files. All were made available to me and proved to be invaluable primary sources.

Numerous handwritten notes and logs dated 1 August 1966, provided almost a minute-by-minute account of the information that came in to the Austin Police Department as the drama unfolded. In addition to documents, the file contains crime scene photos and pictures that were developed from film in Charles Whitman's camera. The crime photos were helpful in piecing together the positions of things and people in the reception area of the Tower, the Penthouse Apartments, and 906 Jewell Street. Whitman's pictures were helpful in forming physical descriptions of Charles and Kathy Whitman during the last weeks of their lives. The Texas DPS file had photos as well.

The *Report to the Governor—Medical Aspects—Charles J. Whitman Catastrophe*, dated 8 September 1966, and footnoted as "Connally Report," summarized Charles Whitman's life, medical history, and death. It included a psychiatric profile, an analysis of his brain tumor, and evidence of his drug abuse. In spite of the wealth of technical information, the commission that investigated the case drew no hard conclusions as to what prompted Charles Whitman to become a mass murderer. After a detailed but ultimately unsuccessful search for a psychiatric or organic cause for the mass slayings, the eminent scientists on the commission could not bring themselves to conclude that Whitman killed because he *wanted* to.

Secondary Sources

The Barker History Center of the University of Texas at Austin has a number of files and scrapbooks entitled "Tower Sniping." The scrapbooks are a convenient source of newspaper articles from 1966 to the present.

The Austin History Center of the Austin Public Library has a file entitled "Mass Murders—Whitman—M8960 (1)" consisting of loose newspaper clippings, mostly from the *Austin American-Statesman*, and copies of a few primary documents from the Austin Police Department file. The center has back issues of the *Austin American-Statesman* on microfilm, which I utilized. Not surprisingly, the *Austin American-Statesman* provided the most complete reporting of the incident and was an invaluable source. Every major newspaper in the world reported the incident and some of the information citing the *Statesman* as a source can be found in virtually any newspaper of the day. The quality of the reporting, however, should not be understated; it was excellent. Below is a list, probably incomplete, of reporters who from 1966 to 1991 contributed to *Austin American-Statesman* coverage of the Tower tragedy.

Jim Berry	Glen Castlebury
Nat Henderson	Derro Evans
Chris Whitcraft	Al Williams
Jack Maddigan	Carol McMurtry
Mike Cox	Sam Wood
Russell Tinsley	Paul Recer
Sara Speights	Jerry Hall
Brenda Bell	Larry BeSaw
Jerry White	Cheryl Coggins Frink
Joe Vargo	Bob Banta

An army of Associated Press and United Press International reporters also covered the incident. They are too numerous to mention. However, one of the reporters, Robert Heard, was actually wounded by Whitman and would later release reports from his hospital room. Additionally, Mr. Heard's first anniversary article for the Associated Press (*Austin American-Statesman*, 30 July 1967) was especially helpful because he located and interviewed at least twenty-six of the thirty-one persons who had been wounded on 1 August 1966. Mr. Heard also provided me with a copy of Fahrenthold and Rider's *Admissions: The Extraordinary History of Brackenridge Hospital* (Austin, Texas: City of Austin, 1984), which deals with the events of 1 August 1966 in Chapter 5. He also faxed me an account of his own movements and wounding on that day.

Other newspapers, magazines and periodicals utilized in my research included:

Palm Beach Post (Florida)	*Dallas Morning News*
Lake Worth Herald (Florida)	*Rosenberg Herald-Coaster* (Texas)
Texas Observer	*New York Times*
Daily Texan	*Summer Texan*
National Observer	*San Antonio Daily Express* (Texas)
Austin Citizen (Texas)	*Los Angeles Herald-Examiner*
San Antonio Standard (Texas)	*Memphis Press Scimitar* (Tennessee)
San Angelo Standard (Texas)	*Sherman Democrat* (Texas)
Time	*Texas Monthly*
UTmost	*Newsweek*
Life	*Esquire*
Playboy	

William J. Helmer's articles in the *Texas Observer* (19 August 1966), *Texas Monthly* (August, 1986), and *Playboy* (October, 1970) were particularly useful. The combination of Helmer's training as a journalist and his being an eyewitness to the event served him well.

As of 1996, no other book has been written about Charles Whitman or the University of Texas Tower incident. There is a peripheral case study on Whitman in Carl Sifakis's *Encyclopedia of American Crime* (New York City: Facts on File, Inc., 1982). Whitman is mentioned often in Jack Levin and James Alan Fox's excellent studies of mass and serial murderers, *Mass Murder: America's Growing Menace* (New York City: Plenum Publishing, 1985) and more recently, *Overkill* (New York City: Plenum Publishing, 1994). Without question, Levin and Fox are America's premier scholars on serial and mass murders. The most detailed treatment, in book form, of Charles Whitman's murders was a single chapter in one of Time-Life's series of books on True Crime that dealt with mass murderers. Unfortunately, the text was largely based on newspaper articles which contained minor errors of fact.

Background material on the histories of the City of Austin, the University of Texas at Austin, and the State of Texas were meant only to put those places in the context of the Whitman murders. Davis and Colson's *Austin: Lone Star Rising* (Memphis: Towery Publishing, Inc., 1994), Richard Zalade's *Austin* (Austin: Texas Monthly Press, 1984), and Clifford Hopewell's *Sam Houston: Man of Destiny* (Austin: Eakin Press, 1987), provided some of the material for the brief discussion of Austin's early history. A concise history of the University of Texas at Austin is Margaret Catherine Berry's *UT Austin: Traditions and Nostalgia* (Austin: Eakin Press, 1992).

Mary Gabour Lamport wrote an autobiography entitled *The Impossible Tree* (Austin: Ginny's Copying Service, 1972), which is a lovely story of her life and family. It is also a story of admirable devotion, faith, and courage. However, her horrible experiences in the Tower take up only a little more than two of the chapters.

Acknowledgments

First and foremost I wish to thank my wife Laura. Writing is an avocation for me; my real job requires extensive travel. Taking on a project like this took me away from her on holidays, vacations, and weekends. Even while we were together at home, my preoccupation interfered with our normal lives together. At any time she could have reasonably asked me to stop. Instead, she provided valuable support. Her *summa cum laude* degree in journalism, her mastery of the mechanics and grammar of the English language, and her considerable skills as an editor made her professionally indispensable. Her name belongs on the front of this book.

Falba F. Turner, my former colleague, patiently listened to endless stories of virtually every person mentioned in this book, and she never told me to just shut up. She read first and second drafts of every chapter as they were written and asked very good questions. I have selfishly exploited her considerable intellectual power.

The cooperation of the Austin Police Department has been superb. Specifically, Lieutenant David Parkinson, presently the head of APD's Robbery/Homicide Detail, very patiently responded to my repeated telephone calls, requests and visits. Never once did he attempt to influence my work, yet he generously shared his considerable knowledge and training in response to my numerous questions. Lieutenant Parkinson also located and contacted Houston McCoy and Ramiro Martinez for me and made those interviews possible. Detective J. W. Thompson helped me track down the full names of APD officers mentioned and greatly facilitated my repeated requests for information. Special Agent James Echols of the Austin Office of the Federal Bureau of Investigation provided valuable insights and technical expertise. He also greatly assisted in my Freedom of Information Act application for FBI files, although the FBI now claims that the file cannot be located. Mike Cox, Chief of Media Relations, and Assistant Commander Enrique Garcia, both of the Texas Department of Public Safety, made possible my review of the DPS files on the event. Coincidentally, Mike Cox, in 1966 a seventeen-year-old reporter for the *Austin American-Statesman*, was one of the first reporters to reach 906 Jewell Street after the sniping incident. He generously provided me a copy of his account of 1 August 1966.

I am indebted and deeply grateful to Houston McCoy of Menard, Texas. My interview with him took most of a day of detailed and sometimes painful recollections. We were able to use the comfortable home of Hugh Bob Spiller for our work. Houston also made available his collection of pictures, clippings and other memorabilia on the Tower incident.

Judge Ramiro Martinez, Justice of the Peace of Precinct 2 of Comal County, Texas, very generously gave of his time for an interview. We drank a great deal of coffee at Luby's Cafeteria in New Braunfels, Texas, and he refused to let me pay for any of it.

Phillip Conner, now Sergeant-Investigator for the Travis County District Attorney, very thoughtfully met with me on very short notice. Mr. Conner was also helpful in dealing with unexpected problems associated with the development of this work.

I did meet for a short time with Mr. C. A. Whitman of Lantana, Florida, who graciously welcomed me to his home. While we did not agree on terms for an in-depth interview, our parting was amicable and I wish to thank him for the time he did spend with me. Lawrence A. Fuess of L. A. Fuess Partners Engineers of Dallas very thoughtfully provided for lunch while I interviewed him in his office.

My former colleague, Dr. Charles Carrick, presently the Superintendent of Scotsboro City (Alabama) Public Schools and an attorney, and Joseph M. Bertrand, an attorney from New Orleans, also provided guidance. Brother David Sinitiere, F.S.C., helped me focus and clarify my thoughts on the writings of Saint Thomas Aquinas.

Dr. Albert Lalonde, a neuro-surgeon and former Chief of Staff of Brackenridge Hospital, welcomed me to his home and reviewed autopsy and other medical reports associated with the Whitman Case.

Other friends and colleagues from the Austin area who provided valuable observations and advice include Norm Hood, who helped me understand the finer points of the arsenal Whitman used from the deck, Karen Pennell, Shannon McGuire, Will Brennan, and Bruce and Val Nordquist. My dear friend, Linda McDonald, often caught mistakes no one else noticed; her irreverence kept me from taking myself too seriously. Pam Lange of Dallas, Texas, gave me much needed advice and help in navigating through the business of publishing. Dr. Richard Sawyer of Iowa City, Iowa, helped me to construct the prediction model used in the discussion of problems associated with predicting who will become a mass murderer. Charles Sidney Stutes of Rayne, Louisiana, reviewed early drafts of the first chapters and helped to determine the direction of the final manuscript.

The staffs of the Barker History Center of the University of Texas at Austin, and the Austin History Center of the Austin Public Library, patiently hauled stacks of files and scrapbooks for my use. Especially helpful was Daniel Barrera of UT's Undergraduate Library. Dan has annotated the Whitman Papers and is an author of note. He made available much of his personal collection. My job takes me to dozens of university campuses throughout the United States and my use of their libraries, most often in the middle of the night, and the kindness of their staffs are appreciated, though they are too numerous to list. The staffs of the West Palm Beach Public Library in West Palm Beach, Florida, and the George Memorial Library of Richmond, Texas, were especially helpful in amassing information for the early chapters.

I was honored to have Dr. James Alan Fox, Dean of the College of Criminal Justice of Northeastern University, take time from a very busy schedule to read my manuscript and provide valuable advice. Mr. Neal Spelce, a well-known news anchorman and reporter for K-EYE News in Austin, kindly gave me a videotape of his broadcasts of 1 August 1991, the 25th anniversary of the Whitman murders. Additionally, Mr. Spelce reviewed the manuscript and contributed a brief review. Mr. Robert Heard, a former Associated Press reporter and presently the editor and publisher of *Inside Texas*, a newsletter about Texas sports, agreed to look over my manuscript and suggested minor changes, nearly all of which I accepted. Jessica Flynn, a journalism major at the University of Texas, made available news programs and videotapes I could not otherwise locate. William J. "Bill" Helmer, a former contributing editor of *Playboy*, provided much needed advice and encouragement. He also contributed directly by reviewing the manuscript and giving me a copy of his recording of live radio broadcasts of the sniping incident.

The staff of the *Lake Worth Herald* of Lake Worth, Florida, very kindly made their back issues available to me. The old newspapers were bound and shelved in a storage area that was barely accessible, and the volumes had to be dusted off for my use. For their trouble I am grateful.

David Reed, a Registered Pharmacist from Rayne, Louisiana, and Jim Davies of Cedar Park Pharmacy in Cedar Park, Texas, were kind enough to provide me with information on Dexedrine and Dexamyl.

The staffs of the Davis-Greenlawn Cemetery of Rosenberg, Texas, the Hillcrest Memorial Park of West Palm Beach, Florida, and the Crestview Memorial Park of Wichita Falls, Texas, were helpful in locating the graves which provided the inspiration for the Prologue.

My agent, James D. Hornfischer of The Literary Group International, and Frances B. Vick, Director of the University of North Texas Press, and Charlotte Wright, Associate Director, could not have been more patient and kind when it came to educating a dilettante of the publishing business.

Finally, I am truly blessed with four children who respect me enough to make our home an environment where this kind of project is possible. Charlie, Mark, Amy, and Anna are the treasures of my life. For the past three years they deserved more of my time. Charlie contributed directly through reviewing and annotating some of the Austin Police Department files. He also reviewed portions of the manuscript as part of an Advanced Placement American History class project at Leander High School, Leander, Texas. Mark accompanied me on picture-taking trips to the Drag and the University of Texas.

Surely, there are others. Their omissions are mistakes of my mind—not my heart.

INDEX